Crime and Calamity in Cholsey

LIFE IN A BERKSHIRE VILLAGE 1819-1919

Barrie Charles

Also by the same author:

Karma and the Helpful Hand

A Pattern of Virtue: The Arduous Life and Mysterious Death of a Corporal-Major in Victoria's Lifeguards

Kill the Queen! The Eight Assassination Attempts on Queen Victoria

Crime and Calamity in Cholsey
LIFE IN A BERKSHIRE VILLAGE 1819-1919

First published March 2013

Dr B. J. Charles
73 Papist Way
Cholsey
Wallingford
Oxfordshire
OX10 9QH

Published on www.lulu.com
Available worldwide through bookshops and online retailers.

Copyright © Barrie Charles 2013

The right of Barrie Charles to be identified as the Author of this work has been asserted in accordance with the Copyrights, Designs and Patents Act 1988.

All rights reserved. No part of this book may be reprinted or reproduced or utilised in any form or by any electronic, mechanical or other means, now known or hereafter invented, including photocopying and recording, or in any information storage or retrieval system, without the permission in writing of the Author.

ISBN 978-1-291-29571-9

Contents

Author's Note and Acknowledgements ... 9

Introduction ... 13

Chapter 1 The Vicar and His Clerk ... 17

Chapter 2 The Swing Riots ... 31

Chapter 3 The Ilsley Family ... 49

Chapter 4 The Coming of the Railway ... 77

Chapter 5 Land Reform ... 91

Chapter 6 Crime and Punishment ... 99

Chapter 7 The Growth of the Railway ... 113

Chapter 8 The County Lunatic Asylum ... 129

Chapter 9 The Philandering Curate ... 147

Chapter 10 The Rise of Democracy ... 161

Chapter 11 The New Century ... 171

Chapter 12 The Great War ... 183

Chapter 13 The Conscientious Objector ... 199

Chapter 14 The War to End All Wars ... 211

Money, Inflation, and Imperial Units ... 225

Chronology ... 227

Sources ... 229

Index ... 241

Illustrations

Front cover: Honey Lane and The Beehive c1906

Fig. 0.1 Cholsey and surrounding settlements in 1830 12
Fig. 0.2 The centre of the village in 1842 14
Fig. 1.1 St Mary's church from the east c1803 17
Fig. 1.2 Cholsey vicarage with the cedar of Lebanon c1904 20
Fig. 1.3 The stone believed to be 'the effigy' 22
Fig. 1.4 Revd Wyatt Cottle 24
Fig. 1.5 Westminster Hall in the Palace of Westminster 25
Fig. 1.6 The writ of mandamus 28
Fig. 1.7 Revd Cottle's grave at the rear of the church 30
Fig. 2.1 The farms in Cholsey c1830 34
Fig. 2.2 Threshing with a flail 36
Fig. 2.3 Setting light to hayricks in 1830 39
Fig. 2.4 A French horse-powered threshing machine 40
Fig. 2.5 Reward poster 43
Fig. 2.6 A Bow Street Runner 46
Fig. 3.1 The Broad Face in Abingdon 51
Fig. 3.2 Sir John Taylor Coleridge 52
Fig. 3.3 Some of the noteworthy signatures from the petition 54
Fig. 3.4 The *York* hulk 56
Fig. 3.5 Sydney Cove in 1821 58
Fig. 3.6 The Ilsley family 60
Fig. 3.7 Abingdon gaol 63
Fig. 3.8 Map of Van Diemen's Land 67
Fig. 3.9 The ruins of Port Arthur in Tasmania 72
Fig. 3.10 Map of the State of Victoria 74
Fig. 4.1 Navvies working on a railway 77
Fig. 4.2 Revd Henry William Lloyd 79
Fig. 4.3 Revd Lloyd's book about his convert 81
Fig. 4.4 Isambard Kingdom Brunel 83
Fig. 4.5 Dowager Queen Adelaide 84
Fig. 4.6 Wallingford Road station c1880 87
Fig. 4.7 Bridge House in Dorchester 88
Fig. 5.1 The tithe map around The Forty 92
Fig. 5.2 The enclosure of many strips into one field at Winterbrook 94
Fig. 5.3 The original course of the brook in the Recreation Ground 97

Fig. 6.1 The Swan Inn in the 1930s 103
Fig. 6.2 Map showing the pubs in the village centre 106
Fig. 6.3 An artist's impression of the County Lunatic Asylum 110
Fig. 7.1 Moulsford station and the new branch line 114
Fig. 7.2 The Railway Tavern, now private flats............................ 119
Fig. 7.3 The railway bridge at Moulsford..................................... 122
Fig. 7.4 Cholsey station c1935 125
Fig. 8.1 Little Stoke ferry and the asylum c1908........................... 130
Fig. 8.2 The County Lunatic Asylum.. 133
Fig. 8.3 Map of the asylum, roads and Little Stoke ferry in 1883 135
Fig. 8.4 Star Terrace, Papist Way 137
Fig. 8.5 Plan of the asylum in the 1870s 141
Fig. 8.6 The Morning Star c1914.. 144
Fig. 9.1 The new Board School and master's house 148
Fig. 9.2 The burning of Washington in 1814................................. 151
Fig. 9.3 Friedrich Wilhelm IV... 152
Fig. 9.4 The battle of Tel el-Kebir 155
Fig. 9.5 Queen Victoria... 157
Fig. 9.6 The Royal Courts of Justice... 159
Fig. 10.1 The old schoolhouse by the church 162
Fig. 10.2 The Red Lion 163
Fig. 10.3 Rules for the election of the first Parish Council........... 165
Fig. 10.4 A school play about the suffragettes in 1908................. 169
Fig. 11.1 An invitation to the Cholsey coronation festivities 172
Fig. 11.2 Honey Lane with, probably, PC Ernest Spratley c1906 177
Fig. 11.3 Boer commandoes 180
Fig. 12.1 The shooting in Sarajevo... 183
Fig. 12.2 Alfred Abdey's Cholsey gravestone............................... 185
Fig. 12.3 George V 188
Fig. 12.4 Lord Kitchener.. 189
Fig. 12.5 The wedding of John Alder and Lucy Abdey in 1913.......... 192
Fig. 12.6 Herbert, William, Alfred, Edwin and Susan Abdey c1906 194
Fig. 12.7 Band of Hope medallion... 196
Fig. 13.1 Bertrand Russell.. 201
Fig. 13.2 An anti-CO poster 202
Fig. 13.3 Dartmoor prison gate 206
Fig. 13.4 Dar es Salaam as painted in 1926 by J. H. Pierneef........ 209
Fig. 13.5 The conscientious objectors' memorial in Tavistock Square. 210

Fig. 14.1 A field kitchen during the battle of the Somme 212
Fig. 14.2 Pte Howse's gravestone 213
Fig. 14.3 Bill Money as a Local Defence Volunteer................................... 215
Fig. 14.4 Lt Carl F. V. Hansen... 217
Fig. 14.5 Mary and Charlie Hansen c1938... 218
Fig. 14.6 A British soldier in a captured German trench 219
Fig. 14.7 The Great War memorial in St Mary's church 222

Illustration Acknowledgements

Permission to reproduce images is gratefully acknowledged as follows.

Cholsey 1000+ and Pie Powder Press: 1.1, 2.2, 4.2, 4.6, 6.1, 7.4, 8.6, 10.4 and 11.1

Ian Wheeler: 8.5 (outline plan)

Jeanne Money: Front cover, 1.2, 1.4, 8.1, 8.2, 9.1, 11.2 and 14.3

Joyce Huntley: 12.5 and 12.6

The Peace Pledge Union: 13.2

Author's Note and Acknowledgements

This book contains, essentially, the true story of the people and events that disturbed the calm of Cholsey parish life over the course of a hundred years. However, the source information is largely based on contemporary reporting in newspapers and the information held in public records and government files, which, of course, are not always error free. Where possible I have tried to consult multiple sources, but this was not always feasible. In addition I may have inadvertently introduced my own mistakes, for which I apologise. I have also tried to divine the thoughts and motives of some of those involved in the events described, something which, by its nature, must at times be speculative, but I hope it breathes some life into the narrative.

It was quite hard to decide what to include and what to exclude as, of course, there were many more crimes, tragic deaths and village events than those related herein. In the main I have used three selection criteria: sufficient source material available in newspapers or other sources; of interest to the modern day reader; and something that fits in with the narrative. I hope the result has produced a selection of stories that will enhance your understanding of village history. The book is largely chronological, in that each chapter begins at a progressively later date. However, each story is taken through to a logical conclusion, so the time period covered often overlaps with that of the next chapter.

Where possible I have used the common terms that were in use at the time, whilst avoiding the rather long-winded and pedantic expressions of a bygone age. Some of the terms may now appear offensive, for example 'lunatic asylum' rather than 'hospital', or 'idiot' rather than 'person with learning difficulties'. If this offends, I apologise, but I felt it added historical reality.

My gratitude goes to the patience of the many staff in the libraries and archives that I consulted during the research for this book, particularly those at the Berkshire Record Office, the British Library and the National Archives. I have also made extensive use of secondary sources for background information and certain details, for which I acknowledge all the authors, as detailed in the 'Sources' appendix.

I am also grateful for help on specific items to Bill Hetherington of the Peace Pledge Union and village historians Judy Dewey, Nev Keating, Jeanne Money, Tony Rayner and Ian Wheeler. I also wish to thank for their assistance my patient draft readers and advisors, David Charles, Maggie Charles, Jeanne Money, Peg Shearer and Elizabeth Rees Lewis.

I hope you enjoy reading this history of Cholsey, and if you have additional information or any comments, then please do not hesitate to contact me at the address shown on the copyright page.

Barrie Charles
Cholsey, Febuary 2013

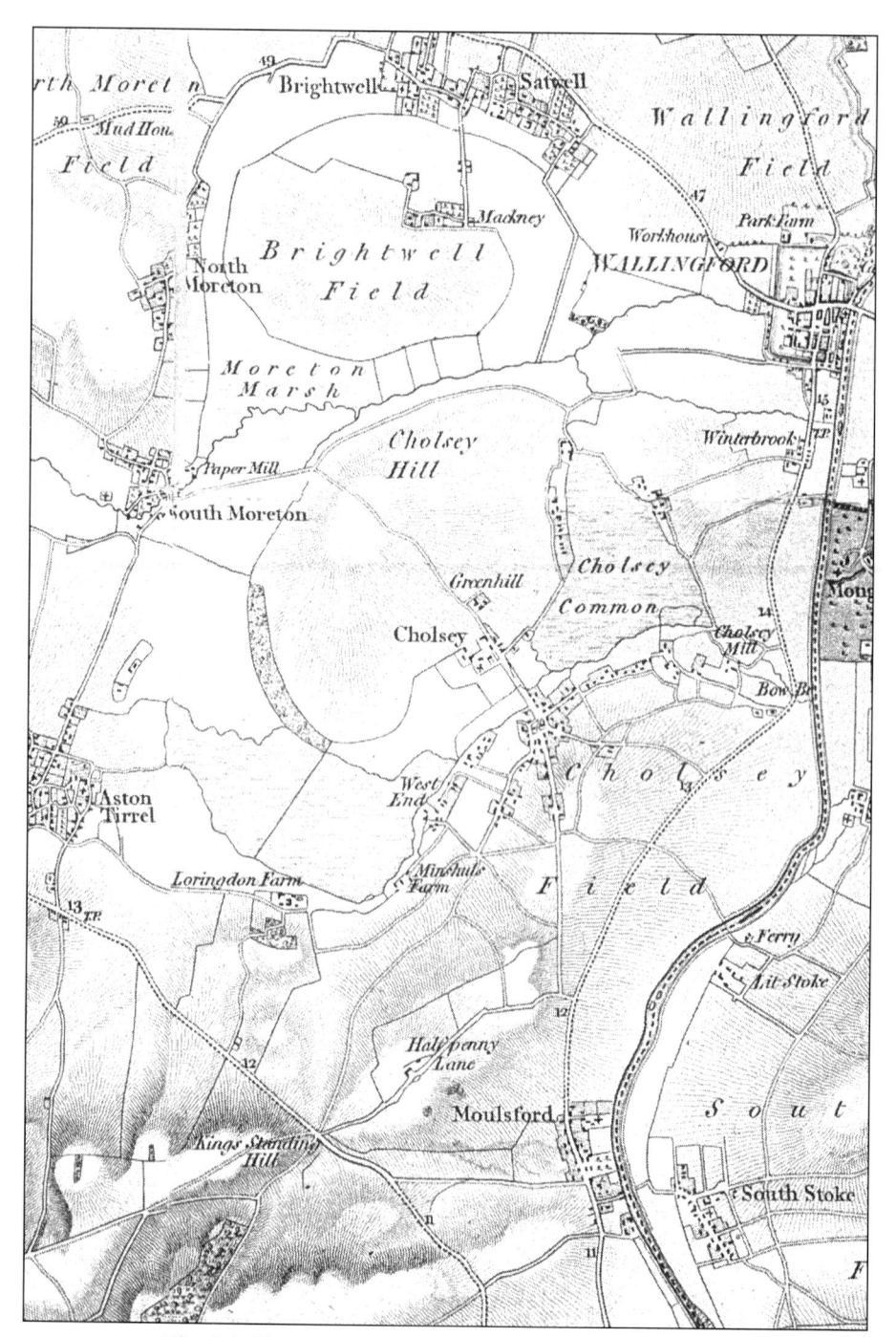

Fig. 0.1 Cholsey and surrounding settlements in 1830

Introduction

By 1819 Cholsey was already an ancient community, perhaps around a thousand years old. The parish was one of the largest in Berkshire[1], extending over 5,000 acres and home to almost 1,000 inhabitants living in about 200 dwellings. To the south and southwest were the Berkshire Downs, a source of wealth from sheep rearing since medieval times. To the west and northwest was a fertile plain of cornfields, known as the 'golden mile', which extended to the county town of Abingdon eight miles away. To the east was the river Thames, a major thoroughfare for trade, and still the best way to transport goods to London, fifty miles distant. Bounding Cholsey to the northeast was the old Saxon borough of Wallingford, the closest market town and for centuries the gateway to the wider world for its smaller neighbour.

Although many of the cottages in Cholsey were grouped in widely dispersed hamlets, the centre of the parish was clearly the village green, known locally as 'The Forty'. Wattle-and-daub cottages and brick and tile dwellings surrounded the open space, while an old thatched hostelry, the Swan Inn, sat at the southern end of the ragged sward. On the other side of Drove Lane[2] from the pub was the village pond, while further east across Honey Lane from the pool were the straw-covered barns of Pound Farm, where the baying of various beasts and the farmyard smells gave the whole scene a suitably rural character. But it was clearly a poor community; many of the cottages were in bad repair, their two or three rooms damp and cold, with nothing but a few broken pieces of furniture on the bare beaten-earth floors. Piles of rubbish lay in roadside corners, and the ditches were clogged and often overflowed, spilling polluted water across the low-lying land.

Five roads converged on The Forty, each often thick with mud in winter and rutted in summer, when each wagon passed in a cloud of dust. Once away from the small village centre, the land was open, largely without hedge or fence, and the ground was still farmed in strips, according to the medieval custom. Drove Lane led across the flat lands to the south and up onto the Downs, crossing the parish boundary at the four-mile post, before continuing to the town of East Ilsley, famous for the sheep fair held every August. Bleating flocks still regularly passed through the village centre

---

[1] Cholsey, along with other lands to the south and west of the Thames, was part of Berkshire until the Local Government reforms of 1974, when it moved to Oxfordshire.

[2] Drove Lane is now known as Station Road.

bound for Wallingford and the road to London, the drovers availing themselves of the local hostelries.

Honey Lane led southeast up out of the village centre towards the neighbouring villages of Moulsford and Streatley, following the straight course of an ancient Roman road. Ilges Lane travelled eastwards from The Forty, passing Pound Farm and providing the most direct route to the mill on Cholsey brook and to the turnpike road to Wallingford. To the northeast was Horn Lane[1], leading to Cholsey Common and the quickest way for those walking to Wallingford, while the street to the northwest was called The Causeway[2], raised above the watery ditches flanking the road on either side, two of the many that criss-crossed and drained the lower lands of the parish. A quarter mile in that direction towards Cholsey Hill sat the parish church of St Mary, supposedly older than the Norman Conquest and on the site of a former monastery. When it was built, the hill would have been an island set in a marshy landscape, reputedly named after a Saxon lord, Ceol's Eye (or Isle). This was now the domain of Cholsey Manor,

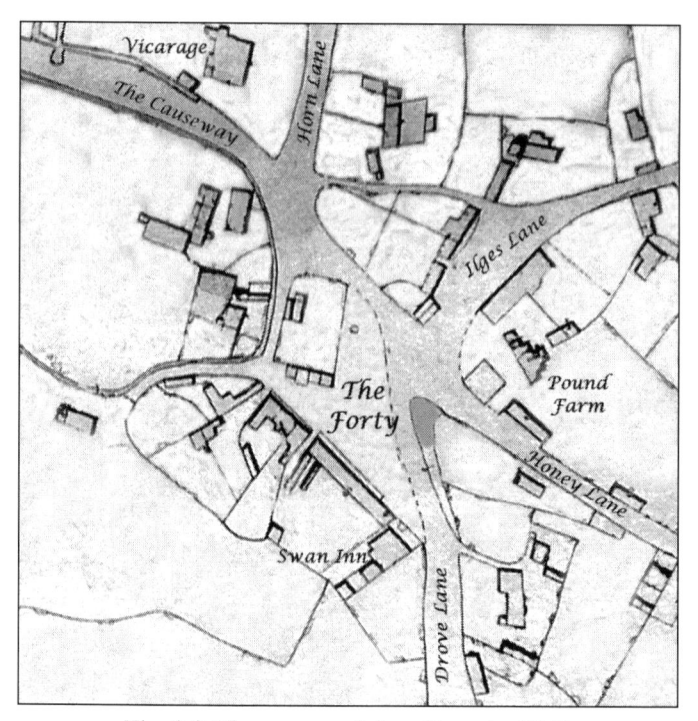

Fig. 0.2 The centre of the village in 1842

---

[1] Horn Lane was the section of the Wallingford Road from Church Road to the Red Lion that is shaped rather like a horn.

[2] The Causeway is now known as Church Road.

whose courts still met to settle village disputes.

Apart from recourse to the Justices of the Peace[1] in Wallingford or the circuit judges for more serious offences, the parish organised its own affairs and had little need for any higher government. The landowners were subject to local taxes to support the church, provide for the poor and maintain the highways, and all such ratepayers managed the affairs of the village through a meeting known as the vestry. They appointed the local officials: the churchwardens to take care of the church and ecclesiastical matters; overseers to administer poor law payments; the surveyor of highways to look after the roads; and one or more parish constables, supported by several tithingmen[2], to keep order. These offices were largely unpaid, and appointments were not always welcome, but as in all the other parishes in the county, they were essential for the smooth running of the community.

One person who was paid was the parson, in this case the vicar, who was entitled to a share of the tithes, the medieval tax originally set at one-tenth of the produce of the land. A rector would receive the greater part of the tithes, but after the Reformation this income was often granted or sold to institutions or individuals who became 'lay rectors'. This was the case in Cholsey and the vicar received just the 'small tithes', a tax on the annual production of crops such as vegetables and fruit, animals and milling.

The tax was passed down to any who rented land and was resented by the villagers, an unearned income for those who already had enough. But this was the order of things, the way life had been organised for generations, and the general view was to suspect any change. Most got on with trying to scrape a living, working long hours at dull repetitive tasks and grabbing what small pleasures were to be had. One of the few joys for women was gossiping with neighbours, and for men what was termed conversation, but amounted to the same thing, at the alehouse. On any day, but especially on a Sunday, villagers would gather on the green, before or after attending church or the devil's attractions at the inn, to gossip about the latest news and to watch the world go by: the parson and his wife out in their carriage; the gentleman farmer riding by on his horse; hordes of ragged local children

---

[1] Justices of the Peace are also known as magistrates.

[2] Originally each group of ten men in the community appointed one of their number to be the tithingman, responsible for order amongst the whole group. By the nineteenth century this connection was lost and a few tithingmen were elected to keep order within particular geographical areas or as general support to the constable.

playing in the dirt; a carter with a load of corn or hay; and, during the week, ordinary labouring folk off to till the fields.

In much of all of this Cholsey was not unusual, just a typical Berkshire village, little altered for centuries, filled with ordinary people struggling to make the most of their lives. But over the next hundred years their way of life would change fundamentally, and their troubles, grudges and misadventures would break through the bucolic surface into crime or calamity. Each event, whether major or minor, would become the next talking point and the people involved the subject of local gossip. This book is a selection of those stories.

Chapter 1 The Vicar and His Clerk

On Sunday 24 July 1819, dressed as smartly as they could afford, local families made their way down The Causeway to the parish church of St Mary. The weather was fine and warm and the five bells[1] in the tall church tower pealed joyfully across the peaceful countryside. To the north, the crops on Cholsey Hill were growing steadily, clearly visible now that the recently-demolished great tithe barn no longer hid the view. As the hour for the service approached, the bell ringers finished their work, and now latecomers only heard the tolling of the ancient sanctus bell. They hurried past the smart carriages left by the well-to-do at the churchyard gate and through the Norman arch into the nave. Most were expecting the traditional unexciting Sunday service. Few in the congregation knew about the drama soon to unfold.

The parishioners settled in their usual seats: the gentry and larger-scale farmers to the front, the tradesmen behind and poorer families at the back. As the coughing and shuffling in the pews subsided, the Reverend Wyatt Cottle, officiating minister for the last eighteen years, came forward to the

Fig. 1.1 St Mary's church from the east c1803

---

[1] Three more bells have since been added making a total ring of eight.

pulpit wearing a solemn expression. Looking towards John Huggins, parish clerk, he began to read an announcement, "As you have admitted several persons into my church, and suffered them to commit sacrilegious depredations without informing me of it, and likewise in several respects not obeyed my orders, I therefore dismiss you from the office of parish clerk." He then ordered Huggins to leave the pew reserved for the clerk and give up his seat to James Smith, who was to be his replacement. Shamed and embarrassed before his fellow parishioners in this close-knit community, Huggins did as he was told.

After the service and all through the following week, people speculated about what the 'sacrilegious depredations' might have been. On the following Sunday, as the congregation assembled, they immediately saw that John Huggins was back in the clerk's seat and were agog as to what might happen next.

When Revd Cottle saw where Huggins was sitting, he came down to confront him, saying, "What do you do there, Huggins? I desire you to turn out, you are not clerk. Last Sunday I read you out, and read James Smith into the office of clerk, so Huggins, turn out!" But John Huggins, having had a chance to think about the situation, felt aggrieved and would not move. The vicar called for help from the Parish Chief Constable, Richard Minshull, but Huggins held the door to the pew closed. Minshull then sought the assistance of three others, and together they dragged the man from the pew as he protested loudly. Revd Cottle urged them on, saying, "Turn him out, turn him out! I will stand the racket."

Such scenes had not been seen before in the congregation's collective memory, but finally John Huggins was thrown out, James Smith took his place, and the service proceeded. But that was far from the end of the matter.

* * *

The Reverend Wyatt Cottle had arrived in Cholsey at the turn of the century and was 63 years old by the time of the dispute with his parish clerk. He was born the son of a landowning gentleman in the middle of the eighteenth century in Monkton Farleigh, Wiltshire. The small village, located about four miles east of the city of Bath, was booming at the time because the honey-coloured limestone produced from its quarries was being used to construct elegant crescents in the spa town. Wyatt Cottle enjoyed a privileged upbringing and in 1775, at the age of nineteen, went up to Pembroke College, Oxford, to train for the clergy. He spent over four years amid the towering spires of Oxford with the sons of aristocrats and gentry, most of whom were destined to follow the same vocation. Amongst those living in the same college at the time was William Pitt, four years younger than Cottle, but destined to become the country's youngest ever prime minister only eight years later. Wyatt certainly knew some powerful people.

Wyatt Cottle graduated in 1782 and was ordained two years later, becoming curate in the village of Ashbury, about nine miles west of Wantage, a deeply rural community on the edge of the Berkshire Downs and within sight of the ancient carved White Horse near Uffington. After four years he was promoted to deacon in the same parish. In 1796 his father died, making provision in his will for his two surviving daughters, but leaving most of his estate in Wiltshire and many properties in Bath to Wyatt and his brother Thomas. Revd Cottle was now a rich man.

Two years later, in February 1798, Wyatt Cottle was married in London at the age of 43. His bride, Lucretia Games, was nearly ten years younger, and gave him one daughter, Charlotte Lucy, and three sons: Henry Wyatt, John Morford and Thomas. The last two were born in Cholsey after their father became vicar at the beginning of 1801. He slowly established himself amongst the local gentry and acquired additional lands and properties, including the Swan Inn and the adjoining cottages on the Forty, which he bought in 1819 for the sum of £210. Throughout his ministry he lived in the large vicarage at the corner of The Causeway and Horn Lane, and perhaps he paid more attention to these living quarters than to his workplace. When the Dean of Wallingford carried out an inspection in 1812, he listed a dozen items that needed attention at the church, including the Bible, which was in a sorry state, plus some of the windows and pews – but found the vicarage to be in good repair.

Before he arrived in Cholsey, Wyatt Cottle took time off to visit the Holy Land and travel extensively in Palestine. Such a pilgrimage would have been a gruelling and expensive undertaking, but would have helped to raise his status amongst the clergy as a man of distinction and piety. However, he was also a tourist, and during a visit to Mount Lebanon he acquired two cedar saplings, which his wife reputedly carried safely home secured in her umbrella to plant in the vicarage garden[1]. In the early nineteenth century cedars of Lebanon were becoming a popular souvenir, and concerns were already being expressed about deforestation. After they settled into Cholsey, the trees steadily growing, the vicarage and garden became places of some refinement. By 1819 Revd Cottle was a well-known man of standing, presiding over a parish which had grown to include nearly 1,000 souls.

---

[1] These Cedars of Lebanon were a feature of the Wallingford Road until 1990 when they were felled for safety reasons. They were planted in 1801, according to an old resident speaking at the end of that century.

Fig. 1.2 Cholsey vicarage with the cedar of Lebanon c1904

John Huggins, by contrast, was from humble origins. He was uneducated, but could read and write, and by 1819 had already been parish clerk for 22 years. He was appointed by the previous incumbent, Revd Evan Evans, when he was only 24 years old, and he felt he had carried out his responsibilities well. The office of parish clerk was established in medieval times and was originally held by a cleric, which is the derivation of the term 'clerk'. It was not a job concerned with writing or administration, but with divine worship. The parish clerk was responsible for leading the singing and ensuring the correct responses by the congregation during the service, so a good voice was the primary requirement. In many parishes where there wasn't a sexton, including at Cholsey, the parish clerk was also responsible for the care and maintenance of the churchyard.

John had taken over the office of parish clerk in 1797 from the man who was now about to replace him, James Smith. James was the son of Bernard Smith, who had been parish clerk for seventeen years from 1779. In 1796 Bernard was thrown into the debtors' prison and Revd Evans dismissed him from his post, initially appointing his son as his replacement. But James was only thirteen years old and Revd Evans found him too young to carry out the task well, and the following year appointed John Huggins in his place. Now, with James Smith aged 36, the tables were turned.

John Huggins had married the year before he became parish clerk, at the age of 21. His bride was Phyllis Bosher, an eighteen-year-old girl from Brightwell. Like most of her generation she was illiterate, but proved very fecund and, over the next 28 years, she gave birth to fourteen children. What's more, they were strong and healthy babies, and all but two survived through their infant years. As time went by they ran out of common names and resorted to drawing from the Bible, naming the last four Naomi, Boaz,

Ruth and Orpah. They lived on The Forty, where John practised his trade as a shoemaker. Although their eldest was 22 by the time of the confrontation with the vicar, and several would have left home to earn a living elsewhere, the small cottage would still have been crammed with children. Six of them were under twelve, and Phyllis was, as usual, pregnant with the next, their thirteenth baby. The older girls would have helped with the housework and looked after the youngest ones, while the boys were sent out to work in the fields at bird-scaring or stone-picking to supplement the family income. At night they would have slept up to four to a bed, the bedchamber divided by a curtain to give some privacy, while during the day the house would have filled with smoke from the open fire as Phyllis heated water for breakfast gruel or some weak tea to accompany supper, while John worked in a corner of the room.

By chance, James Smith was another shoemaker, also living on The Forty. It was one of the easiest professions to enter, with only a little capital required, and was the most popular skilled occupation in the country. The result was that it did not pay well, and John Huggins needed his income from being the parish clerk to help support his family. The emolument was £1 6s per annum, equivalent to just 6d per week, although this might have been supplemented by other rights and entitlements. Even the pay would have been useful, as John may only have earned ten or fifteen shillings a week from his trade and would have had fixed outgoings, such as the rent for his cottage. On more than one occasion he had to fall back on the parish to support the family; such as in 1813, when the overseer allowed one of his sons a smock frock. Being parish clerk also gave him some standing in the community, a position of respect that John was angry to now have threatened.

* * *

One Friday towards the end of May in 1819, a group of men crept through the quiet churchyard and into the dimly-lit church. They were carrying picks, shovels and other implements. The two in the lead were brothers: James and John Hunt[1]. James was something of a historian and had surveyed the great tithe barn just before its demolition. John was a whitesmith[2] and iron founder with a useful business in the village.

In the floor of the confession room at one end of the church was a particularly fine stone that was carved with an effigy, probably a fourteenth

---

[1] It is possible that James and John Hunt were cousins rather than brothers.

[2] A whitesmith was a worker in tin, pewter or other light-coloured metals.

century lady. Who knew what historical treasures might lie beneath? The men set to lifting it with crowbars, and then dragged it aside. They started digging. The earth was soft and, as fast as they dug, the sides crumbled and began to refill the hole. Eventually they reached a depth of four feet where they uncovered some large bones. Then their shovels rang out as they hit the hard sides of a vault.

But they got no further. At that point the door to the confession room opened, and Robert Hardy, a local gentleman, came in. Seeing what they were up to, he demanded to know who had authorised the excavation and told them to stop at once. In the face of his demands, they were forced to give up on their clandestine research.

Fig. 1.3 The stone believed to be 'the effigy'

John Huggins knew about this episode, but heard no more until nearly two months later. Then, in fact, it was Revd Cottle's wife who intimated to him what was to come. She said that he had allowed certain persons to enter the church and commit sacrilege, and for that her husband intended to turn him out of his office. He denied being involved, but a few days later a note was delivered from the vicar, with the same text as was later read out before the congregation. After serving faithfully as parish clerk for 22 years, John felt ill-treated and humiliated. Not having been given any chance to defend himself against the accusations, he was determined not to give in without a fight.

As well as being dismissed from his office unjustly, John also felt that his violent ejection amounted to an assault. He might be poor but justice, at least in theory, was available to all. In this he was encouraged by the two men who led the digging operation in the church: James and John Hunt. James Hunt lived on The Causeway and, as well as being an amateur historian with a letter published in 'The Gentleman's Magazine', was a small-scale farmer. John Hunt was a well-known tradesman with premises in the East End of the village. A few years later he would be asked to recast two of the church's bells, and he also forged the heaviest bell for the parish church of nearby Blewbury. Alongside his name the latter is inscribed 'Nil

Desperandum[1]', perhaps related to the fact that he was declared bankrupt soon after.

With the support of others in the village, John Huggins sought out a Justice of the Peace and made his complaint. He was taken seriously, and the incident was listed for the next county Quarter Sessions. In addition to his complaint of assault against Revd Cottle, Huggins accused Richard Minshull and the other three people who helped him: Richard Robards, William Moore and Joseph Button. Richard Minshull of Home Farm was the closest friend of the vicar, the owner of 260 acres and also the lay rector, a churchwarden, overseer and constable. Richard Robards or Roberts was a farmer living in Drove Lane[2] who owned 120 acres of land and was also a constable. William Moore was a baker with a shop on The Forty, while Joseph Button was a victualler and farmer who owned a parcel of land on Horn Lane (and may well have been the landlord of the Chequers[3] too). They were both also tithingmen.

The summer Quarter Sessions had only recently finished so those involved had to wait several months before the hearing. As autumn approached speculation amongst parishioners must have continued, a ready topic of conversation as they worked hard to bring the harvest in.

* * *

On 19 October 1819 the Michaelmas Quarter Sessions opened in the county town of Abingdon. John Huggins would have walked the nine miles from Cholsey, or perhaps cadged a lift from a friend or some carter. During his lifetime he probably never strayed much beyond the village where he was born and neighbouring Wallingford. So after the quiet of the countryside, the crowded streets of Abingdon must have seemed exotic and exciting. As well as being the county town of Berkshire, Abingdon was important as the junction of the Wilts & Berks Canal and Thames waterways. The numerous tradesmen were augmented by all the lawyers, jurymen and witnesses visiting for the court hearings. Each Quarter Sessions began with a Grand Jury, and the twenty-three men chosen considered the cases listed and, with guidance from the magistrates, decided whether there was a case to answer. Where they decided positively, a 'true bill' was issued to indict the accused to appear before the court.

---

[1] Nil Desperandum means 'never despair'.

[2] The farm was probably what is now Kentwood Farm.

[3] The Chequers is now the Memories of Bengal in the Wallingford Road.

John Huggins waited nervously until his turn came to be called. Finally he stood before the bench, officials and the jurors sitting in closed session, and was asked to explain his accusation. He was allowed to call witnesses to back up his case. Although daunted, he was pleased that neither Revd Cottle nor his supporters were present during this time. At the end of his evidence, the jurors decided there was a case to answer. Revd Cottle and the others were indicted.

The indictment was that:

on the first day of August in the fifty ninth year of the Reign [etc.] ... and in and upon one John Huggins in the peace of God and our said Lord the King there and then being did make an assault on him, the said John Huggins, then and there did beat wound and ill-treat so that his Life was greatly despaired of and other wrongs to the said John Huggins then and there did to the great damage of the said John Huggins and against the peace of our said Lord the King his Crown and Dignity.

Perhaps the assault was rather exaggerated, but against all expectation, the Crown had adopted his case. However, justice was not going to be swift. Part of John's claim was for reinstatement as parish clerk and this was beyond the powers of the Quarter Sessions. The case was referred on to the Court of King's Bench, the highest criminal court in the land. The Crown v Cottle case and the humble Huggins were about to make the national press. Revd Cottle and his accomplices were not taken into custody, but recognisances[1] were demanded at a total cost of £40 for Wyatt Cottle, £100 for Richard Minshull, £80 for Richard Roberts, £20 for William Moore and £40 for Joseph Button.

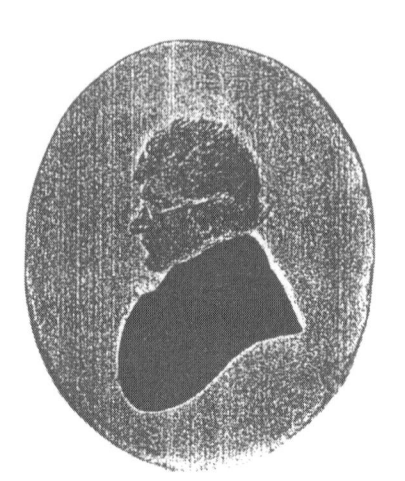

Fig. 1.4 Revd Wyatt Cottle

The Court of King's Bench dated from the twelfth century and heard both civil and criminal cases. The latter were mainly appeals and special cases from the lower courts, either the county Quarter Sessions of the local Justices of the Peace or the assizes, which were the courts that dealt with more serious crimes under the jurisdiction of circuit judges. Because the King's Bench hearings were in London, a long way to travel from distant parts of the realm, much of its business was conducted through

---

[1] Recognisances were bonds paid into court to ensure they appeared when summoned.

the medium of affidavits[1] rather than demanding that all the evidence be heard in person. On 3 November, at some expense, John Huggins travelled to Oxford and made his written statement before a Commissioner for Oaths.

The Court of King's Bench met in Westminster Hall, the ancient and cavernous hall in the Palace of Westminster that forms part of the Houses of Parliament. It is not clear whether John Huggins ever attended any of the hearings of the case, but if so he would have been overawed. First was the long uncomfortable journey, perhaps on the fast post coach from Wallingford which only took seven or eight hours, but more likely using less expensive means of transport: a slower coach, on foot, or using the wagon of some carter, which might take a couple of days. The dirt, smoke, noise and tumult of London would have been a shock to John, and the massive buildings around Westminster awe-inspiring.

Westminster Hall itself was over 700 years old and designed to impress with the majesty and power of the King's authority. The walls were six feet thick, it covered an area eight yards by twenty-two, and the magnificent ceiling reached forty feet above the ground. The King's throne and table used to stand in the hall, but now they were hidden behind the wooden

Fig. 1.5 Westminster Hall in the Palace of Westminster

---

[1] Affidavits are sworn statements.

screens enclosing the Court of King's Bench, where the proceedings were conducted in relative peace. But outside in the great hall, the vast space thronged with lawyers, litigants, spectators and Members of Parliament making their way to or from the chambers.

On Monday 8 November John Huggins' appointed counsel, Mr Cross, stood up in the court and moved for a rule to show cause why a writ of mandamus[1] should not be issued calling upon Revd Cottle of Cholsey to restore John Huggins to the office of parish clerk. The details of John's affidavit were presented to the court, causing some merriment amongst those present, used as they were to graver matters. The court granted the rule and set a hearing for the following week.

But Revd Cottle and his friends were putting all their effort into marshalling their defence, and their counsel, Thomas Smith of Reading, asked for a postponement while affidavits were gathered from a dozen witnesses scattered across the country. The defence team were in no hurry; the court's Michaelmas term came to an end and, as the Hilary term began in January 1820, statements were still being sworn. The work of the court was delayed slightly by the death on 29 January of George III, Shelley's 'old, mad, blind, despised, and dying king'. George IV acceded to the throne, now officially head of state rather than Regent, the position he had held for the last ten years during his father's insanity. On 12 February the King's Bench finally issued an order that all affidavits in the Cottle case had to be submitted by 18 April; the hearing would not now be until the Easter term.

John Huggins' accusation was that he had been assaulted and dismissed without cause. He denied being privy to sacrilege in the church, asserted that he had always carried out his duties responsibly, and claimed that he had neither been told of any deficiencies in his conduct prior to his dismissal nor been allowed to answer any accusations.

Revd Cottle's account couldn't have been more different. He said that Huggins was often intoxicated; on one occasion he had to refuse him the sacrament at communion, and on another he caused great embarrassment at a funeral. One Saturday Huggins spent the whole of the night at a public house and in the morning was so drunk and bruised from fighting that he was unable to carry out his duties. He had often reprimanded his clerk for these failings, but had been tolerant because he knew the man had a large family to support and needed the work. The reason that he had delayed in taking action after the sacrilegious act was that he had only been told by Robert Hardy about it on 8 July. He immediately confronted Huggins, who did not deny involvement, but behaved insolently and just laughed when

---

[1] A writ of mandamus is a court order requiring the carrying out of some duty.

told he would be dismissed. Further, Richard Minshull did not assault the man, rather it was Huggins who threw the constable to the ground when he tried to lead him away from his seat.

Joseph Hunt, a land-owing gentleman who had lived in Cholsey for thirty years, praised Revd Cottle's character of integrity, uprightness and the highest respectability. He said the vicar would never show harshness, indeed he was too lenient and had not responded to earlier calls by many inhabitants to dismiss his clerk. Richard Minshull supported this character assessment and claimed that Revd Cottle never spoke the strong words attributed to him in turning out the clerk. He had also seen Huggins drunk on several occasions and said that he mismanaged the churchyard, leaving it in an improper and indecent state, even with bones left lying on the ground.

These witnesses made much play of the fact that the vicar had customarily been the sole person to decide who should and should not be parish clerk. James Smith, the clerk in 1796 and again now, supported the fact, as did his father, Bernard Smith, who now lived in Peckham. Thomas Pither, a butcher and farmer, gave evidence of John Huggins' involvement in digging inside the church. He claimed that after the event he had met the clerk in the Chequers public house and Huggins had said that he had been hard at work in the church with Mr Hunt and others, and had then described what they had done. The butcher alleged that after saying to Huggins, "I suppose it was a good job for you," he received the reply "I was well paid for it and had as much beer as I could drink and some to carry home."

As well as defending himself against the charges of unfair dismissal and assault, Revd Cottle also made his own accusation of trespass for the incident in the church, accusing John Huggins, John and James Hunt, Joseph Hopkins the elder and N. Whittock. The hearing to consider the reinstatement of the clerk took place on 16 May. Mr Taunton spoke for the prosecution and Mr Nolan for the defence, but, despite all the evidence from Revd Cottle's supporters, the court did not believe him. A couple of weeks later, on 3 June 1820, the writ of mandamus was issued.

Wyatt Cottle was forced to comply, and a few days later responded with his grovelling agreement: 'I Wyatt Cottle ... Do in obedience to the said Writ most humbly certify and return to our sovereign Lord the King that I have restored John Huggins in the said Writ named into the place and Office of Parish Clerk ...'

But that was not the end of the matter; there was still the question of the assault and trespass, and the court appointed an arbitrator to resolve the whole sorry business. It all dragged on for many more months and it was

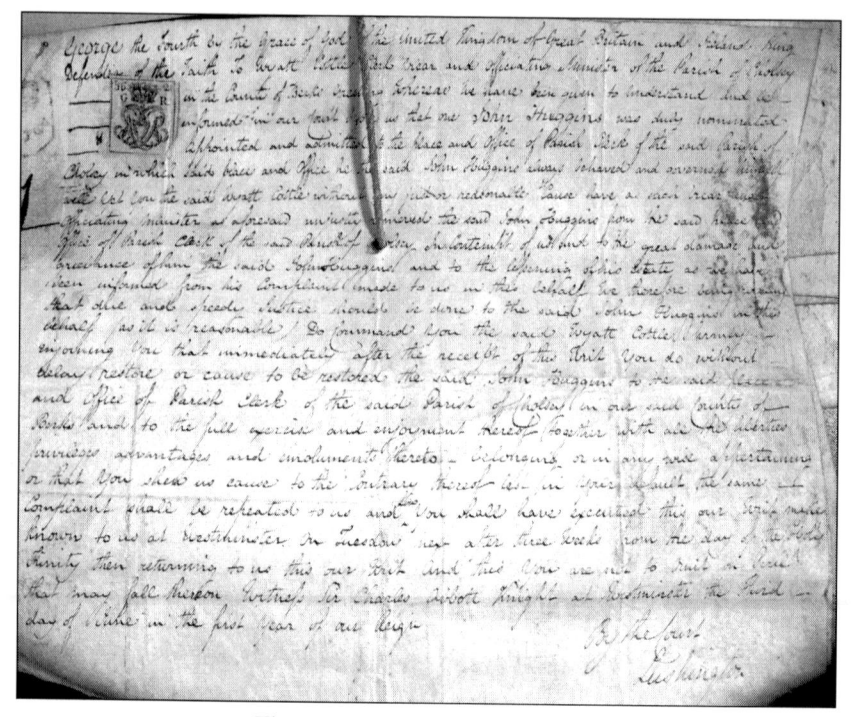

Fig. 1.6 The writ of mandamus

only in late autumn that the award was issued. The verdict was decidedly in John Huggins' favour.

The vicar and his four assistants were all found guilty of assault. Revd Cottle was ordered to not only meet his own costs, but also to pay for those of the four other defendants. John Huggins would resign his office as from 8 December, but would receive in compensation from Revd Cottle the sum of £96, which was to be paid by 1 January. On the question of trespass, John and James Hunt were found guilty, but John Huggins and the other two were exonerated. For the trespass the arbitrator only awarded one shilling in damages to the vicar, whilst ordering the vicar to pay all the costs of the three cleared defendants.

So John Huggins was completely vindicated and received a sum worth more than seventy years' pay as parish clerk, and far more than he could ever earn at his trade in a year. He must have been jubilant, and probably forever retold the tale over the succeeding years. For the vicar, he had at last rid himself of this troublesome clerk, for a mere hundred pounds or two.

* * *

That was the end of the parish clerk affair, but events in the following years showed that Revd Cottle was not so warmly regarded by his co-defendants as was written in their affidavits. Less than three years later, the vicar was back in court; this time a civil matter about an unpaid blacksmith's bill. The blacksmith was William Moore, 78 years old and the father of the William Moore who was accused with Cottle over the assault. The two old men couldn't sort out their differences amicably and resorted to the assizes to resolve the argument. The verdict again went against the vicar and he was ordered to pay £11 8s.

In 1828 Wyatt Cottle fell out with his so-called close friend and associate from the Huggins affair, Richard Minshull. It was an argument over the tithes and this time Revd Cottle was the plaintiff. The substance of the dispute was that Richard Minshull had been unjustly taking an income from the annual hay harvest along with his entitlement to the much larger 'great tithe'. Counsel for the plaintiff called several witnesses aged over 70 years who attested that the hay tithe customarily belonged to the vicar. Richard Minshull's counsel held that an even older document from the diocesan archives in Salisbury would show differently, but that his witness had gone there and not yet returned. The judge admonished him for not being better prepared and awarded £63 damages to Revd Cottle, three times the value of the tithe.

Revd Cottle was by then an old man of 73. The previous year his wife Lucretia had died whilst on a visit in Wiltshire, aged 63. She was buried in the Cottle ancestral village of Monkton Farleigh. By then their three sons had left home, Henry and Thomas to follow their father into the church and John to become a doctor. Their daughter Charlotte was still unmarried and probably continued to live in the large house with her widower father, while Henry returned in September 1827 to act as curate in Cholsey for a short while before becoming rector of Watford in Northamptonshire.

Five years after his wife, one May Sunday, Wyatt Cottle himself died. He was buried five days later in a fine grave to the west of the nave which is marked: 'Sacred to the Memory of The Revd Wyatt COTTLE L.L.B., 31 years vicar of the Parish, who departed this life May 27th 1832, Aged 77 years.'

A month earlier his son Thomas had became curate of the chapel at Moulsford under his father, and the following year he also became curate at Cholsey. He could not continue to occupy the vicarage, however, as it would belong to the new incumbent. On 24 and 25 July 1832 the contents were sold by auction. These included ten bedsteads with feather bedding, eight mahogany wardrobes and chests of drawers, and numerous other furniture, crockery and kitchen utensils. Also included in the sale were

Fig. 1.7 Revd Cottle's grave at the rear of the church

brewing equipment, a two-year-old bay colt, a phaeton[1] and horses, eight pigs, a cow and six stocks of bees.

Despite the welcome payout as a result of his legal action, John Huggins could never imagine owning so many possessions. He never again came to the attention of the newspapers and continued working at his trade in the village for the rest of his life, dying at the age of 70 in June 1845. He just missed seeing the comeuppance for his successor as parish clerk. In 1846 James Smith, now 63 years old, was reprimanded for not keeping the church clean. The following year, in a court before the archdeacon in the vestry room, following strict ecclesiastical procedure so as to avoid any repeat of the Huggins debacle, James was dismissed. John's wife Phillis must have been amused to witness these events. A pauper supported by the parish on 2s 11d a week, with her large family scattered across the country, she died on 21 March 1853, aged 75. She was buried, like her husband, in an unmarked grave.

So ends the story of the poor shoemaker who challenged the ruling gentry over a minor upset, took the case all the way to Westminster, and won. However, the poor working men of the countryside did not often prevail over their wealthy employers, as the events of 1830 demonstrated.

---

[1] A phaeton was an open four-wheeled carriage.

Chapter 2 The Swing Riots

Early in the afternoon of Monday 22 November 1830 Elizabeth, the young wife of John Potts, was standing by the gate of the workhouse on the Wantage Road in Wallingford when she saw seven or eight men approaching from Brightwell through Slade End field. They were carrying bludgeons. The mass vandalism and violence that had been sweeping the country over the last few days had arrived. She heard one of the men, William Champion, declare that there would be no more machinery on the neighbourhood farms and that they intended to break any they found. Elizabeth asked if any more men were following behind, and William replied, "There will be about a thousand of them by and by."

A few minutes later Elizabeth's husband John spotted the men coming along Picked Piece[1] towards the town and going into the Cross Keys public house. The previous day most of the town's law-abiding citizens had been sworn in as special constables and divided into companies led by a captain. John went to raise the alarm. Champion and his ragged band moved on to St Mary's Lane where they went into the French Horn public house. They boasted of the numbers they were collecting to the cause and the fight to come, when a cry went up that a group had arrived in the Market Place. When he heard that in fact they were a body of special constables armed with staves, Champion said, "Blast my eyes, I will smash the bloody buggers' heads, six at a time!"

The band of wreckers headed out of the town, followed by one of the specials, and crossed into Cholsey parish at Winterbrook,. On the turnpike road the gang met William Greenwood, a Cholsey tenant farmer, and Champion asked him for sixpence to buy a pot of beer. He refused and walked on, and Champion called after him, "Have you not got a threshing machine? If you have it will soon be broken to pieces." Another of the gang shouted, "You have and we'll break it." At about 4 p.m., close to Winterbrook Gate, they met Revd James Hazel of Clapcot[2] and asked for money. He exhorted them not to cause any damage and gave them two sixpences.

---

[1] Picked Piece was the section of land to the west of the Cross Keys beside the road to Wantage.

[2] The parish of Clapcot was on the north side of Wallingford.

The band then repaired to Wakefield's public house[1] in Winterbrook for more ale and some bread and cheese. William Keeling, one of the special constables, followed them in and asked them to avoid any violence and not to return home through Wallingford. Champion said, "We are not going to injure anyone, nor set fire to any ricks, but we are going to break all the machines we can find." He also said that they would go back to the market town, "Damn my eyes, I don't care if there are one hundred constables, for I have not molested anyone."

Soon afterwards they left and headed for Orchard End[2]. A large body of constables was waiting for them and one, Richard Arding, went up to David Hulcup, one of the wreckers, saying, "In the King's name, you are my prisoner." Hulcup held up his bludgeon, but the constables attacked the men with their staves, seriously injuring Hulcup and some of the others. Nine men were taken into custody.

* * *

The unrest that had exploded across the country sprang from the plight of agricultural labourers, driven to desperation by the powers that regulated their lives. Much of their wherewithal to survive was controlled by the parish, working in concert with the county Justices of the Peace, and daily life was dictated by the interactions between three main groups: the gentry, the farmers and the workers. Everyone was taught to respect their place in the hierarchy, and children learnt to recite the catechism: 'To submit myself to my pastors and masters, and to order myself lowly and respectfully to all my betters.'

The gentry typically consisted of the parson, the squire, and other wealthy gentlefolk. They were expected to be charitable and act for the good of the community, but not of course to the detriment of themselves, and they ruled through the meetings of the vestry in the parish and the Quarter Sessions in the county. The farmers worked the land and employed the labourers, sometimes just one or two and sometimes in larger numbers. The workers consisted not only of the labourers, but also the small tradesmen, such as the blacksmith, shoemaker, publican and shopkeeper.

In Cholsey the gentry were few in number, because of its rural character and the lack of a squire, most land being owned by interests outside the parish. Solicitors, doctors and other professionals tended to migrate to

---

[1] William Wakefield was the landlord of the public house more commonly known as the Nag's Head, now a private house on the Reading Road in Winterbrook.

[2] It is unclear where Orchard End was, although a house with this name exists in Brightwell.

Wallingford, leaving just the parson, Revd Cottle, and perhaps the odd retired cleric, annuitant or medium-sized landowner in the gentry class. For this reason, the larger tenant farmers filled the gap and had positions of some importance in managing the affairs of the village.

About three-quarters of the 240 or so working men in Cholsey toiled on the land. In many parts of Europe, peasants often owned a small piece of land and could exist largely by subsistence farming. But in England such people were few in number, and most worked for wages, perhaps supplemented by access to common or waste land, a small plot for vegetables and possibly a chicken or a pig. Set on Cholsey Hill, Cholsey Farm was the largest employer in the parish. It was the property of the Lord of the Manor, originally Lord Kensington, but the title and lands were bought by George Payne Esq. sometime before 1825. Neither of them ever lived in Cholsey.

By the nineteenth century the heart of the parish was clearly centred around The Forty, but the farms were mainly located in hamlets spread out around the periphery. North of the church and Cholsey Farm were Greenhill, Hillgreen and Hithercroft farms; towards Wallingford were Winhurst and Winterbrook farms. South of the church were Pancroft, Barn Elms, Minshulls and Lollingdon, whilst closer in to the village were to be found Blackall's, Pound, Drove Lane and Honey Lane farms[1]. The large farms might employ a dozen adult labourers plus half-a-dozen boys. In addition to these, many smallholdings of just a few acres were dotted about, mainly worked by a single family employing at most one or two labourers. The farmers running all of these enterprises were largely tenants, or owned just a minority of their holdings and rented the rest.

Apart from the manor land, most of the parish was still free of enclosure with large open fields divided into strips, usually 220 yards (a furlong) long and traditionally 22 yards (a chain) wide, separated from the next by long mounds. Such a strip was an acre of land, with a furlong the length a team of oxen could plough before resting, and an acre the amount they could plough in a day. However, in Cholsey many of the strips were narrower than a chain and some wider. A large farm might encompass many different plots spread around the parish, whilst some villagers might own or rent a single strip.

---

[1] Some of these farms no longer exist and some have changed their name. Cholsey Farm is now Manor Farm; Minshulls was later called Rectory and is now Westfield Farm; whilst Drove Lane is now Kentwood.

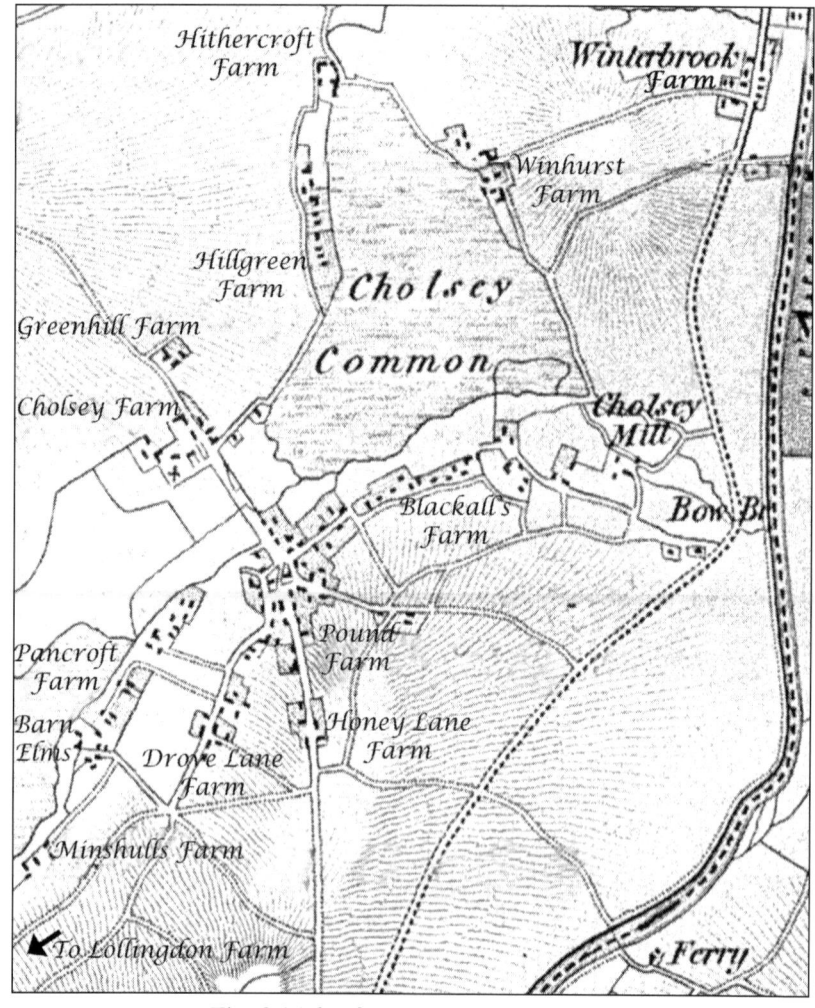

Fig. 2.1 The farms in Cholsey c1830

Much of the earth was a rich fine loam and worked in a four-year rotation. After fallowing came the wheat, followed the next year by beans, then barley, and then back to fallow. Once every eight years broad clover was sown to enrich the soil. The wheat was threshed and the grain taken to the mill on Cholsey brook, which stood near to the Thames, to turn into flour for bread. The beans were harvested in August when the pods turned black and the seeds usually fed to the horses and pigs, although in poor times they were milled and mixed with the flour. The barley was normally sent to Wallingford, which was famous for its sixteen malting houses and Mr Wells' brewery, reputedly the largest in the country. Lands to the north and east of the parish were rather gravelly and were often laid to sainfoin[1] or

---

[1] Sainfoin is a purple-flowered leguminous forage crop suitable for dry alkaline soils.

grass for grazing by sheep. Turnips were also grown on this land for the benefit of the flocks, or carted away as feed for horses or pigs. They were eaten by the poor too, who also had access by tradition to common land and could sometimes gather bean stalks to use as fuel, the resulting ash being saleable as compost.

The working man's food staple was bread, perhaps supplemented by potatoes, onions and vegetables grown on a small piece of garden. In good times there might also be butter or cheese, and perhaps a little bacon. A typical breakfast might have been bread with broth flavoured with herbs or bacon scraps, or gruel made from oats or barley[1]. At midday dinner might be cabbage, bread and butter or cheese, with perhaps bacon for the wage earner and the children; while supper could be potatoes, more gruel, or bread with butter or cheese and onions. A typical labourer might eat 1½ lb of bread and 10 oz of potatoes a day, although a greater proportion of bread was preferred as potatoes were seen as inferior food and involved the trouble of heating water over the open fire. However, a few leaves from a twist of tea might be used to provide an accompanying weak but warming beverage.

Free flour could be obtained by gleaning missed corn ears after harvest and the diet could be supplemented by gathering nuts and berries or searching for edible mushrooms. Snaring the abundant rabbit population was also seen as a right by most rural workers, although the law termed it poaching if and when they were caught. More favourably viewed was the netting and trapping of avian pests: sparrows, crows, rooks and pigeons. Blackbird or pigeon pie would have been a welcome change to the monotony of the family's usual diet.

In 1795 there was a landmark decision affecting wage rates at the Pelican Inn in Speenhamland, a village on the outskirts of Newbury. Berkshire Justices of the Peace met to discuss the fact that the current labourer's wage was generally insufficient to meet the needs of an 'industrious' family man. Wages were typically set locally by the magistrates, perhaps at 10s a week for a married man and 8s for a single labourer. However, the meeting did not decide to increase this pay, but rather to allow the use of the poor rate to supplement wages. Paupers were traditionally supported by the parish through the poor rate under the scrutiny of the vestry and the overseer, and now these funds would also be used to supplement the incomes of those with large families or facing periods of unemployment. In many ways this decision led to much of the misery that followed.

---

[1] Gruel was a sort of watery porridge.

The 'Speenhamland System', as it was known, was taken up widely throughout southern England. It included a specification of the support to be offered: 'When the gallon loaf[1] shall cost 1s, then every poor and industrious man shall have for his own support 3s weekly either produced by his own or his family's labour, or an allowance from the Poor Rate.' For family men the rate was 4s 6d and the allowance rose or fell in step with the price of bread. During the Napoleonic Wars the price of bread rose steeply, but wages also held up because of the shortage of manpower in the countryside. However, after the battle of Waterloo in 1815, up to a quarter of a million men returned from the front desperate for work. The price of wheat fell amid a general economic depression and farmers tried to cut back their costs. The standard of living of the average rural worker steadily deteriorated.

At the same time mechanisation was improving productivity for the larger farmers. Separating the seed from the corn was traditionally a labour-intensive process that took most of the winter, carried out by men using flails on the barn floor[2]. It was repetitive and gruelling work, but paid well and lasted over the months when there was little other farming work available. However, through the early part of the nineteenth century threshing machines, often horse powered, gradually spread, taking only a fraction of the time and a fraction of the labour.

Fig. 2.2 Threshing with a flail

---

[1] A gallon or half peck loaf was at the time the common measure of bread and weighed 8lb 11oz.

[2] A flail was two sticks joined by a flexible knot.

Earlier in the eighteenth century many labourers, especially single men, were hired for the year and lived in as farm servants with their accommodation and food provided. As the nineteenth century progressed, the practice declined and most worked as agricultural labourers paid by the day or the week and laid off when there was no work, which could mean most of the winter, when life was at its hardest. In addition cottage industries, such as weaving, straw plaiting or the manufacture of tools by local blacksmiths, gradually became unprofitable as industrialisation progressed. Incomes were squeezed and unemployment increased, and agricultural workers had little to fall back on.

Many were forced to go cap in hand to the parish for help. Not only did this sap the dignity of the labourers, but it put increasing demands on those who paid the poor rate, not just the large landowners, but also the small farmers and tradesmen. The increase in support for paupers also encouraged overseers to emphasise the words 'industrious man' in the Speenhamland system and refuse help to those who held rebellious views or those the rulers of the parish felt were not trying hard enough to find work.

Meanwhile the larger farmers became wealthier because of increased productivity and reduced labour costs. They aspired to be gentlemen, relinquishing any hands-on work and leaving the management of the men to the farm bailiff[1]. Much of the cost of supporting the agricultural labourers had been shifted to those who paid the poor rate. In Cholsey there were just a handful of large landowners and tenant farmers, but many who owned smallholdings and had to pay the tax.

Although the action by the workers was against the farmers in terms of breaking machines and demanding higher wages, it was rather the gentry who they primarily blamed. In addition to the rent due to the landowners, tenant farmers were also obliged to pay tithes. This hated tax went to the vicar, Revd Cottle in Cholsey, who was already a wealthy man, and the lay rector, Richard Minshull and sometime after his death the Comtesse de Broc, neither of whom did anything to earn the income. It is not surprising, then, that the parson and his well-fed gentleman cronies were the focus of much of the labourers' anger.

Enclosure was another factor behind the riots. Parish by parish, by local agreement or Act of Parliament, the old system of farming strips was giving way to enclosed fields. While this increased efficiency for farmers by consolidating far flung pieces of land into much larger plots, it also had

---

[1] A farm bailiff was the agent of the landowner, perhaps acting as foreman to the workers, paying the hands and keeping the land clear of poachers.

negative effects on the poor. Common and waste lands were often lost, and access was denied to what were once open strip fields. As well as the loss of gathering and grazing rights, fenced and hedged land made poaching more difficult.

The result of these changes was that, by the end of the 1820s, many labouring families were hungry and some close to starvation. Then came a series of poor harvests. In July 1828 the rains were so violent that fields were flooded, hay washed away and the corn laid flat. In 1829 there were only four fine days between 16 June and 20 September, and on 6 and 7 October snow fell. Harvest time was when labourers worked longer hours and earned a little more to pay for additional necessities such as clothes and shoes. As a result of the reduced harvests, not only was food in short supply, but working families had less money to buy it with. Then came the terrible winter of 1829/30, the worst for a hundred years, when, between 20 December and 7 February, thick snow lay on the ground and the temperature was rarely above freezing.

At the Berkshire Quarter Sessions in January 1830 Charles Dundas MP, chairman of the magistrates, said, "The poor are in a most miserable state, and I fear it is too generally the practice to beat them down so low, as well in wages as parochial allowances, as to leave them scarcely sufficient to maintain even their existence. The consequence is that they are almost driven to the commission of dishonest acts." But nothing was done to remedy the problem and Colonel Dundas would later be a key figure in the pursuit of the rioters and would pass some of the most severe sentences on the guilty.

The leader in the *Reading Mercury* accompanying the Quarter Sessions speech said: 'If a scheme for the promotion of pauperism had been intentionally devised, it could hardly have been done more effectively than by our present Poor Laws, which go on from year to year increasing the national burdens and aggravating the very evils they sought to cure. They unfortunately derive support from an interested class, who, by paying their labourers out of the rates, contrive to throw on others the charge of paying their servants. The peasantry are thus doomed to a state of perpetual helotage[1].'

Summer 1830 was also cold and wet. In Paris, over 'three glorious days' in July, a second revolution overthrew Charles X. Talk of French agitators crossing the channel became commonplace. The previous month George IV had died, to be replaced by William IV, and at the following election the Whigs, the forerunners of the Liberals, gained fifty seats. Those who

---

[1] Helotage was serfdom or a state midway between slavery and citizenship.

supported the labouring classes were hopeful of change brought about by parliamentary reform, but then on 2 November the Prime Minister, the Duke of Wellington, delivered a speech in which he said bluntly that not only would he not propose any reform, but he would actively oppose such a possibility. The autumn had seen another unimpressive harvest and with winter approaching, the working classes, hungry and desperate, had had enough. The only surprise was that a revolt did not happen earlier.

* * *

The unrest, which came to be known as the Swing Riots, had begun in Kent earlier in the year, with threatening letters sent to farmers signed by the mythical Captain Swing[1]. Arson attacks began in June in Orpington, and hayricks, barns and even whole farms were burnt to the ground. The first threshing machine was broken in a village near Canterbury towards the end of August 1830, and the movement gathered pace through October. Initially the attacks had been midnight forays under cover of darkness, but now large gangs roamed the countryside in broad daylight, demanding higher wages and extorting money or refreshments.

Fig. 2.3 Setting light to hayricks in 1830

---

[1] The name might have arisen from 'swingel', the part of a flail which strikes the corn to release the grain.

In November the troubles reached Berkshire and Oxfordshire, which became two of the worst affected counties. Mr Sharp, a landowner who had acquired the farm of Mr Freeman in the village of Fawley, near Henley, received a letter from 'Kent Swing': 'I understand you are the little King at Fawley now, and Pope is the Queen, and you and him have said that you and him would fetch the fat off Mr Freeman's men, which I understand you will: but mind yourself as you go to market, old red-face … we mean to give Fawley a bit of a rout out … and remember, without you alter your hand, we shall soon make you glad to do it.'

Arson attacks were made on Berkshire farms on 12 and 16 November, and on the 18th a mob went on the rampage in the Thatcham area, blowing horns and destroying machinery through the night. The next day they continued through Aldermaston and other parishes breaking machinery and demanding money, beer and food. At Brimpton, a mile south of the Bath Road, Revd Edward Cove was ready for them, having assembled 100 local tradesmen and special constables. The mob of around 150 approached three abreast down the street and Mr Cove confronted them, announcing that he was a magistrate and they must disperse. As they continued to press forward, he read the Riot Act, "Our Sovereign Lord the King chargeth and commandeth all persons being assembled immediately to disperse themselves and peaceably to depart to their habitations, or to their lawful business, upon the pains contained in the act made in the first year of King George for preventing tumult and riotous assemblies. God Save the King." As his words died away the mob laid into the constables and a free-for-all began with sticks, sledgehammers and fists. Some of the defenders were knocked to the ground, but many of the mob ran away and the constables gradually got the upper hand. A dozen of the rioters were captured and taken to Reading gaol.

Two days later, the day before the trouble in Winterbrook, the riots spread to Oxfordshire. On that Sunday, 21 November, it became known

Fig. 2.4 A French horse-powered threshing machine

that Thomas Newton, a large farmer of Crowmarsh, was about to make another attempt at obtaining an Act of Parliament for enclosures in the parish of Bensington[1]. A large crowd, estimated by some at over 1,000, gathered in the churchyard after morning service to await the fixing by the farmer of a notice on the subject. When no one came, about 200 stormed off to his premises in Crowmarsh, broke open the barn and destroyed the threshing machine. Subsequently the mob went to Ewelme, Bensington and other parishes and committed similar acts.

Through the second half of November, unrest spread around the country. Apart from the trouble in Winterbrook, Cholsey appears to have escaped attacks and none of the inhabitants were arrested for riot, although the events all around must have been of high concern. Perhaps Cholsey labourers were in a slightly better state than in neighbouring parishes. Enclosure was still a long way off and the parish was predominantly made up of large open fields. Having one's own land was more common, with 28 land-owning electors living in the parish, and over 100 tenants working at least one of the acre-size strips. Perhaps a third of working class families could grow their own crops, and all had access to 460 acres of down and common. Two ancient commons, in East Moor and West Moor[2], were still in existence, although only a few inhabitants had legal commoners' rights.

Nevertheless there were still plenty of poor in the parish, many of whom had to go begging to the overseer for help to ward off starvation. Most went cap in hand, but some were obstreperous, such as Maria Taylor. Earlier that year, on a Monday in June, she had gone along to the church to see William Goodchild, a deputy overseer, and asked for relief. She was a single woman with an income of only 7d a day, but Mr Goodchild decided that she was capable of earning more and refused any support. "Be damned if I won't have it," said Maria, snatching a shilling from the table and running off. She was brought before the magistrate but was unrepentant, saying she would do the same thing again under the same circumstances. She was sentenced to fourteen days' imprisonment with hard labour. At least in prison she was offered regular meals.

On Friday 19 November, when news of the unrest in the south of the county would have been the talk of the village, Edward Durbridge, 29, thought that he would also take matters into his own hands. Whilst working

---

[1] Bensington is now known as Benson.

[2] East Moor was the larger piece of land, also known as Cholsey Common, situated to the northwest of the present Wallingford Road just outside the village, while West Moor was to the southwest of West End.

at Barn Elms Farm he took a sack of barley and hid it in a hayrick. Unfortunately, the son of the owner, John Hunt, spotted the sack and set a man to watch. Edward was seen collecting the goods and when his house was later searched, some of the barley was found. At the Quarter Sessions in Reading the following January he was found guilty and, as this was a second offence, sentenced to seven years' transportation[1].

After the trouble in Wallingford on Monday 22 November, regular night patrols were instituted and no strangers were allowed to enter the town without being challenged. The following morning at 8 a.m. a mob arrived in Streatley at Farmer Froome's. They had been roaming the area all night and demanding from each of the farms 5s and a signature on a paper promising increased wages of 12s a week for married labourers and 9s for single men. Mr Froome gave them the money and the mob enlisted his three labourers, who had been at work threshing, and broke their machine. The men did the same at another farm in the village before moving on to Basildon. Soon afterwards they were surprised by a troop of soldiers and eleven were taken prisoner.

At 9 a.m. the following day a crowd of 100 men or more gathered in Aston Tirrold, shouting, "More money for labour!" Not all the labourers were involved in the disturbance, but when William Pope was accompanying the parish constable Thomas Herbert to Wallingford to be sworn in as a special, William was dragged back. The mob went round the farms of the village and those in Aston Upthorpe, demanding wages of 2s a day now and 2s 6d after Lady Day (meaning the winter and summer rates). At Henry Slade's farm they were met by his wife and asked her for beer. She said, "You coming in this riotous manner will not induce me to give you beer; if you came in a peaceable manner I might. I am not at all daunted or afraid of you." Their leader, James Bennett, said, "Hush, how would it be if you had your farm set on fire?" Charlotte Slade said that she hoped they wouldn't, and the mob left.

When they arrived at Charlotte's father-in-law's farm, John Slade asked them what they wanted.

"To break your machines," said Bennett.

"What do you want to do that for?" asked Mr Slade. "I am obliged to hire men out of the parish to work mine."

"We are going to break everyone's machines," replied Bennett, "but we won't do you any harm."

A call for beer then went up, which Mr Slade provided, and some of the men asked for an advance in their wages.

---

[1] Transportation to the penal colonies in Australia is described later in Chapter 3.

"I will give you what the magistrates allow," said Mr Slade.

"Down with the magistrates!" shouted the mob.

The response of the authorities to the troubles was uncompromising. Initially it was left to the local magistrates and constables to deal with the problem, but as the contagion spread, the new Home Secretary, Lord Melbourne, mobilised the yeomanry and called out regular forces in support. The protestors were poorly organised and moderate in the steps they were prepared to take to fight for their cause. From Newbury a detachment of the Grenadier Guards and several hundred farmers and gentlemen swept through the surrounding villages capturing the ringleaders. By the end of the month the open rebellion was over.

In Berkshire the prisoners were taken to Reading or Abingdon gaol to await trial. The people of Newbury witnessed a particularly heart-rending scene when the vans to convey the men to Reading drew up in the marketplace. Under the supervision of a troop of Lancers and the yeomanry, with sabres drawn, they were brought out in batches while their womenfolk fought their way to the front of the crowd for a parting word, perhaps the last for ever. One poor woman, with eight children and a baby at her breast, only managed to press the manacled hands of her husband as he took his seat.

A special commission was appointed to try those held and proceedings began on 27 December 1830. There were 138 men on trial and Reading thronged with witnesses, lawyers and concerned relatives. On 5 January 1831 the commission moved on to Abingdon, where there were a further 47 prisoners, including some of the Wallingford and Aston Tirrold ringleaders. Four men were tried for the disturbances in Wallingford and Winterbrook: William Champion, his brother James, William Greenaway and David Hulcup. They were charged with conspiring with diverse others to break threshing machines, to create riots and disturb the peace, to the terror of His Majesty's peaceable subjects.

Fig. 2.5 Reward poster

After the evidence had been heard, Mr Carrington, speaking for the defence, pointed out that no machines had actually been broken and no assaults made by the men, although they themselves had been severely beaten by the special constables. Two farmers from Berrick spoke of the good character of the two Champions. The jury found all four guilty;

William was sentenced to twelve months' imprisonment with hard labour, and the other three men to six months' each. They appeared grateful for the judge's leniency.

Most of those charged with the insurrection at Streatley were acquitted, but Thomas Hanson was found guilty of breaking three threshing machines and sentenced to transportation for fourteen years. The four ringleaders from Bensington were given seven years' transportation. The six men charged after the Aston Tirrold disturbances escaped lightly, with two months' imprisonment for James Bennett and the others discharged upon entering into their own recognisances to keep the peace in the amount of £20.

Over the eleven days of trials many other Berkshire men received similar fines or periods of imprisonment, but 43 men were sentenced to transportation and three received the death penalty. In the wider country, over 600 were imprisoned, around 500 transported and 19 executed. Following numerous petitions for clemency, two of the Reading men facing death had their sentences reduced to transportation. But on 11 January 1831 William Winterbourne, the leader from Kintbury of major disturbances in West Berkshire, was taken from his cell in Reading gaol to the scaffold high up on the west wall facing the ruins of the abbey. An immense crowd watched in expectation while a white cap was pulled over his face. As the prison clock finished striking twelve noon, the lever was pulled and he dropped and struggled his last, a suppressed groan rising from the crowd. A few moments later vendors began shouting out their wares; pamphlets claiming to be Winterbourne's valedictory speech in which he admitted that the sentence was just.

* * *

The result of the crackdown was that protest went underground. Disaffected labourers returned to making forays under cover of darkness, with dozens of ricks and barns burnt down across the country in January 1831 alone. Despite the victory of the authorities, farmers and the ruling classes remained fearful of another uprising, and attempts were made to alleviate the suffering of agricultural workers. Promised wage increases were maintained, poor law payments made more generous, and attempts to squeeze more out of labourers abandoned. What's more, the hated threshing machines that had been destroyed were not replaced and the adoption of new devices was halted. Although the summer of 1831 was again quite wet, the weather conditions were not as bad and the harvest improved. Gradually the fire-setting reduced and relations became more amicable.

Nevertheless the plight of the agricultural labourer was still precarious and some continued to turn to rural crime to relieve their lot. In November

1831 James Cock was caught stealing two fowls from William Goodchild in Cholsey. He was later sentenced to six weeks' imprisonment with hard labour. A year or so later John Randall and John Cripps were accused of stealing wood from Mr Washbourne of Cholsey Farm, although the charges were dropped just before the trial.

Anonymous protests continued too, although the motive behind the Cholsey arson attack of December 1832 was not clear. It was during a general election, the first after the Great Reform Act, which abolished many of the 'rotten boroughs' and redistributed parliamentary seats according to population. Wallingford lost its two seats and now would elect just one member from a constituency that also included Cholsey and other local parishes. Feelings were running high against the Whig candidate, Mr Eyston, who was accused of gross corruption. Contrary to the national position where the Conservatives had opposed the Reform Bill, the Conservative candidate, Mr Blackstone, was a supporter of reform, anti-corruption and believed in the abolition of slavery in the colonies.

Voting was scheduled to take place at Wallingford on Monday 10 December[1], but the previous day the talk in Cholsey was of a local disaster. The parish contained fifty-nine electors, most of them wealthy gentlemen and landowners, but James Powell was different. He called himself an agricultural labourer, but was now eligible to vote thanks to the three acres of land which he owned in six strips in the common fields. At 2 a.m. on the Sunday morning his family was awoken by the smell of smoke. An outbuilding of their farmhouse that contained hay was on fire. They barely had time to leave before the thatch had caught and the whole house was ablaze. In a few minutes their home and all their possessions, together with those of their next door neighbour, were consumed.

A Justice of the Peace from Streatley, William Stone, was at the scene later that day and confirmed to his satisfaction that it was indeed arson. Mr Stone felt that the motive was associated with the election, but whether it was James Powell's intentions in this regard or some other harm he had caused, is not clear. Recently Mr Stone had investigated several cases of fire-setting, and as before he immediately wrote to the Home Secretary, Lord Melbourne, requesting that the government issue a reward for the apprehension of the culprit or culprits. The sum of £150 was authorised, to be matched by local money, and it attracted one of the country's foremost detectives, Samuel Taunton of Bow Street.

---

[1] Elections at that time took place on different days in different constituencies over a period of a month or more.

Colloquially known as the Bow Street Runners, these agents of Bow Street magistrates' court had been the foremost law agents in the capital, and more widely in the country, until the establishment of the Metropolitan Police three years earlier. They were often paid not by the court or the government, but by the rewards of grateful citizens, and, until the regular police established a detective division, they still continued their investigative work. Samuel Taunton was one of their most senior members, having been a Principal Officer for more than twenty years.

Fig. 2.6 A Bow Street Runner

But, as with most cases of arson, it appears he had no luck in tracking down the arsonist. Meanwhile, in the election, Mr Blackstone won comfortably, by 195 to 151 votes. The *Berkshire Chronicle* was triumphant, saying that the district had been 'emancipated from the fetters which a low and corrupt faction have for so long imposed upon every honest and independent elector'.

Before and after this election, partly in response to the Swing Riots, the government had started to look at the implementation of the poor law. However, they were probably more concerned about how to reduce what were seen as the onerous rates of taxation on landowners than to improve the plight of the poor. The end result was the Poor Law Amendment Act of 1834, which established new entities called Poor Law Unions, which would look after the destitute from a collection of local parishes. Able-bodied men and women would no longer be allowed to receive outdoor relief and could only be supported after entry into purpose-built workhouses. These were meant to be useful houses of industry, but soon became dispiriting and monotonous semi-prisons where families were split up and men segregated from their wives.

The Wallingford Poor Law Union was established on 2 June 1835 under the control of a Board of Guardians, and the existing Wallingford workhouse on Wantage Road in the town was extended to incorporate inmates from neighbouring parishes. The ownership of the poor houses held by Cholsey Parish was transferred to the new Union, who sold them in August 1836. The choice for the destitute of the parish was now stark. No longer would those on low wages be able to augment them with poor law payments. It was either earn enough to survive or be consigned to the workhouse, for who knows how long. Perhaps this choice was a spur to the confrontation that happened in Cholsey in August 1835.

For as long as anybody could remember, groups of Irishmen had roamed the country around harvest time seeking work. Many found employment, as farmers needed many extra hands to bring all the crops in. But the availability of this cheap labour sometimes prevented local people earning extra wages from the long hours, income that was crucial to supporting the family through the hard winter to come. The end of July was very hot, with the temperature often in the high 80s, and a group of Cholsey agricultural labourers decided that they were going to do something about the forthcoming annual Irish invasion.

On Sunday 2 August the confrontation came. A party of about twenty Irishmen arrived, expecting to secure work as in previous years. A larger body of Cholsey men declared that they were not welcome, but the Irish armed themselves with reaping hooks and a furious fight ensued. It is lucky that nobody was killed in the incident, and one of the tithingmen, who came to try and quell the disturbance, was seriously injured by a slash to his thigh. The affair was later investigated by William Stone of Streatley and another Justice of the Peace, but no one in particular could be identified as causing the breach of the peace and nobody was prosecuted.

It is not clear how successful the village vigilantes were in protecting their incomes that year, but it was not the last time that desperate labourers took the law into their own hands.

Chapter 3 The Ilsley Family

It was cold and dark when William Parsons crept into James Ilsley's room at 4 a.m. on that morning in January. The year of 1835 was just five days old, but the two had already hatched a plan which they hoped would see their fortunes improve with the new year. James stole out of the bed that he shared with Charles Marcham, trying not to wake the other man and boy who slept in his room at Frankum's boarding house[1]. At the age of twenty there was no room for James with his parents, and the lodging was all he could afford, given his meagre income. James and William, who was a year younger, left the house together and headed out across Cholsey Common.

It had been mild so far that winter, so there was no snow or ice to slow their progress. As they navigated by the light of the half moon, William, full of bravado, clutched the sycamore stave that they had cut as a weapon. They soon reached the place where they intended to hide and wait for their victim. William had now been working for Thomas Edward Washbourne of Greenhill Farm[2] for almost two years, and knew that Monday was pay day. Soon Elijah Baldwin, the farm foreman, would be coming from his house at Hill Green on the edge of the Common across those fields carrying the necessary money. They lay in wait.

At half past five Elijah reached their hiding place and they sprang out. William knocked him to the ground. But he was only stunned for a moment and, despite being over 50 years old, he jumped up and fought the two young men, calling out loudly, "Murder!" They threw him to the ground again and William held him by the throat while James rifled his pockets. He pulled out a silver watch and two purses. William was distracted by the booty, and Elijah again broke free and managed to grab his stick. Seeing that James had what they had come for, William gave up the fight and they both ran off. When they were a safe distance away, they counted the money. There was £6 11s, over a quarter's wages for William, and in addition the silver watch would fetch a tidy sum.

Elijah ran and woke his nephew Job, who lived nearby. Elijah said that he thought he recognised Parsons, and Job went out to look for him. He soon found him and accused him of being one of the attackers, but Parsons

---

[1] Frankum's was probably in Ilges Lane.

[2] Greenhill Farm was just to the north of the current Manor Farm, on the other side of the road. Manor Farm was then known as Cholsey Farm and was also worked by Mr Washbourne at that time.

said, "No, I was just coming from Wallingford." Elijah came up and confirmed that it was indeed him, but Parsons denied it so hotly that Job let him go.

Elijah then went to Greenhill Farm and told Mr Washbourne what had happened. The latter went to fetch the Cholsey constable, John Bristow, and together they went to Frankum's boarding house. By the time they got there, William had gone back to bed, but he was roused and the room searched. Underneath his pillow was a pair of trousers. In the pockets of the trousers was a silver watch and two purses. The constable took William into custody and put him securely into the village lock-up on The Forty. Over the next few days, the events were pieced together and James Ilsley joined his friend. By the order of a Justice of the Peace, they were then taken under guard to Reading and lodged in the gaol to await the Lent Assizes.

* * *

James Ilsley was the eldest of the four surviving sons and two daughters of Joseph and Sarah Ilsley. They had married in Wallingford in 1812 and moved to Cholsey with their family around 1820. Joseph's father originally came from the village, but Sarah's parents lived in Dorchester, where she had remained until she was 22, when she gave birth to an illegitimate daughter, seven months before her marriage. All the men, on both sides of the family, were labourers.

By the time of James' crime, Joseph and Sarah's children were aged from three to twenty. The family was poor, uneducated and rather unintelligent. Nothing unusual in that, but what was not commonplace was that all four sons turned to criminality to escape their condition. Often during James' youth the family had to fall back on the parish when no work was available, such as in 1819 when the parish bought his father a pair of shoes. By 1832 the family was receiving a shilling a week in support.

People said that the Ilsleys were descended from lords who came over with the Norman conquest. The Hildesley family occupied Little Stoke Manor in the seventeenth century and gave their name to the village of East Ilsley where they owned lands, and reputedly also to Ilges Lane in Cholsey. But what wealth there might have been had long since dissipated, and Ilsley was now not an uncommon name in the county. The Cholsey family had no wealthy relations either, and perhaps it was frustration and desperation that led James to robbery.

In fact it was his slightly younger brother Joseph who was first up before the courts. Aged seventeen, he had been accused of larceny at the Quarter Sessions the previous year. The theft was just of an iron pot and an empty sack from Mr Thomas Dodd, a farmer and gentleman of Moulsford who employed another Ilsley family living in that village. Joseph senior was also accused of receiving the goods, but the jury was not convinced and the pair were acquitted.

But it was for a much more serious offence that James now languished in Reading gaol. The assizes were held only twice a year, usually in Reading in March and in Abingdon in July, so the two young men had plenty of time to get used to their new quarters. The regular meals of gruel and bread were welcome, more than they had often managed on the outside, but life was very tedious. Before dawn a bell rang and they had to rise from their straw mattresses, tidy the bedding and wash, before being escorted to breakfast. A second bell then rang for divine service, after which they were put to work. As prisoners on remand they were not expected to engage in the hard labour of driving the treadmill, which involved the equivalent of climbing more than 10,000 feet during the eight-hour winter working day, but they would have been kept occupied in some equally pointless task. An hour was allowed in the middle of the day for dinner and outdoor exercise, and the prisoners were put back in their cells a quarter of an hour before sunset, to face the long night alone with their cell mates.

William and James had two months to contemplate their rashness. The charge was highway robbery, still a capital offence, although the numbers suffering the ultimate penalty had declined of late. But outside the gaol gate, as a reminder, stood the scaffold for the well-attended public executions. Opposite a similar gallows in Abingdon stood the Broad Face public house, whose strange name derived, so people said, from the bulging of the features caused by strangulation at the end of the rope.

On Saturday 28 February the circuit judges made their entrance into Reading. The Deputy Sheriff of the county rode out to greet them at the county boundary, and the High Sheriff with his Javelin Men[1] joined them as they

Fig. 3.1 The Broad Face in Abingdon

---

[1] Javelin Men were retainers appointed by the Sheriff who traditionally kept order in the courts.

approached the town. With the numbers swelled by local gentry on horseback and in carriages, the party entered the county town to the sound of trumpets, a regular yearly spectacle for the townsfolk. They proceeded to the Town Hall and opened the commission. That night the inns were overflowing with visiting lawyers, witnesses and court officials. On Sunday the judges in their red robes attended divine service at St Lawrence's church, and then on Monday proceedings in the Crown Court opened at nine o'clock.

Once everybody was assembled in the courthouse, the King's proclamation against vice and immorality was read. Mr Justice John Taylor Coleridge[1] then summarised the cases scheduled for the assizes, commenting, "I am sorry to see such a preponderance of charges for highway robbery; whether this results from lenient punishments having been awarded I cannot say, but if nothing but very severe punishment can prevent these crimes, that must be inflicted." Before each trial took place, the Grand Jury considered the accusation to see if there was a prima facie case to answer. They did indeed issue a 'true bill' against James and William.

Their case came up on the Wednesday, and they were led into the dock, the object of scrutiny by the public, jurors, lawyers and the bench. They pleaded not guilty. The victim Elijah first gave evidence, which was corroborated by his nephew Job. Mr Washbourne and the constable then described how they had apprehended Parsons and discovered the stolen goods. William Garlick, who worked on the roads, described how he had seen the two prisoners by a ditch near some sycamore trees on the Saturday, which may have been the source of the weapon that Parsons carried. James Clifford, a carter who worked for Mr Washbourne and one of the men that Ilsley shared a room with, described how the two were conferring together on the Sunday evening when he went to bed at eight o'clock. He had also heard Parsons come into the room at 4 a.m. and saw them go out together. The man Ilsley shared a bed with, Charles Marcham, who also worked for Mr Washbourne, did not wake up until later, but said that at 5 a.m. he found the bed empty. The ten-year-old

Fig. 3.2 Sir John Taylor Coleridge

---

[1] He was the nephew of Samuel Taylor Coleridge, the poet.

who also shared the room, William Powell, gave evidence that Parsons returned at about 6 a.m.

In his defence, William said that he was not involved in the attack, but had got up early in order to meet a man in Wallingford. On his return through the meadow where the attack took place, he heard a noise and saw a man running off. Soon after, he kicked against something and picked up the two purses and the watch, before returning to his bed. When asked, James muttered miserably that he had nothing to say. Neither of the accused called any witnesses.

The jury considered the case for half-an-hour before reaching a decision. Compared to many other cases, this was a long time. The evidence against William was overwhelming, and perhaps they were considering whether there was enough to implicate James Ilsley. But they did find both men guilty.

The judge immediately placed the black silk cap upon his head and passed the sentence of death. He addressed the prisoners solemnly, "In consequence of the increased and increasing number of highway robberies, it was absolutely necessary to visit the case with the highest penalty of the law, and to make an example that might deter others from commission of a similar case. The premeditation you have shown, and the violent manner in which you proceeded to commit this very heavy offence, leaves me no chance of holding out to you the least hope. I have now only to recommend you to employ the short space of time allocated to you in preparing yourselves for the awful change you are about to undergo. In a short period you will be summoned before your maker, and I earnestly advise you to avail yourselves of the valuable assistance I am sure you will receive, that you might not go into that presence unprepared."

The date of execution was set for seventeen days' time.

* * *

James's family were horrified by the sentence and there was considerable consternation in Cholsey that the sentence was too severe for the two young men. Some men of influence in the village contacted the Member of Parliament for Berkshire, Mr Walter (a liberal and perhaps more sympathetic than the Conservative MP for Wallingford, William Blackstone), to see if he could intercede on their behalf. Mr Walter was concerned and began to see what he could do. A colleague, the Member for Maldon in Essex, Thomas Barrett Leonard, took up the case and wrote to the Home Secretary, Mr Henry Goulburn, warning him that he planned to ask a question about the case in the House that very evening, Wednesday 11 March. Mr Goulburn sought further details urgently.

There was some sympathy in the Commons for the plight of the convicted men. The previous year a bill had been presented which would have repealed the death penalty for robbery, but it had been dropped in the Lords pending a more systematic revision of the law on capital offences. When Mr Justice Coleridge was contacted, he said that he had already ordered a respite[1] on the executions the previous Sunday. He pointed out in his reply to the Home Secretary's query that the case 'was one of highway robbery, with evidence that satisfied me of deliberate concert beforehand, and preparation to put down all resistance by violence, and a good deal of cruelty in the execution'. He continued, 'I thought an example, at least to the extent of passing the sentence of death, might be useful.' But, he claimed, it was only a warning and wrote 'I was, of course, very unwilling to execute the sentence, especially on two individuals'.

So the death sentence was to be commuted, but only to transportation over the seas for life. This caused more anguish, as the parents of the convicted duo realised that although their sons might live, they would never see them again. A petition was raised in the village. The large piece of parchment attracted 73 signatures from property-owning householders in Cholsey and the vicinity. It was a roll call of the local trades and professions with 25 farmers, five bakers and grocers, four boot and shoemakers, four carpenters, three blacksmiths, two whitesmiths, two bricklayers and three

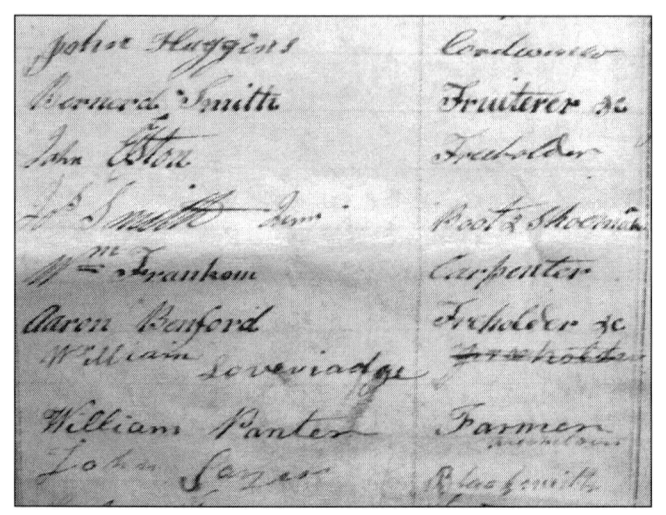

Fig. 3.3 Some of the noteworthy signatures from the petition

---

[1] The 'respite' refers to a postponement of sentence.

victuallers, as well as the schoolmaster, the dissenting minister[1], a brandy merchant, a corn dealer, the beadle, deputy constable and the parish clerk. It was explained that there was no signature from the Church of England minister as the parish currently had an absentee vicar. But where were the signatures of the curate, Thomas Cottle, and the rest of the gentry? It was the artisan population and lower middle classes who were sympathetic.

The document was sent to the Home Secretary via Mr Walter, who was still MP for Berkshire despite a change of government. Sir Robert Peel had only been leading a minority Conservative government over an interim period and, following elections, the Whigs were back in charge. The new Home Secretary, Lord John Russell, refused any further reduction in the sentence.

By the beginning of May their fate was clear, and James and William were taken chained together on the long slow journey down to Portsmouth. No doubt, before they set off, James and his parents exchanged a tearful last goodbye, never to meet again. Once they reached the port, the immediate fate of the two men became clear as they were taken aboard the hulk *Leviathan*. This old ninety-gun warship, which had fought at the battle of Trafalgar, was now a floating prison. The three decks were divided into cages made of iron bars where up to 600 prisoners were housed, as tame as rabbits from discipline and a state of semi-starvation. The lowest deck was reserved for new arrivals and James and William stumbled, encumbered by their chains, as they were led down into the gloom. No light came through the portholes facing the wharf and a lack of ventilation made the foul cold air suffocating. The bedding and walls crawled with vermin and each morning the deck was sluiced with salt water, creating a mouldy dampness that fed sickness and weakness of spirit. They were told by their new cell companions that the consequent high death rate - around one in three died - was welcomed by the local doctor who received six guineas for each body rendered for dissection.

James and William found themselves in a place of abject misery. The nights were the worst, cramped together with their coughing, foul-smelling comrades, most only interested in survival and minimising their own discomfort. When, during the day, they were released into the fresh air, it was a great relief, but the work was hard. Soon after their arrival the blacksmith had attached a heavy iron weighing about four pounds to their right legs. Wearing this heavy encumbrance, they were expected to cart timber or carry out other heavy work in the dockyard, despite their

---

[1] 'Dissenting' was the term used for non-conformists.

weakness. After a few months, the iron was replaced by a 'basil', a much lighter ring, as a reward for good behaviour, and walking became much easier. For those more inclined to bad behaviour, the lash awaited, with the enthusiastic flagellator intent on cutting the malefactor in two with each stroke, so his back became a gory red pulp.

Every now and again a 'bay' ship would anchor at Spithead[1], ready to take a cargo of convicts to New South Wales. Despite their trepidation, each time the two young men hoped that they would be taken aboard the tender out to the ship, but each time they were passed over. They knew that some men, ghosts of their former selves, had remained on the hulk for years. At last, after 24 weeks in their wet and putrid lodging, their turn came. On 19 October 1835, 160 convicts were offloaded from the *Leviathan* and taken out to join the *Recovery*, their transport to the other side of the world.

The *Recovery* was a three-masted bark of about 300 tons. Not a large ship, and in addition to the *Leviathan* cargo it would hold a further 120 convicts from the *York* hulk, a guard from the 28th Regiment made up of 29 officers and men, along with eight women and four children from their families, plus a full crew. The master was Thomas Johnson and the surgeon superintendent was Alexander Neill. The latter was responsible for the health and good conduct of the prisoners, and would receive a bonus of ten shillings for each convict delivered alive, an incentive introduced earlier in the century to reduce the appalling death rate.

Fig. 3.4 The *York* hulk

The departure was delayed by some trouble amongst the convicts, including two who managed to get intoxicated with wine, and some were sent back to the hulks. Finally, eleven days after they had boarded, James heard the creaking of the anchor chain and the ship began to slice through the water. The accommodation for the convicts was not dissimilar to that of the Leviathan, but once they were underway, the prisoners were allowed

---

[1] Spithead is an area of the Solent, off Portsmouth.

up on deck from time to time. Four days into the voyage, the wind grew and seasickness became a major problem for a time, not helped by the greasy cocoa that was served for breakfast.

James and William were issued with two sets of clothing, trousers and shirts labelled 'A' and 'B', to be worn alternate weeks, plus some primitive bedding, cooking and eating utensils. The convicts were divided into 'messes' of six men, each electing a mess captain responsible for the tidiness and conduct of his messmates. Between 6 p.m. and 6 a.m. they lived and slept in cells six feet square, which housed four or five convicts, allowing a width of eighteen inches each for sleeping. The only light and ventilation came from grated hatches, which were battened down during storms. Water seeped through the seams between the timbers of the ship as it wallowed through the seas, and the foul contents of the bilges swept in waves from one side of the deck to the other, wetting everything in their path. In hot weather in the doldrums, the atmosphere below could become unbearable, the only thought of each man a cup of the brackish slop that passed for water and at that moment tasted like nectar. On deck, near the bow, were the 'heads', holes high above the sea which were used as toilets. But down below there were only buckets, and the smell mixed with the sweat of 280 men and the rotting timbers to make a suffocating miasma.

The routine was the same every day. Those chosen to be cooks would be roused in the small hours to light the fires under the coppers of cocoa, which took four hours to heat. The prison doors were opened at sunrise and the convicts called up by division, bringing their bedding to stow somewhere on deck. The convicts, naked, were then called forward one at a time and a bucket of seawater was thrown over them. All on board also washed themselves and their clothes in seawater, drinking water being far too precious, and the dried salt on the skin chafed against the clothing. Cocoa and biscuit[1] or gruel were issued to each mess captain for breakfast. At 9 a.m. the decks would be washed with seawater, sometimes with added vinegar or chloride of lime as a precaution against infection. Following prayers, convicts were divided into groups to exercise, chained together under the watchful eye of the redcoats, carry out allotted tasks such as picking oakum[2], or attend the school, where James started to learn the rudiments of reading and writing. Other tasks were carried out on set days of the week; for example, washing clothes, cutting hair and shaving beards.

---

[1] Not today's biscuit, but compressed bread which, once damp, often became home to small grubs.

[2] 'Picking oakum' refers to the process of pulling hemp fibres from old ropes to be used for caulking

The main meal was at midday, and the food was more generous than in the hulks, being nominally set at two-thirds of the navy ration, provided none had been pilfered by the crew.

Soon they left land far behind and were out on the ocean, following the trade winds. On 15 November the island of Madeira was in view and on the 25th they passed close to the Cape Verde Islands. The equator was crossed on 6 December and on the 16th the island of Trinidad[1] was sighted. Their journey was long and without stops, but at least they were lucky with the weather. In the tropics the temperature never rose above 80 degrees, whilst in the cold Southern Ocean, it rarely fell below 50 and, as it was the summer season, the storms were not severe. From Trinidad the ship headed in more of a south-easterly direction, but made no landfall at the Cape Colony, as many transports did. That meant no fresh vegetables, and James longed for the taste of fresh food. By the end of the voyage nine convicts were suffering from the effects of scurvy, despite the ration of lime.

The *Recovery* finally sailed between the dangerous twin heads that lead to Port Jackson and Sydney on 25 February 1836. Not one of the prisoners had died, the only casualties being a soldier and one of the children, both of whom died of some kind of brain condition. The convicts were locked down below and most of them had to remain on board for another twenty days while each was assigned to a settler. Australia was set up as one big open prison. People like James remained convicts and subject to convict

Fig. 3.5 Sydney Cove in 1821

---

[1] This is not the Trinidad in the Caribbean, but a small rocky island in the South Atlantic under the sovereignty of Brazil.

discipline, but only the worst were held in prison. Rather they became the property of one of the free settlers for a time, providing unpaid labour in return for food and shelter. So, after five months on board and over a year living in some kind of cell, James was ferried to dry land to start his new life. Initially he found that he could not stand up straight, staggering like a drunk until he regained his land legs.

Sydney was a well-established town, but he was not destined to remain there and was soon travelling through the strange countryside into the outback north of Sydney. The white population of the whole enormous state was only 77,000, so the land was largely deserted. It was the tail end of the Australian summer and still hot in the middle of the day. Everything was different, with the seasons back to front and different constellations in the sky at night. As far as the eye could see were gum trees, with strange peeling bark and leaves that did not drop in autumn, but stayed ever-grey. Occasionally James saw animals that hopped rather than walked, and birds that ran instead of flew. Everywhere was a wary silence, as if the land was waiting for something to happen. The birds that could take to the air did not seem to sing, except for one particular creature that let out a loud cackle as if laughing at the puniness of the white man.

Over the ensuing months and years James learnt about his new home from those who had been there for some time. Over a third of the population were convicts like him, and many of the rest had once been transported but were now free men. James became the servant of Charles Cowper, an important landowner and a man of some renown in the state. Seven years after James arrived, Mr Cowper was elected to the legislative council and after 1856 was often the Premier of New South Wales. He was knighted in 1871.

In his new home James kept out of trouble and steadily became more and more useful to his employers on the farm. Although he was still a convict, food was more plentiful than back in England, and James gradually became more comfortable with his lot.

* * *

Back home in Cholsey, life did not get any easier. The cottage where James' parents lived in Honey Lane had belonged to the parish for housing the poor. But recent legislation had created the Wallingford Poor Law Union, and ownership of those five thatched cottages plus the poor house on Ilges Lane was passed to the Union. The management board decided that the accommodation was no longer needed as those who could not look after themselves would be housed in the Wallingford workhouse, and in August

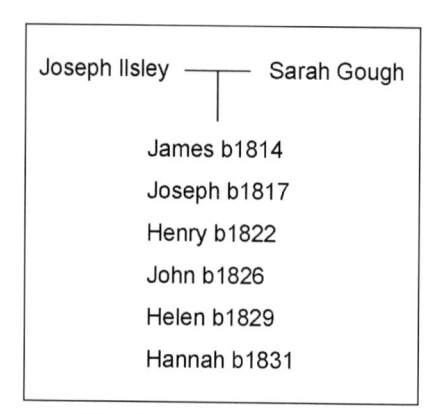

```
Joseph Ilsley ——T—— Sarah Gough
              |
         James b1814
         Joseph b1817
         Henry b1822
         John b1826
         Helen b1829
         Hannah b1831
```

Fig. 3.6 The Ilsley family

1836 the cottages were sold, creating a period of uncertainty. Luckily, Joseph senior and Sarah were able to remain in Honey Lane.

In June 1840 Joseph junior was married in Cholsey church. His bride was Sarah Savage, the 21-year-old daughter of a labourer from Dorchester. Joseph became a labourer on the railways, and the couple moved around following the work. In 1841 they were to be found in Thorn Hill, a few miles south of Wootton Bassett in Wiltshire. That year they had their first child, christened James, and another was born in Elham, near Folkestone in Kent, in 1843. A year earlier, Joseph senior died at the age of 55, leaving Sarah a penniless widow.

In February 1844 Henry Ilsley was accused of stealing a grey gelding from Richard Good, a general dealer in Cholsey, and also three quarters of beans from Thomas Howard Hodges in Moulsford, but was acquitted. Two months later, his brother John, then aged seventeen, was convicted of stealing a pair of shoes. John was out of work and hungry, and he took the shoes from the shop of Ann White, blacksmith, selling them later in Wallingford for 4s 6d. He was sentenced to three months' imprisonment with hard labour. John was still in gaol when his two remaining brothers, Joseph and Henry, committed their next criminal exploit. He was never to see them again.

* * *

On the night of Midsummer Eve, 23 June 1844, Joseph and Henry Ilsley did not go to sleep. Instead, around 1 a.m., they left the house and hitched up Joseph's cart. Henry was now 22 years old and Joseph was 26, and both were fed up with their hand to mouth existence. They were soon joined by two accomplices in another cart: John Pulbrook from Didcot and Charles Wilkins, who had been accused with Henry of stealing the horse four months earlier. The four had spotted an opportunity for enrichment.

The night was clear and the half moon illuminated the scene as the two carts made their way slowly over Cholsey Hill. The dew shone off the burgeoning crops as they came carefully down the steep hill, along Hithercroft Road and under the new railway bridge into South Moreton. At the entrance to the village by Anchor Lane, they turned their carts and dismounted. The four men walked a short way down the High Street and then turned into Mill Lane. About 200 yards down the lane were some buildings belonging to Mr Kirby, who farmed around 500 acres. After checking there was nobody about, they borrowed a ladder that was leaning against a hayrick and used it to climb up and break into a barn. Inside were 600 fleeces of wool.

They took it in turns to carry the fleeces back the quarter mile to where their carts were parked outside the village. Taking one of Mr Kirby's wagon cloths to cover the haul, they pushed the barn door closed and prepared for their escape. At around 3 a.m. they trotted back the way they had come, breaking into a gallop once they were beyond the railway bridge. By then the sky was lightening and the eastern horizon was glowing red, making the two hurrying carts all too visible. At that time of year people were abroad early. Henry Wilson, a labourer, was in his garden a furlong from Anchor Lane and heard them pass by. John Somerset was in the vicarage in Cholsey washing his master's gig[1] when he saw the carts come down the Causeway.

They continued on through Moulsford, where they were greeted by William Brown, an acquaintance and a local sweep, who was driving his cart in the opposite direction. They kept to the Reading Road, passing through Streatley, over the Basildon railway bridge and into Pangbourne. By then Joseph had dismounted and was running alongside so that they could keep up the pace. At the tollgate the keeper remarked that they seemed in an awful hurry, and Joseph swore at the man. They drove on through Reading and finally, at around seven o'clock, stopped at a public house, where the tired horses were given some hay and the men drank a quart of beer. Somewhat rested, they continued through Wokingham until they came to the house of William Warren, a fellmonger[2].

Joseph showed him the fleeces, but at that point they could not agree a price, and drove off further down the London Road to the Three Frogs public house. John unhitched his wagon and the four drank some more beer, before deciding to accept the price offered. The fleeces were loaded onto Joseph's wagon, and he returned to the fellmonger's house. He was given two sovereigns on account, the remainder to be paid the following Saturday. It was still only 8 a.m. William Warren's son promised to return the wagon to the alehouse once it had been emptied, and Joseph walked back to the Three Frogs. Now that they had some money in their pockets, the four young men spent several hours enjoying what the pub had to offer.

---

[1] A gig was a light two-wheeled carriage pulled by a single horse.

[2] A fellmonger was a dealer in hides and skins, especially sheepskins.

Back in South Moreton, the theft had been discovered. Shadrach Wilcox turned up for work sometime before 5 a.m. that Monday, and immediately spotted that the ladder had been moved. He noticed several bits of wool by the yard gates and, on trying the barn doors, found that they were unbolted. He immediately went to fetch his master, who lived in a large house opposite Mill Lane. Mr Kirby estimated that 80 fleeces were missing, and also noticed that the wagon cloth was gone. He immediately dispatched several of his men in various directions to make enquiries and inform the authorities. The Wallingford policeman soon received intelligence on the route that the thieves had taken, and hurried to Reading to make contact with his colleagues in the town.

Meanwhile, the four young men finally left the Three Frogs around noon and set off in their empty carts back towards Reading and home. They threw the stolen wagon cloth into a field as they passed. But they did not get much further. In Reading they were stopped by the police. Brought before the Superintendent of Police for the town, Henry Houlton, they all denied any wrongdoing. Joseph claimed that his cart had only contained flats[1], and that he had given them to a man in Wokingham, although he did not know his name. John Pulbrook said that his cart only contained grass. On examination, the carts revealed small pieces of wool. Later in the day, the Superintendent discovered what had happened and went to Wokingham, returning with the fleeces and a wagon cloth clearly labelled 'Kirby'. On the following day Mr Kirby identified the goods as his. The four men were conveyed to Abingdon gaol to await trial.

The Summer Assizes were due in just two weeks' time, which was just as well for the prisoners as the ancient and insanitary prison had seen several cases of smallpox over the previous six months. Some of the new men on remand had natural immunity to the disease through exposure to cow pox, and the others were inoculated with a vaccine as a precaution. One man went down with the illness, but the Ilsleys were not affected.

The assizes were opened by Mr Sergeant Atcherley in Abingdon on Wednesday 10 July 1844. The Ilsleys' turn came on the Saturday. When the four men were brought into the dock, it was clear which two were brothers. They both stood 5 feet 8 inches tall and resembled each other, although Henry was clean shaven and darker with black hair, while Joseph's hair and whiskers were brown. Ranged about them were the court officials, lawyers, the jurymen and the public, who, apart from the friends and relations of the accused, were looking forward to an entertaining drama.

---

[1] A flat was some sort of stackable container. For example, 'butter flats' were large wooden boxes built to hold butter, but often also used for other purposes.

Fig. 3.7 Abingdon gaol

The case took several hours of the court's time. The Ilsleys were represented by Mr Pigot, while Mr Williams defended John Pulbrook and Charles Wilkins, meaning that each of the prosecution witnesses was cross-examined twice. Mr Kirby and Shadrach Wilcox testified to the theft, and then a long line of witnesses described the passage of the escaping villains: Henry Wilson in South Moreton; John Somerset and Thomas Dearlove in Cholsey; William Brown in Moulsford; William Newman in Pangbourne and the two public house landlords near Wokingham. In addition, another carter heading through Cholsey towards Reading saw them both on their way to South Moreton and later when they overtook him near Basildon railway bridge. William Warren the younger testified to the sale of the fleeces to his father and Superintendent Houlton described the arrest of the prisoners and the recuperation of the stolen goods.

The evidence was overwhelming and there was little that the defence lawyers could do. Following the summing up, the jury immediately found all the prisoners guilty. Charles Wilkins had a previous conviction for larceny received six years earlier, for which he had been whipped, and this weighed against him. All four were sentenced to be 'transported beyond the seas', Charles for ten years and the other three for seven. Two more of the Ilsley brothers were destined for Australia, where the regime had become much harsher than when their older brother was sentenced.

*   *   *

For their mother, Sarah Ilsley, that was two more sons that she would probably never see again. It was even worse for Joseph's wife and children. Not only would they have no husband and father, but also no breadwinner, so that they would have to fall back on the parish for support. There was time for them all to say their last goodbyes, as the governor had to alert the Home Secretary, Sir James Graham, to the recent smallpox outbreak and await permission to move the prisoners.

All four convicted men were taken under guard to Millbank Penitentiary in London at the end of July. The large grey forbidding prison housed over 700 convicts and sat on marshy ground by the Thames to the south of the Palace of Westminster[1]. The living conditions were much better physically than those in the hulks, but instead the torment was psychological as they were put into isolation, separated from each other and all the other convicts. Luckily, the two Ilsley brothers and John Pulbrook did not have long to wait for a ship to the Antipodes, but, because of his longer sentence, Charles Wilkins was taken instead to Pentonville Penitentiary. There he would spend two years in the so-called 'separate system', where each prisoner lived in total silence and isolation, something that drove many men mad. After that he was transported to Victoria to serve the rest of his sentence.

A month after they arrived in Millbank, the other three were chained to a gang of convicts and taken out through the gates and down to a lighter moored at the dock. They were ferried down the Thames and put aboard the *Sir Robert Peel*, a 610 ton sailing ship bound for Van Diemen's Land. In total there were 254 convicts on board, guarded by 52 soldiers of the 50th, 58th and 99th Regiments. In addition to the master William Champion and his crew, there were also fourteen women and children, the families of some of the soldiers. The surgeon superintendent was John Arnold Mould, in contrast to his name a stickler for hygiene and cleanliness. The prison deck was dry-holystoned[2] every day, and frequently fumigated and sprinkled with chloride of lime. Any moisture was mopped up, stoves were lit when it was cold, and the ventilation in still weather was improved by rigging up windsails above the hatches to divert air below.

The result was that illnesses amongst the convicts were few, with just one death from consumption. It was a different story amongst the guard and their families, who accounted for more than half of those on the sick list, despite their smaller number. The surgeon railed against the 'indolent and untidy habits of these people', making especially derogatory comments about the Irish, blaming the filth for their infections. A month after

---

[1] Tate Britain stands on the site of the Millbank Penitentiary.

[2] In dry-holystoning, sand was sprinkled on the deck and then scoured with a piece of freestone (typically sandstone or limestone).

departure, one of the children contracted cholera and later died. The disease spread to four of the convicts, but there were no more deaths. Most of the illnesses were indeterminate fevers, but there were some cases of nyctalopia[1], which the surgeon put down to reading in too bright a light and tackled by prescribing purgatives.

The ship made rapid progress through the Atlantic on the usual route, turning to the east and passing by the island of Tristan da Cunha before briefly stopping at the Cape for provisions. The run through the Southern Oceans was also quick and uneventful, and the ship hove into Hobart harbour on Boxing Day, just 108 days after leaving London.

It took a long time to process and unload the convicts. They were brought up from below in small batches, and each man was interrogated by convict clerks who wrote all their details in large black ledgers. How old were they, were they married and who were their family? Where were they tried and for what offence? The process of getting the convict to explain how they had transgressed was seen as the first stage in rehabilitation. Detailed descriptions were written, right down to the scar under Henry's right eye and the mole on his neck. The idea was to identify the 'bolters', people who tried to flee their imprisonment.

Finally Joseph and Henry were taken off the ship and after a further delay were put on another destined for their 'probation station'. The system was different from that experienced by James Ilsley, with each prisoner going through a period of hard labour before they were allowed to engage in more constructive work. The most awful 'punishment stations' were Port Arthur and Cascades on the Tasman peninsula, where the life was designed to be as painful and dispiriting as possible. But Joseph and Henry had been model prisoners on the journey, and their conduct was graded by the surgeon as 'actively helpful' and 'well behaved' respectively, and both were marked as 'specially recommended'. So instead, on 1 February 1845, they boarded a ship to take them forty miles down the coast to Dover and the Port Esperance station. John Pulbrook, who was described as 'impertinent', was sent to Saltwater Creek on the Tasman peninsula, which boasted a convict-worked coalmine with appalling conditions.

Port Esperance might have been less awful than some places, but they were still worked hard. The place was densely forested, devoid of settlers and only easily accessible by sea, and the convicts were largely engaged in farming and construction. The huge trees had to be cut down and the

---

[1] Nyctalopia is an inability to see in low light, probably caused in this case by a lack of vitamin A.

undergrowth cleared to provide the fields which then had to be cultivated, and the Ilsleys, as farm labourers, were probably put to this work. Others such as bricklayers, carpenters and general labourers were assigned to building work on the station.

Again the Ilsleys tried hard not to upset the authorities, and their twelve months of probation came to an end when they 'emerged from the gang' on 26 December 1845, the anniversary of their arrival on the island. They returned to Hobart and became Probation Pass Holders third class. As such they could be employed by settlers, who would be responsible for their behaviour and welfare. Away from prison, their movements were still restricted and they had to carry their pass at all times. But as Passholders third class, they would receive the full nominal wage; classes one and two had some of their money banked against good behaviour.

Joseph and Henry were initially housed in the prisoner barracks, known as the 'Tench', which accommodated all who could not find work, and were employed by the government in stone breaking or other public labour. In April 1846 they were sent to Macquarie Harbour, 100 miles or so away on the west coast, where they both became constables. It might seem an unlikely occupation for members of such a criminal family, but it was in fact quite a common assignment. The authorities knew that getting the convicts to police each other usually worked. It was also far from a sinecure, with most employed to patrol the same beat repeatedly through night shifts that ran from 8 p.m. until 6 a.m. The pay of 1s 9d per day was little enough to cover the cost of food and lodging, never mind clothing to protect against the rain and cold of the southern winter that was just setting in.

The two brothers were together in Macquarie Harbour for over a year without falling foul of the authorities, but then, in April 1847, Joseph was sent back to become a constable in Hobart. A month or two later, without the steadying influence of his younger brother, he went on a drinking binge and failed to turn up for his night-time duty. He was sentenced to three days' imprisonment with hard labour, but then was allowed to return to his job. A few months later he changed jobs to work for various settlers. Henry had also erred and in August spent four days in solitary with no pay, but then in September and October of 1848 they were each granted their Ticket of Leave. This freed them from the control of a particular master and allowed them to seek work independently, although they were still classed as convicts.

Continuing in lock step, the following year they both got married, and to two sisters. It was three years earlier, soon after he arrived in Hobart from Port Esperance station, that Joseph probably met Sarah Eliza Stanley, who was then only seventeen. She lived on George Street with her father, who had been transported in 1811 for horse stealing, and her mother, who was born in Sydney in 1800. Nine months later, while Joseph was in Macquarie

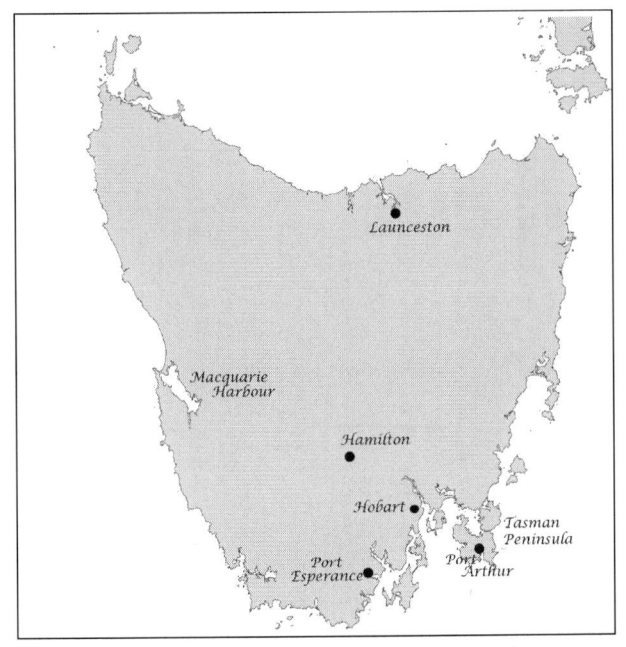

Fig. 3.8 Map of Van Diemen's Land

Harbour, she gave birth to an illegitimate child, christened James Raymond. Her family stood by her; indeed James was baptised on the same day as Sarah's youngest brother.

When Joseph returned to Hobart and wished to resume the relationship, she insisted that they be married. He faced a quandary: if he applied for permission to marry, as all convicts must, they might discover that he was intending to commit bigamy. So instead, he did not apply for permission, but declared to the minister that he was a free man. They married on 29 March 1849 in St Andrew's Presbyterian Church in Hobart. Unbeknown to his new wife, Joseph had committed another crime.

Henry, being single, did apply for permission and his marriage took place at St John Baptist chapel in the hamlet of River Ouse, near Hamilton, 70 miles north of Hobart, on 17 October 1849. His bride was Charlotte Amelia Stanley, Sarah Eliza's younger sister, who was seventeen. Earlier that year in May, both men had been recommended for a conditional pardon. The outlook looked bright for the two brothers, but soon everything would go badly wrong for Joseph.

* * *

Meanwhile, back in England, Joseph Ilsley's first wife Sarah and her children were in the workhouse. Wallingford Union workhouse was a large building on the Wantage Road that held up to 400 inmates. Once admitted, Sarah and her family were not allowed to leave without permission; if they did so then they would be arrested for stealing the coarse workhouse uniform, the only clothes they were permitted to keep. The daily routine was strict; inmates rose at six or seven o'clock for breakfast and retired to the mass single sex dormitories at 8 p.m. The work, from 7 or 8 a.m. to 6 p.m. with an hour for lunch, was mainly associated with running the institution, with Sarah assigned to clean, wash or cook. Her youngest child, Mary, would probably have been allowed to sleep in the dormitory with her. But James and Thomas, being over seven years old, would probably have slept somewhere else and would have seen their mother only rarely.

Mary was born two years after Joseph Ilsley was transported and clearly was fathered by another man. The unknown man could have been Matthew Baldwin, a sawyer[1] living in Drove Lane in Cholsey. In any case he was to prove to be Sarah's route to escaping the workhouse. In November 1851 Matthew's wife (yet another Sarah) died at the age of 33. Less than nine months later, in another act of bigamy, Sarah Ilsley, claiming to be a widow, married Matthew at Cholsey parish church. She became stepmother to Matthew's existing seven children, as well as mother to her own three and then another five that were born to both of them over the next nine years[2].

The last of the Ilsley boys still in England, John, was in trouble again soon after his brothers had left those shores. He had gone to work for Mr Simmons of Home Farm in Basildon and was living there with some of the other workers. In May 1847 he offered to take a pocket watch belonging to a fellow labourer, Jeremiah Brooker, into Pangbourne for repair. On Monday 18 May John disappeared from his employ, taking with him a waistcoat belonging to William Wise, who also lived in the same house. John went to Pangbourne, picked up the watch, and a few days later pawned it in Reading for five shillings using the name James Wakefield. The following Saturday Jeremiah Brooker caught up with him and took him to Superintendent Houlton, the same man who had arrested John's two brothers.

At the trial a month or so later, John claimed that he had bought the waistcoat from a man in Basildon whose name he did not know, and said he knew nothing about the watch. The jury found him guilty, and the chairman of the magistrates, noting his earlier conviction, sentenced him to eighteen months in gaol, saying, "You appear to be one of those incorrigible persons

---

[1] A sawyer was somebody who earned a living by sawing timber.

[2] Matthew Baldwin may have been the nephew of Elijah Baldwin, the man who James Ilsley attacked in 1835.

on whom punishment has but little effect, but under the discipline now pursued in the county gaol, the Court trusts that you may yet be reformed."

The new Reading gaol, opened in 1844, was a cross between Pentonville Prison and Windsor Castle, with four large turrets and castellated walls. The imposing building was the largest in town and dominated the eastern approach. When the outer doors slammed shut, John said goodbye to the outside world and virtually all human contact, as the gaol used the 'separate system' pioneered at Pentonville. He was examined by the visiting surgeon, assigned a cell, bathed, and put for a minute or two into a refractory cell to instil some fear of the punishment regime. These cells were pitch black with ventilation and heating controlled by a warder to ensure maximum discomfort.

The prison was built with four wings emanating from a central hub, with the 60-odd cells of each spoke arranged on several floors either side of a wide corridor. The landings were reached by an open staircase such that the governor could see every cell door from his central location. All the cells were 13 feet long by 7 feet wide by 10 feet high and equipped with warm air heating to maintain a steady 54 degrees Fahrenheit. Inside John found a table and stool, a hammock for sleeping, a cistern of water and a copper bowl. Each day he was allocated six gallons of water for drinking, washing, cleaning and all bodily functions. There was a gaslight, a Bible and a prayer book.

For the period of his sentence John did not leave his cell except for a daily exercise period, when he walked around a yard some distance from the next prisoner, and attendance at chapel, where each prisoner sat in a separate compartment such that he could only see and hear the chaplain. Every day was spent in silence, speaking being a serious offence, along with making signs to other prisoners, attempting to look out of a window, or folding the bedclothes incorrectly. Lights out was between 8 p.m. and 6 a.m., with the prisoners given some kind of manual labour to undertake in their cells during the morning and afternoon periods. At least the meals were regular, with a pint of oatmeal gruel for breakfast and supper, and a pound of bread and a pound of potatoes for midday dinner. Mondays, Wednesdays and Fridays were special, with the potatoes replaced by one and a half pounds of scouse[1].

The mental punishment must have been hard, but at least John suffered less than most as far as physical hardship was concerned. Reading gaol

---

[1] Scouse is a stew made with mutton and vegetables.

lacked facilities for hard labour, with just ten positions in the pump room, where convicts had to hand crank water up to the tank in the roof. The visiting justices complained bitterly of this deficiency, but it was only many years later that it was remedied.

After John was eventually released, it is not known where he found work, but he may well have remained in Reading. In 1846 his sister Ellen had married Michael Pike, a painter and glazier, in Reading, and lived close to the city centre. His other sister, Hannah, was still a spinster and lived close by in Welldale Street, where she earned a living as a dressmaker. It seems probable that his mother Sarah also moved to Reading, where she lodged close to her two daughters and earned a living as a nurse[1]. She died in 1852, a few years after John's release.

In April 1854 John found a more worthy occupation, and joined the Berkshire Militia. The country was awash with war hysteria as hostilities were about to break out in the Crimea between the Turks, British and French on one side, and the Russians allied with the Prussians on the other. The militia was a part-time reserve force, with a three- or four-week camp once a year. John signed up on 8 April as a recruit from Cholsey, giving his age as 23, four years lower than it actually was. Six months later a warrant was issued for the militia's 'embodiment', and on 1 January 1855 the regiment assembled in Reading, ready for action. But nothing happened for some considerable time, while the soldiers were billeted in the town and practised on the Forbury parade ground. With over a thousand mainly young men on the loose, there was often trouble with the townsfolk.

Finally in September the militia received orders to embark for Corfu, where they would free up regular forces. Three companies of 800 men marched to Reading station on Wednesday 19 September led by the band, and another 800 the following day, all to the cheering of several thousand spectators. They sailed on the *Saladin* from Portsmouth to Corfu, and ended up spending eight months on the island. The regiment were not called on to fight, but nevertheless there was considerable loss of life due to a cholera epidemic, with 50 men dead and a similar number of women and children. John Ilsley survived, although he was several times in hospital.

After the war ended, the regiment returned to Reading in June 1856 in pouring rain, to a less than enthusiastic welcome. A couple of weeks later the men were paid off and the militia returned to being a part-time force. John sometimes complained of having a pain near his heart, and in March 1857 he was discharged as a casualty with a payment of 18s 6d. He found

---

[1] This would be as a servant to help families with young children.

work at the Katesgrove Foundry as a labourer, and all went well for the next year.

On Good Friday, 10 April 1857, John Ilsley finished work early at four o'clock, and went home for a wash and some tea. He then went out for a walk, and a little before eight o'clock met James Green, a gamekeeper, with his family. John knew him well, as they had both worked for Mr Popham of Purley Park a few years earlier, where John was a cowman. They all repaired to the Roebuck public house and had some beer together. About half-past nine, while still quite sober, John suddenly slipped off his seat. He emitted a snore as if asleep, but then lay quite still. He was lifted up and a doctor was sent for, but he was quite dead. The inquest the following day, in the same public house, ascribed his death to the rupture of a blood vessel of the heart. He was 30 years old.

* * *

So by 1857 at least one of the four criminal brothers was dead; but what had happened to the other three in Australia? The eldest, James Ilsley, had been a model convict in New South Wales working for Charles Cowper and in 1844, the year that his two brothers embarked for Australia, he was granted his Ticket of Leave. He moved down to Albury, near the Victoria border in the south of the state, and in 1848 he was granted a conditional pardon. This meant that he was a free man, provided he did not try to return to England. In 1855, aged 37, he married Ann Eleanor Peters, a widow. Her husband had died in a farming accident some months before, and James took over a ready-made family of seven children, with another on the way. The eldest was only fourteen, and James and Ann had at least a further three children together.

Around the time of his marriage, James purchased some land at Jindera, ten or twenty miles to the north of Albury, at a cost of a pound an acre. He was known by the name Hilsley in Jindera and became a respected landowner, purchasing further plots over the years. He was elected president of the Jindera Farmers' Union and was asked more than once to enter public office, but always declined. He died in 1897, aged 82. Perhaps he never revealed his true identity, as his death certificate records his parent's names as 'unknown'.

Earlier, back in Van Diemen's Land in 1850, Joseph's deception over his marriage was discovered. He had committed perjury, a serious crime, and in October 1849 his Ticket of Leave was revoked. He was sentenced to spend a further twelve months on probation, this time in Port Arthur.

Fig. 3.9 The ruins of Port Arthur in Tasmania

Port Arthur punishment station was a large settlement holding a thousand convicts at the southernmost tip of the Tasman Peninsula. The chief superintendent boasted that the work given to the convicts was 'the most incessant and galling that the settlement could produce'. Apart from breaking rocks in chains, men were yoked together as human ploughs on the land and forced to carry two-hundred-foot-high giant blue gum trees from the forests down to the saw pits on their shoulders. If one man tripped, the whole weight bore down, crushing the others in the party. Escape from the hell hole was virtually impossible, with the choice being between swimming across shark-infested seas or crossing the narrow isthmus of sand, guarded by armed soldiers, that linked the outpost to the mainland.

Joseph's new wife sent a petition to the governor asking for a reduction in his sentence, but the request was refused. In January she gave birth to another son, Frederick Joseph, and sent another petition soon after, which met the same fate. But, with good behaviour, the regime ameliorated for a convict in Port Arthur, and Joseph managed to earn 51 days' reduction in his punishment period through 'task work'[1]. He finally emerged in August 1850, and one might have expected that he would avoid trouble after the experience. But a few months later he was convicted of burglary and absconding, and his overall sentence was increased by eighteen months.

This time Joseph was sent to Cascades punishment station, a smaller establishment on the north side of the Tasman Peninsula. Again the work was hard, with the principal tasks being land cultivation and the felling and sawing of the blue gums. Ships now often docked close to Cascades in the

---

[1] 'Task work' refers to additional tasks undertaken voluntarily.

bay, which was more sheltered than at Port Arthur. Goods and people were then transported between the two using a sort of tramway that switch-backed four miles over the wooded hills and used convicts as its motive power.

After Joseph Ilsley emerged from the Cascades punishment station in October 1851, he found that his wife and children had gone. The governor had declared their marriage null and void, because the ceremony had not taken place with the colony's official permission, and Sarah Eliza had reverted to using her maiden name of Stanley. She had left Hobart with her family for Victoria.

In 1851 gold was discovered at Clunes in Victoria, with further large discoveries later that year at Ballarat and Bendigo. Like many others in Van Diemen's Land, Sarah's father William decided to chance his luck and took his family to Bendigo. He didn't spend long as a miner, but the family settled in the area. Sarah adjusted to her new situation quickly, and in January 1852 she married John George Craig in Shepparton. Joseph's children both took the surname of Craig, little remembering their biological father. Sarah went on to have another five children with John Craig, and another three with a third husband whom she married after John's death. She died in 1888. According to a family story, she was once held up by Ned Kelly when travelling in a Cobb & Co. stagecoach in the area. He did her no harm, perhaps because she was in the same sewing circle as his sisters, with whom she got on rather well.

Meanwhile Joseph Ilsley finally became a free man in August 1852 when the remainder of his extended sentence was remitted. No more is known of him after this date, with nothing in the official records. Perhaps he changed his name, or perhaps he also headed for the gold diggings where he died, like many others, without anybody knowing his true identity.

Henry Ilsley fared much better than his brother following his marriage to Charlotte in 1849. Their first child was born the following year, and he was granted a conditional pardon on 30 July 1850, meaning he was free to go where he liked in search of work. Soon after, Henry left for the mainland following his wife's family, probably to seek his fortune. Certainly in 1855, when his second child was born, he was to be found in Back Creek in Victoria. Back Creek was near the gold diggings in Beechworth, Omeo and Bright, and only 40 miles from Albury in New South Wales. Perhaps he was in contact with his brother James and they met up, or maybe they were completely oblivious as to what had happened to each other.

Henry Ilsley and his family continued to move around, with children born in Bendigo in 1860, Lexton in 1862, Inglewood in 1866 and Mount

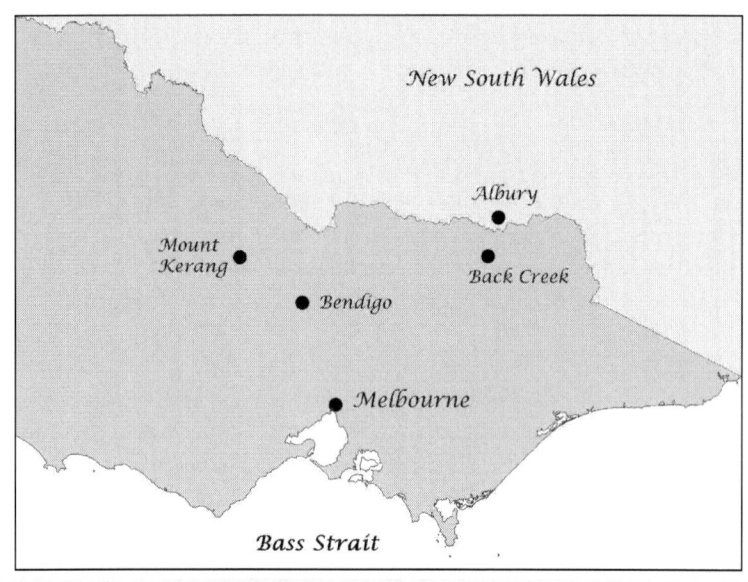

Fig. 3.10 Map of the State of Victoria

Kerang in 1869. All of these towns were in the middle north of the state, quite some distance from Albury. They finally settled in Kerang, where their last child was born in 1874. Henry found employment as a groom and became well known in the community. In 1882 his wife caused an upset by accusing the teacher at Kerang State School of ill-treating her son Henry junior, aged eleven. A doctor provided a certificate showing that he had been severely beaten, with excessive bruises and abrasions to the buttocks.

Henry Ilsley died on 13 January 1888 of apoplexy[1], aged 66, and was buried in the town cemetery. A month later, his widow caused more controversy. At ten o'clock on the evening of 13 February 1888, the township was startled by the pealing of the fire bell. The family's four-room weatherboard cottage near the showground was on fire. The bright glow attracted a crowd as the Kerang fire brigade tried to deal with the blaze. But there was insufficient pressure in their hose to play it on the burning building, and the strong wind soon reduced the building to a pile of blackened embers. The cause of the fire was a mystery, as luckily there was nobody in the cottage at the time, nor indeed much in the way of furniture. Or perhaps not just luckily, as house insurance with the Commercial Union resulted in a payout of £75 for Charlotte. Whatever the origins of the fire, Henry's widow continued to live in Kerang for another 38 years, dying in 1926 at the age of 94.

---

[1] Apoplexy was a sudden death, usually caused by a stroke.

By the time of her death, it was nearly a century since the four brothers from Cholsey started their criminal exploits. The law and fate dictated that they led very different lives, mostly far from home, and they would have been soon forgotten by the people of their home parish. The villagers' attention would have turned elsewhere; in particular, to a major construction project at the end of the 1830s, which would be pivotal in determining the future importance of the village.

Chapter 4 The Coming of the Railway

In the spring of 1838 Cholsey was overrun by an army of foreigners, an invasion of a size perhaps not seen since the arrival of the marauding Danes in 1006 AD. The new legion numbered several hundred and were called navigators[1], commissioned by the Great Western Railway Company to lay a permanent way slicing the parish in two. With pick, shovel, muscle and sweat they came to dig a cutting through the hill southeast of the village and to build a brand new river crossing close to the village of Moulsford. The contracts were let in April of that year, to William Chadwick to construct the bridge, and to James Thomas Bedborough, John Ramsbottom and Thomas Jenner to build the line from there to the hamlet of Didcot. Each hired an army of labourers to carry out the work.

The navigators came from all over the country, attracted by the high wages on offer for heavy work against tight deadlines. They had a lawless and fearsome reputation, and many in the village were afraid of what might happen. Already towards the end of that month of April, trouble had exploded on the works at Ealing. A large body of Irishmen had arrived offering to work for less than the Scots and English already in employment,

Fig. 4.1 Navvies working on a railway

---

[1] Navigator was originally the term used for those who built the canals; later shortened to 'navvy'.

and a fierce battle erupted which was only quelled by the arrival of the cavalry in the form of the 12th Lancers, who separated the warring contingents using the flat of their swords. Arrests were made by the hated 'Peelers'[1] and the men then went on strike. Over the following days further confrontations ensued until an uneasy peace returned.

The next month the contractor for the Sonning cutting ran into financial difficulties and couldn't pay his workmen. When the news was broken to them, they smashed everything in view on the site and then, hoping to gain recompense, they marched on Reading, a thousand strong. The angry workmen gathered on the Forbury, and the Mayor pacified them temporarily by promising they would be paid, whilst waiting for the arrival of a squadron of Horse Guards from Windsor. An uneasy week passed, during which the men lived off the charity of the townsfolk, freely or not so freely given. Finally they were persuaded to return to the works on the offer of one to two weeks' pay guaranteed by some of the leading citizens, confrontation with the cavalry being the other alternative.

So it was with some trepidation that villagers greeted the new arrivals coming to carry out the works in Cholsey over the next months and years. Those charged with keeping the peace, the unpaid parish constables and Justices of the Peace, wondered what they would have to confront. As it turned out, there were no major incidents, just the usual problems associated with drunkenness.

In fact, the works brought much appreciated extra money to some in the village. Many of the navigators lodged with the locals, and the pubs saw much increased business, especially on a Sunday. The keeping of a day of rest in the works was one that caused great public concern. A certain Francis Trench of Reading wrote to the *Berkshire Chronicle* that he had observed much Sabbath-breaking on the stretch near the town, by which 'God is dishonoured and public feeling scandalised'. Revd Henry William Lloyd, newly-appointed vicar of Cholsey, was concerned to ensure that no such thing happened locally, and in the main he was successful. But the navigators did not use their leisure to attend his services, rather they spent the time in the pubs. The forced closure of these between 3 and 5 p.m., to coincide with evensong, did little to increase the congregation. Indeed, Joseph Willmott of the Brentford Tailor[2] was fined in November for continuing to sell beer during these hours.

Revd Lloyd spent time with the workmen trying to mend their ways, but the first and last time he saw many of them was at their burial. Accidents

---

[1] 'Peelers' refers to the Metropolitan police, established by Sir Robert Peel in 1829.

[2] This Brentford Tailor was on The Forty, a short distance from the Swan Inn.

were common, and the first death came in August when Edward Edney, a Moulsford man of 27, was killed. The following June, William Hulse, a native of Gloucestershire, died and was buried in Cholsey, but the most celebrated funeral occurred in March of 1839.

John Starling hailed from Weeting, near Brandon in Norfolk, and was born in the early years of the century. He came from a poor family of agricultural workers in this deeply rural part of the country, but left the area to seek his fortune after the death of his wife. Finding he could earn a good wage working on the construction of the new railways, and without any family ties, he gave himself over to a hedonistic lifestyle, spending his money as quickly as it came. Without a care for the future, he styled himself 'Happy Jack', and that was the only name he was known by in the neighbourhood. Most of his cash went on drink and, as he later told the vicar, "I have often taken on the Saturday night two pounds, week after week, and on the Monday morning have not had sixpence left, and in the course of the week have pawned some of my clothes for more liquor." In Cholsey he paid for his lodgings in advance, so at least he was provided with food and shelter.

Revd Lloyd met John Starling in June 1838, when the works were only two months old. He lodged with two or three other railwaymen in a house on The Forty and was at home when one day the vicar called to give out some religious tracts. He admonished the man for his sinful lifestyle, but Jack only replied angrily that he did not know he had many sins to answer; he paid everyone what he owed, bore no grudge to anyone, and did not know that he was worse than others. Most of his friends were the same. The navigator took his hat and left the house in a hurry.

But Jack had developed a nasty cough, and soon after the encounter he went to the Radcliffe Infirmary in Oxford for treatment. It was consumption, and another clergyman at the hospital impressed on him the horrors of hell, which now awaited him in the near rather than distant future. Returning to Cholsey, he had to give up work and became more

Fig. 4.2 Revd Henry William Lloyd

fearful as to what future awaited his immortal soul. Jack invited the vicar back and asked if he would read to him. Revd Lloyd became a frequent visitor; they would sit by the fire, Jack in the wooden high-backed armchair with his black dog lying by his feet. The vicar spoke of how Jack had only been feeding himself with 'the empty husks of worldly pleasures', and that salvation lay in dedication to the Lord. Jack now thought himself a great sinner and doubted that such a one could meet with mercy. Privately, Revd Lloyd was of the same opinion.

Jack was no longer happy and continually reproved another railway man who slept in the same room for blaspheming and swearing, to such an extent that the man left the lodgings. He told the vicar that he had been an undutiful son and never sent anything to his father, and asked a neighbour to write to his parents to tell them of his illness. He began praying constantly, and seemed no longer to have any joy or peace.

The vicar attended Jack regularly for five months, but then in February he was confined wholly to his bed. On the 26th he saw him for the last time, the clergyman sitting on the wooden chest by his bed trying to raise his spirits by talking of the glad tidings of salvation. Early the following morning, as Revd Lloyd was writing at his desk in the vicarage, he looked up to see the woman with whom John lodged crossing the street to his house. He had died at 5 a.m. The funeral was fixed for the following Sunday, four days hence, so that other railwaymen could give their respects. It soon became apparent that such was Jack's popularity that the ceremony would be extremely well attended and quite a spectacle.

Sunday 3 March was a sparkling early spring day and by mid afternoon an immense multitude of railwaymen had gathered on The Forty outside the cottage which held Jack's remains. They were dressed in white smock-frocks and had white ribbons tied around their hats as a mark of respect, although there was more joking and laughing than solemnness in their manner. But even this large crowd was greatly outnumbered by the spectators from Wallingford and the surrounding villages who had come to watch the railwayman's funeral, and were estimated by the local paper as between two and three thousand. A procession of about two hundred navigators followed the coffin from The Forty to the churchyard, where the spectators parted to allow the cortege to pass into the church. Every corner of the building was filled for the service, with many crowding outside by the doors and windows.

Revd Lloyd was not going to let pass this rare occasion when he had the attention of the navigators. He took the unusual step of preaching a sermon, hoping that with his words 'the seed now to be sown by the hand of man, may be watered by the dew from heaven; and, taking root in the hearts of my hearers, may spring forth, and bear fruit abundantly, to the honour, the praise, the glory of his holy name'. The vicar warned particularly against disregard for the Sabbath and the sin of drunkenness, reminding his audience, who grew increasingly impatient, of the fire and brimstone that awaited them if they did not change their ways. After perhaps half-an-hour or forty minutes of admonition and warning, Revd Lloyd concluded the ceremony with a hymn and released the mourners back out into the sunshine for the committal of the body.

* * *

All through 1838 and the first half of 1839 the navigators made excellent progress. By July 1838 the cutting had already grown to a huge slash through the hill, with the spoils carted by wagon eastward and westward to form the necessary embankments over the marshy ground. The chief engineer, Isambard Kingdom Brunel, was obsessive in trying to ensure that the railway was almost completely level, so that few stretches built were on the original ground rather than in a cutting or on top of an embankment[1]. By August 1839 it was fully expected that the new bridge across the Thames would be finished for Christmas and that the new section of line would open in the spring. Then the rains came. Unprecedented amounts fell through the late summer, autumn and winter, and the land purchased for the mining of gravel for ballast was flooded and unworkable. To keep the work moving forward, they dredged the Thames for gravel instead. In early 1840 at last a partial section of single track was finished, which allowed an engine and trucks to be deployed to help with completion of the work. Cholsey people had their first sight of the iron monsters that would soon be in regular use through the parish.

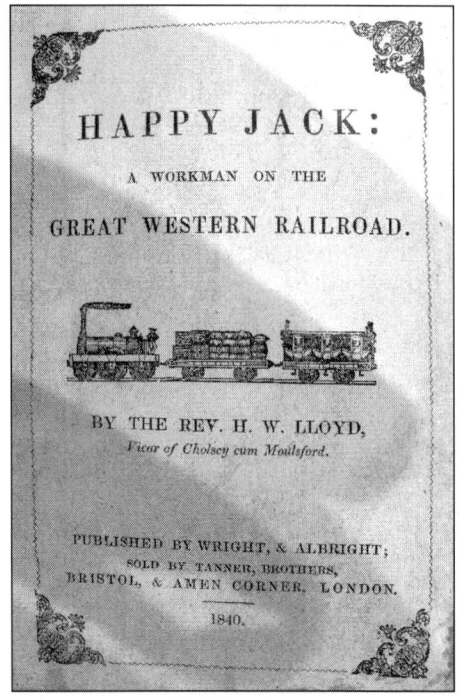

Fig. 4.3 Revd Lloyd's book about his convert

---

[1] The line was sometimes later referred to as 'Brunel's billiard table'.

With the spring the rains eased and the contractors could complete their work. The first section of the Great Western Railway had opened between Paddington and Maidenhead in June 1838, and the plan had been to open the whole of the next section through to Steventon. Instead, because of the delays, the line was first extended to Reading, which opened on 30 March 1840. Finally on Monday 1 June, it was the turn of the section through Cholsey to open for public use.

Excitement started to build on the Saturday, when it became known that the directors were coming to inspect the new section. At 12.30 p.m. a set of first class coaches pulled into Steventon station hauled by the locomotive *Charon*, and Mr Brunel, together with several directors and ladies, descended to inspect the works. The journey from London had only taken an astonishing one hour ten minutes. Sunday and Monday were fine days, and thousands of spectators gathered at Steventon, along the line, and at the new station in Cholsey field to witness the opening. Steventon was styled Oxford Railway Station, providing links to the university city via the turnpike road, while the station in Cholsey parish was initially called 'Moulsford' and then a few months later, 'Wallingford Road'[1]. Two other stations opened that day on the new line, at Goring and Pangbourne[2]. The initial service consisted of eight trains a day, with three on Sundays, and was immediately popular, with around 2,400 tickets sold just on the new section of line each week. To carry such numbers would have required hundreds of stage coaches, and the routes that competed with the new railway now saw rapid decline. However, those feeding the stations saw an improvement, as did the turnpikes leading to them, and the toll collector in Winterbrook on the Wallingford to Reading road saw a substantial jump in his takings.

The locomotives that drove the trains were an awe-inspiring sight to the villagers, used as they were to nothing more powerful than a horse or an ox. Mounted above the large pair of driving wheels was the long cylindrical boiler with an open cab at the rear and a tall chimney stack at the front. Of the twenty or so engines in Brunel's possession at the time, only the four in the Star class were reliable[3]. Those in charge of the locomotives needed great skill to avoid bursting a cylinder or bending a connecting rod. Most of the drivers were tough, experienced men from the north of England, who worked in all weathers to coax the beasts into action for 44 shillings a week.

---

[1] Remnants of the original Wallingford Road station, near to the bridge across the Thames, are still visible from the A329 Reading Road bridge across the railway. See the map in Fig. 7.1.

[2] Didcot opened after the branch line to Oxford began operation in 1844. Tilehurst station opened in 1882.

[3] One of these locomotives was the *Morning Star*, commemorated in the public house on Papist Way, which was given its name sometime before 1878.

Behind the polished brass of the engines and dressed in their uniforms of white corduroy jacket, trousers and cap, freshly laundered every Monday, they were a stirring sight.

By Act of Parliament the Great Western Railway could set its own laws as to what happened to the passengers who ventured onto its properties. Only first class passengers were really wanted; second class travellers were tolerated in the hope that next time they would travel in first; whilst third class was only available in open coal wagons on selected goods trains after dark. At the station the traveller was sold a ticket, hand-written with the date, destination and train. On the platform the ticket was inspected by a policeman, impressively dressed in the regulation uniform of 'rifle-green' tailcoat with brass buttons and tall leather-crowned top hat. The conductor then assigned the passenger to a carriage, taking no notice of any expressed desires of the traveller. The accommodation owed a lot to the legacy of the stage coaches, with luggage tied to the roof and only those paying the most having any comfort. The second class carriages had roofs, but open sides, so that on stormy days they filled with rain, and in the winter, with snow. On more than one occasion passengers were taken out of the carriage frozen solid and left outside the station to recover or die.

Fig. 4.4 Isambard Kingdom Brunel

Once all the passengers were inside, the doors were locked, regardless of the fact that overheating axles or flying cinders could set the wooden carriages alight. In 1842, 53 passengers on a French train burnt to death in just such an incident. At each station the guard would only let out those passengers with tickets for that destination, oblivious to all other calls of nature, hunger or thirst. Railway accidents were commonplace. There were no signals and no regulation of which engines should be using the track, other than the timetable. Policemen patrolled beats 2-3 miles long beside the line checking for problems and could signal danger to the drivers, but the engines took over a mile to stop once they were up to their full speed of 40 or more miles an hour. Brunel happily admitted that the brakes were 'tolerably useless'. Trains crashing into broken-down engines were a common occurrence.

In addition drunkenness was a frequent complaint against the railwaymen. The conductor was nominally in charge of the train and supposed to ride with the driver to ensure that the latter did not get too drunk. But on one occasion, the driver of an up train[1] from Slough left the engine in the charge of the fireman and made his way back along the roofs of the carriages to the guard's van, where he happily sat down with the conductor to quaff a gallon flagon of ale, much to the horror of the passengers present. He made the return journey to the front just in time to handle the arrival at Paddington. But even sober drivers could do nothing when the problem was on the track, such as when some points were left wrongly set by two policemen who had repaired to the pub, causing the down train to swerve into the carriage sheds at Maidenhead and cause untold damage before being finally brought to a halt.

Despite the dangers, those who could afford it began to use the railway in large numbers. They were encouraged by the first member of the royal family to use the Great Western, who chose to start her journey in Cholsey. The Dowager Queen Adelaide, the widow of William IV, had been on a tour of Buckinghamshire followed by a visit to the Archbishop of York's residence at Nuneham. On Saturday 15 August 1840 she travelled by carriage from there to Wallingford Road station, where a specially prepared royal train awaited her. The ornately appointed state carriage had a crown mounted on the roof and was furnished with silk hangings, Louis XIV sofas and a rosewood table. It was flanked by two other saloon coaches for her entourage. She was welcomed by the Chairman of the Great Western Railway Company, and in charge of the locomotive *Charon* was Brunel himself. Brunel liked to show off the technical superiority of his wide gauge railway, describing the so-called standard gauge as only suitable for coal trucks. The train positively flashed along, and the journey to Slough

Fig. 4.5 Dowager Queen Adelaide

---

[1] 'Up trains' were those heading for the London terminus, in this case Paddington, while 'down trains' were travelling in the opposite direction.

took a mere 38½ minutes, an average speed of nearly 50 mph. Perhaps the journey was rather bumpy, as Brunel subsequently arranged for the four wheels of the oversize coach to be augmented with a further four before Queen Victoria rode in it two years later. From Slough Queen Adelaide proceeded by more conventional means to her residence at Bushey.

The royal visit was an early example of how the railway was causing Cholsey to feature in newsworthy events, albeit as a bit player in a larger drama. Injuries were commonplace on the railway, and the first fatal accident at Wallingford Road station occurred just two years later. It concerned a certain Robert Munday, a man of 78 who lived in Islip, northeast of Oxford. On Sunday 28 August 1842 the widower had been visiting his son in the nearby village of Elsfield, before setting off to walk home alone. Although still working as an agricultural labourer, he had grown rather feeble-minded, and his son became worried when he learnt from his sister that their father had never reached his destination. After making enquiries, it was discovered that instead he had been spotted in Marston heading for Oxford. No more was known of his subsequent movements.

The new railways were often used as footpaths by travellers, providing as they did a dry, level and direct route between settlements, much preferable to the often muddy, twisting and rutted roads and paths. Dusk came early on Wednesday 7 September as a thunderstorm rolled in from the Downs across the railway line at Cholsey. A labourer working near the station saw an old man walking on the up line and warned him of the danger, but he took no notice. At 7.30 p.m. the stoker on the approaching luggage train was the first to see the pedestrian, and sounded the whistle. Whether because of deafness or the thunder that was rolling at the time, he seemed not to hear. The buffer of the locomotive struck him in the back and killed him instantly. The engine was stopped, but there was nothing to be done. The inquest was held in the Royal Hotel[1] behind Wallingford Road station two days later, at which point the man's identity was still unknown. But his son was alerted by the publicity and came to identify him, so that, on Monday 12 September, the unfortunate man could be buried in Cholsey churchyard under his rightful name.

Many more deaths occurred on the railway at Cholsey over the succeeding years, but the railway also featured in criminal cases of national importance when the station was used for escape by the malefactors and

---

[1] Built by Brunel, this hostelry was more commonly called the Railway Hotel or Railway Tavern, but was known for a period as the 'Royal Hotel' following Queen Adelaide's visit. It is now converted into flats and known as 'The Gables'.

pursuit by the police. One particularly noteworthy case happened just four months after the railway opened.

* * *

The young man descending from the second class carriage at Wallingford Road station late on the afternoon of Friday 25 September 1840 was of a dashing appearance. He wore a blue cap, a rose-red neckerchief and a cloak of blue velvet, and his luxurious mustachios resembled those of a military man, although he had never been in service. William Davey did, though, have about his person a swordstick and a pair of heavy duelling pistols, together with the wherewithal to fire them. His financial situation had led him to a desperate decision and he was heading for Dorchester-on-Thames, his original home, with murder in mind.

The Daveys were well-known landed gentry in the neighbourhood, able to trace their origins back to the sixteenth century. They were Roman Catholic, and suffered from some persecution in the early days, but from the eighteenth century onwards they prospered. They had long occupied the manor house at Overy, southeast of the town, where they farmed extensive land holdings, gaining fame for their advanced agricultural practices. William's grandfather, also called William, introduced a four-course rotation system, was praised for his ploughing, and made several advances in crop yields and animal husbandry. He was a founder of the Oxford Agricultural Society, and George III was said to have visited his model farm.

William's grandfather married the daughter of the steward of Stonor in 1784, and they had a daughter and four sons: (another) William, John, Robert and George. The young man who descended from the train was Robert's son, but he had lost his father in 1823 when he was only five years old. Four years later his mother died too, and his uncle John became his guardian. John and his wife Elizabeth were childless, and treated their nephew as their own son, looking after his schooling and welcoming him into their home during the holidays. Robert's will provided funds for William's maintenance, but his primary inheritance came from his grandfather, who died in 1831. The will left £6,000 to his favourite grandson, to be held in trust until his majority.

John Davey felt that he had grown close to his nephew and had named him as his own heir in his will. But their relationship changed after William reached the age of 21 in September 1838. Coming into his own money and living in London, he became reckless, living a lavish lifestyle at a large and fashionable hotel near Bond Street. In the summer of 1839, as William squandered his fortune, they argued and fell out to such an extent that there was no further communication between them, apart from the occasional letter. William had threatened his uncle, so John was a little worried when he appeared at his house in the middle of September 1840. The young man said that he was now short on funds and asked for money. Rather than invite him into the house, John sent for his brother George, who lent him £40, advising him to take greater care of this money. John shook his nephew's hand when he left, and thought that they parted on somewhat better terms.

That had been ten days earlier and William Davey now had an altogether different view as he set off northwards along the turnpike from Wallingford Road station. He refused the offer of a ride from the driver of the horse-drawn omnibus that ran through Cholsey from Mouslford to Wallingford; it was still light and he needed it to be dark for what he had in mind. Several noticed the young man in his striking attire as he passed through Wallingford Market Place around half-past six. An hour later he paid the toll to the keeper as he crossed Shillingford Bridge, taking the turnpike road to Dorchester. After passing over the bridge spanning the river Thame[1] into the town, he turned sharp left down Bridge End road. A couple of hundred yards later he reached Bridge House[2]. It was nearly eight o'clock as William let himself through the gate into the walled garden of his uncle's residence. He concealed himself amongst the laurel bushes that grew close

Fig. 4.6 Wallingford Road station c1880

---

[1] The river Thame flows into the Thames at Dorchester.

[2] This large house became the presbytery to St Birinus, the Catholic church established in 1849 by John Davey in the grounds of his house.

by the path.

John Davey had been attending a vestry meeting in the town when he returned to his house about half-past-eight. He came via the garden gate, locking it behind him, as was his habit about that time of an evening. Then, as he walked along the path by the bushes, he heard a noise. A French boy was staying with the family at the time and John Davey thought that it was some kind of game. He reached forward and struck the laurel bush with his cane, when suddenly there was an explosion and he felt a violent pain in his chest.

Thinking he had only moments to live, John shouted "Murder!" as loudly as he could and ran for the house. His servant Mary came running and helped him examine the wound. By a strange fortune the bullet had struck one of the metal buttons on his coat and the skin was not broken, although the following day the doctor treated a livid bruise on his chest 3 inches in diameter. When Mary went outside to where the perpetrator had struck, she found only footprints leading to the gate, which was once again unlocked.

William Davey ran down the street and hurried across the fields to the bridge across the Thames at Little Wittenham, despondent that his plan did not seem to have worked. He retraced his steps south through Wallingford and Cholsey, but continued on past the station to Streatley, where he stopped at The Bull for a pint of ale. It was now after 11 p.m. and he walked on through the night, arriving at Reading in the early hours, his boots and trousers covered in mud from the appalling roads.

Meanwhile John Davey had alerted his brother George, who made enquiries locally and discovered a witness who had seen William loitering in the neighbourhood. George rode off in pursuit with a friend, travelling down to Cholsey where they waited for the early mail train at Wallingford Road station. At Reading he saw his nephew on the platform and called to the conductor to unlock the carriage door. But by the time this was done, William had boarded and been locked into another coach, so George judged it

Fig. 4.7 Bridge House in Dorchester

safest to resume his seat. At Paddington they finally caught up with their quarry, grabbing hold of the man and calling for help. A struggle ensued until James George, a railway policeman, ran up and managed to secure the accused, without having to draw his truncheon. They searched William and found the pistols, one of which had clearly recently been fired.

Joseph Collard, the chief police inspector at Paddington, escorted the prisoner in handcuffs back to Cholsey on the next down train and thence to Dorchester, where he was examined by a magistrate. He was remanded into custody, and Inspector Collard delivered him personally to Oxford gaol later that same evening. A week later William Davey was brought before a full bench of magistrates at the gaol and a thorough examination made. Mr Hedges, solicitor at Wallingford, appeared for the prosecution, whilst William defended himself. Numerous witnesses were called who testified to the accused's progression from Cholsey to Dorchester and back, and after six hours the bench committed the prisoner to appear before the next assize court on the capital charge of 'shooting with intent to kill'.

William had five long cold months in Oxford gaol to contemplate his situation, as the Lent Assizes were not held until Wednesday 3 March 1841. For that trial he fielded a whole defence team, led by Mr Sergeant Ludlow, but it did him little good. A dozen witnesses again testified to William Davey's journey to and from Dorchester, from Jacob Talbot, a labourer in the stables at Wallingford Road station, to James Palmer, the governor of the Wallingford Union Workhouse. The defence called no witnesses and instead Mr Ludlow threw doubt on the identification of his client by the witnesses and questioned whether the gun was actually loaded with a bullet. Without the intention of murder, the charge could not hold. In the end the jury agreed with him, and only found the prisoner guilty of shooting with intent to cause grievous bodily harm. This saved William from the gallows, but the judge, finding no sign of contrition in the outlook of the prisoner, sentenced him to fifteen years' transportation.

William Davey was taken to the hulk *Justitia* berthed at Chatham on the Thames Estuary. He languished there for over two months before being put aboard the *David Clarke*, bound for Van Diemen's Land. The journey took five months, with particularly awful weather in the southern ocean, where it was wintertime. For some reason the surgeon failed to issue the usual lemon or lime ration, and scurvy became widespread, which he treated with nitrate of potash in lime. Bleeding gums, loose teeth and ophthalmia, which can lead to blindness, were rampant, but only one convict died during the voyage. Following disembarkation William was given two years of probation in the labour gang at Rocky Hills. This isolated station had just been opened on the east coast of the island and was so poorly managed that the entire staff were dismissed after an inspection in 1846.

William's behaviour was in general good, and he passed through the usual stages of becoming a Pass Holder in October 1843, receiving his Ticket of Leave in October 1847, and being granted a Conditional Pardon in July 1850. Not long after his release from the gang he was given permission to marry, and his wedding to Jane McDonald, a free woman, took place on 21 November 1845 in Launceston. Once William was free, it would appear that they stayed in the town and lived a quiet life. They seem not to have had any children and they died when still quite young; William in 1865, aged 47, and his wife two years later.

Back in Dorchester his uncle John lived almost as long, dying in 1863 at the age of 76. He had changed his will, and in any case had donated much of his money to worthy causes, particularly the establishment of a Catholic chapel in the town, St Birinus, which opened in 1849. In 1898 Edward Charles Davey, first cousin to William, published a memoir of the Davey family. It was comprehensive in detailing the long history of the farming dynasty, but failed even to mention the events that exiled the black sheep of the family to the other side of the world.

Earlier, in Cholsey, after the stir caused by William Davey's arrest and trial in 1840, talk returned to more parochial concerns, particularly the changes proposed for the village's farming, land and taxes.

Chapter 5 Land Reform

On Wednesday 4 October 1837 Cholsey Farm was packed with visitors. After fourteen years managing Cholsey's largest agricultural enterprise, Thomas Washbourne was selling up. Under the hammer were 200 ewes, thirteen rams, 600 lambs, 21 cart horses, eleven ploughs, eight carts and countless other livestock and equipment. Born in 1791 in Highworth, Wiltshire, Mr Washbourne had become an important member of the community. Arriving in the village in 1823, he was immediately appointed an overseer and then Revd Cottle's churchwarden. After the latter's death he continued in post as the parish churchwarden. Although he had often been the prosecutor in thefts from the farm and other crimes, he was generally a kindly person and well known for his sunny smile. But now, at the age of 45, Thomas was leaving the farming business and Cholsey to move with his family to Shaw-cum-Donnington, near Newbury, where he would become a land agent and valuer.

Thomas had spotted a lucrative opportunity arising from the Tithe Commutation Act, which had become law the previous year. The payment of tithes in kind was to be halted; all landowners would in future pay their obligation in money. In some parts of the country cash tithes were already used, but in Cholsey Parish the change had yet to happen for most of the land, the biggest exception being the manor fields which were exempt from payment. Thomas became a land agent specialising in carrying out the detailed commutation work necessary. He first found plenty of employment in neighbouring parishes, but in 1841 it became Cholsey's turn.

Thomas Washbourne embarked on the major undertaking, first employing William Baillie of Newbury to carry out the task of mapping the lands. The survey work was completed accurately and carefully, and the following year the resulting map, which measured about 10 x 4 feet, was delivered to Mr Washbourne. The map met the highest standards and was later affixed with the Commissioners' seal; only one sixth of all tithe maps achieved this level of quality. While the mapping was in progress, one of the tithe assistant commissioners, Thomas James Tatham, held various meetings with interested parties in the parish. Having considered the proofs offered, he announced an award which detailed all the lands exempt from all tithes, such as Cholsey Farm, and others exempt from the small tithe, such as Lollingdon. No agreement had been reached on the amounts involved, so he imposed a rate. The great tithe, payable to the current impropriatrix[1],

---

[1] An impropriator is a lay person who enjoys an ecclesiastical benefice (income from a church office) as their own property.

Louise Minshull, would be nominally £675 per annum, and the small tithe and other amounts due to the vicar would be £219 12s 6¾d. The total for both parties was the equivalent of production from the tithable lands of the parish of about 850 bushels[1] of wheat, 1,500 bushels of barley, and 2,170 bushels of oats, using the seven-year average price of these grains.

The next stage was to record the details of each plot: its size, ownership, who the occupier was and what it was used for. Each was numbered on the schedule and written in the appropriate plot on the map. With about 2,600 strips spread over the common fields of Cholsey, the cataloguing took a long time. The tithe due for each plot from each owner was then calculated at an average rate of about 6s 4d per acre, but varied up or down depending on the strip's possible crop yield, such that the grand total was equal to the tithes to be paid. These amounts were actually not fixed, but rather were a par value known as the corn rent, which was translated into an actual rent using the corn price published by the government each year.

It wasn't until 1845 that all this work was completed and the resulting draft was deposited at the Chequers public house for inspection. A meeting to hear objections was held at the Railway Tavern on Saturday 26 April, and the final version was approved by the tithe commissioners on 3 September. Thomas Washbourne made two copies of the map for lodging with the parish and the diocesan officials, and sent the original to the commissioners

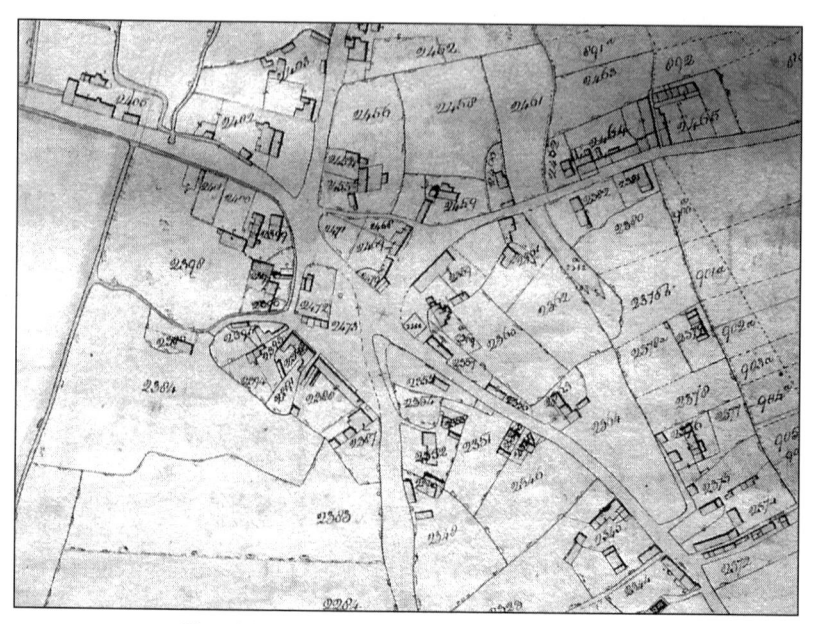

Fig. 5.1 The tithe map around The Forty

---

[1] A bushel was eight gallons or about 36 litres.

in London. Some changes were made subsequently to individual tithes as lands were merged or changed, but the commutation decision essentially set the tithe rent-charge for the best part of the next hundred years[1]. Although it was the 88 owners listed who were responsible, it was rather the 111 occupiers who would have to pay the charge.

Although no doubt the change was widely discussed and grumbled about, it was a minor affair compared to what came a few years later. The General Enclosure Act of 1845 allowed for enclosure without a specific Act of Parliament under the auspices of permanent commissioners. Thomas Washbourne was not involved in managing the fraught question of enclosures for the parish. He had moved to Oxford and was now carrying out work on enclosures in that county. Later he would move to London, but he kept fond memories of the village and returned to Cholsey before his death in July 1855. Alongside his two wives and two of his children, he was buried in a chest tomb close to the church.

The process of enclosure in Cholsey was carried out by William Bryan Wood, a land surveyor from Barnbridge, near Chippenham, who used Mr Washbourne's excellent tithe map as a starting point. Discussions amongst the major landowners began not long after the commutation of tithes, and by 1848 they had reached agreement. Enclosure was clearly in the interest of the largest freeholders, greatly increasing efficiency by substituting many scattered strips with a larger field that could be worked in much less time. A provisional order was made by the Enclosure Commissioners on 19 December based on the consent of owners of two-thirds of the land. Only agreement amongst the five biggest landowners was needed to reach this target, and on 8 February 1849 the commissioners announced via advertisements in the local press that they intended to proceed with enclosure. The detailed award by the commissioners was not completed until two years later, but work began much earlier to implement their decisions.

The execution of the enclosure plan totally changed the landscape of the parish. Ownership of the farming strips was swept aside and each landowner was assigned one or more consolidated fields in their place. Each was to be enclosed, and the award spelt out who was responsible for the erection of a fence or the planting of a hedge. The 2,600 or so separate strips were reduced to fewer than 200 fields and plots.

---

[1] Tithes came to an end in the twentieth century. The Tithe Act of 1936 replaced tithes payable to the owners, who were compensated with government stock, with annuities payable to the government. The Finance Act 1977 finally extinguished the whole system.

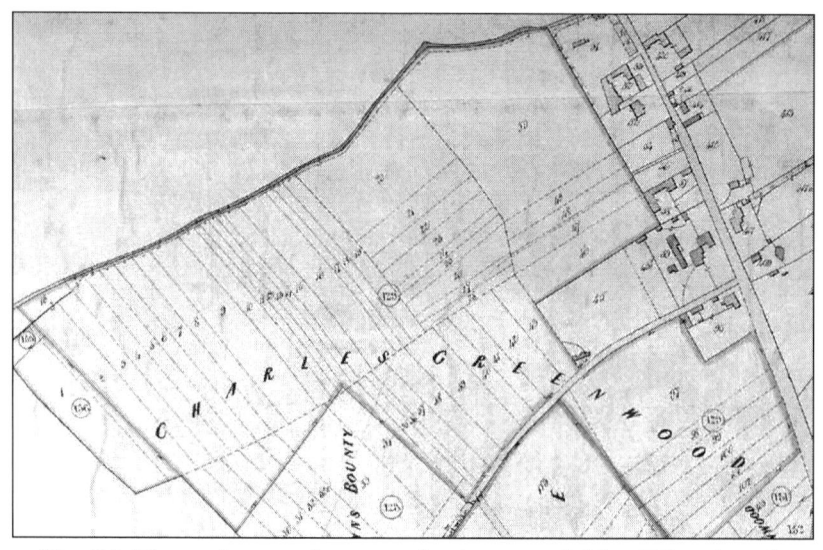

Fig. 5.2 The enclosure of many strips into one field at Winterbrook

Not only was the agricultural system radically altered, but so was the way the villagers got about. Five roads and twenty-one footpaths and bridleways were to be closed, including the main route to Wallingford that went by Cholsey Mill to the turnpike, and Bier Way, the bridleway to Moulsford which crossed the railway at what had already become known as 'Silly Bridge'. In their place were three new footpaths, eleven new private roads and five wide public roads, including a direct long straight joining Winterbrook to the village centre, to be called the Wallingford Road, and its continuation beyond Drove Lane to the Downs and hence to Ilsley, to be known as West Field Road and then Ilsley Road.

Some time before the enclosures took place, smaller landowners were worried about what it would mean to them. They would bear a share of the surveyor's and other costs, and the expense of fencing a small field could be high. In October 1849 William Wood met with the farmers in the Railway Tavern to present their allotments, so that they could spread manure at the start of the new season. Apparently, most of those present were happy with the allocation, but by then many of the smallholders had already sold out. In the final allocation there were only 60 owners left. Many of these were non-residents, such as the Countess de Broc, Queens College Oxford and Revd Thomas Wintle, Rector of Tidmarsh, near Reading. However, by far the largest owner was James Morrison, with nearly a thousand acres of land assigned to him.

James Morrison was a self-made man, born in 1790 the son of an innkeeper in Middle Wallop, Hampshire. Starting as an employee of a London haberdasher, he married the owner's daughter and expanded the business. By the 1820s he was already a millionaire and invested widely and wisely to gradually become one of England's richest men He bought up huge swathes of the country, purchasing Basildon Park in 1838. Some time earlier he bought the lands on Cholsey Hill to become the new Lord of the Manor, fields that were outside the commissioners' remit. By 1850 he owned more than a third of the surface area of Cholsey parish.

Prior to the enclosures, at least seventeen small landowners sold their holdings to Mr Morrison. Many more, who previously rented strips as tenants, also lost the ability to grow their own crops, and the commons in West and East Moors disappeared. The plight of the landless was recognised to a small extent, with the allotment of ten acres in three parcels of land to the Churchwardens and Overseers for the benefit of the labouring poor[1]. These were not free, however; they attracted a rent charge of £16 10s, the net value of their crop potential, being 15.7 bushels of wheat, 27.8 bushels of barley and 40 bushels of oats. For a typical plot of 10 rods, allowing 160 plots in all, the rent amounted to about 2s per annum, not a lot, but still a sum to be found. However, in this Cholsey was lucky; many parishes had no allotments for the poor at all, while others had land rented by farmers at much higher rates. Also allocated by the commissioners for their benefit were two chalk pits on the new West Field Road, available for the liming of their pieces of land.

Twenty years after the Swing Riots, the plight of the average labourer was little improved. The average weekly wage was still only about 8s per week, barely changed from 80 years earlier, with Berkshire one of the most poorly paid counties in the country. In the north of England wages had risen, as workers moved to the industrial towns for higher pay, but in the south the surfeit of agricultural labourers continued. Supply and demand had replaced the Speenhamland system in keeping wages low. Although the cost of foodstuffs had dropped somewhat, with flour now costing 1s 8d a stone, still it was hard to get by. Many women and children had to exist on bread and lard accompanied by vegetables from the garden and weak tea, with the scraps of bacon and cheap meat saved for the labourer. The bread was also sometimes made from poor quality grain, including barley, as acknowledged by one vicar in Dorset who wrote to *The Times* pitying their lot: 'Fed like fowls, sheltered like beasts, they are expected to hallow the Sabbath, reverence the Game Laws, and hold their tongues.' For those who fell below even this level of subsistence, the workhouse beckoned. One in seven people in the county was a pauper.

---

[1] These 'allotments' are still extant on the Wallingford Road, Station Road and Ilges Lane, although the latter two are somewhat reduced in size since parts were sold off by the parish for development during the twentieth century.

Not surprisingly, many were upset with the new enclosure arrangements that favoured the better off again, and unrest grew in the neighbourhood, with fire-setting became common once more. On 8 December 1849 a barn at Lollingdon was targeted and burnt to the ground, and only thanks to a large group of locals and the engine from Aston was the fire stopped from spreading. Ten days later, perhaps as a sign of ill omen, workers constructing a new section of Papist Way at the end of Honey Lane uncovered four skeletons at a depth of three feet. More were discovered in the following week, but there was nothing to indicate how old their interment might be. One skeleton was very tall, another doubled up, and none had coffins. Some local antiquarians suggested that they dated from the civil war, others that they belonged to the fallen of the battle of Aescesdûn, between the Danes and the Saxons of King Alfred[1].

Despite the upset and unrest, work continued. As well as changing the fields and rights of way, the commissioners also changed the watercourses. The brook was almost completely rerouted from its source south of the railway to its exit into the Thames. This meant the stream ran farther west on its northerly passage and no longer fed the ditches that ran beside The Forty and along the Causeway, and many meanders and tributaries with which the parish abounded were filled in[2]. For the benefit of the Parish Surveyor of Highways, two gravel pits were created, one situated off the West Field Road, and the other near to Papist Way.

By the end of 1851 the works were finished and landowners and farmers were becoming used to their new domains. Poorer people now had less access to land for their own benefit and were arguably worse off, but the process of change over the previous years had seen no major crime wave. On 22 September 1849 the *Reading Mercury* reported that during the last three years nobody from the parish had been brought before the magistrates, an exemplary record for crime. The claim was denied the next week, with the figure put at fifteen, but nevertheless five a year is not much. However, an alternative explanation for fewer arrests was that those involved were becoming less easy to identify. Something would have to be done.

---

[1] Aescesdûn is thought to be the old name for the Berkshire Downs and the battlefield is supposed to be near to Aston Tirrold. Alternatively, Honey Lane follows the line of an old Roman Road, so the skeletons could have been even older.

[2] The line of the old brook is still visible in the slight depression lined by trees that crosses the Recreation Ground just beyond the mound.

Fig. 5.3 The original course of the brook in the Recreation Ground

Chapter 6 Crime and Punishment

The arsonist of Lollingdon Farm was never caught, and a wave of minor crimes in Cholsey at the beginning of 1850 went unsolved. The house of Richard Neal, a farmer, was broken into and property worth £8 stolen. Then during the night of 23 March his poultry house was raided and three fowls taken. On the same night John Larkcom's butcher's shop door was forced and a sheep's head plus other victuals stolen. Two days later Dr Arnould's house in Winterbrook was burgled, but nothing was taken on that occasion.

More generally, in the early 1850s doubts grew over the effectiveness of a rural police force based on the parish constable. By then the Metropolitan Police had existed for over twenty years and had proved the potential for professionals to cut down crime. Following this example, the Police Acts of 1839 and 1840 allowed for the establishment of county constabularies 'for the preservation of the peace and protection of inhabitants' in such places as the Justices of the Peace felt that the existing system was insufficient. The funding would come 75% from a new county police rate and 25% from central government. But Berkshire and many other counties failed to avail themselves of the Act.

The old method of voluntary policing could trace its roots back to the Anglo-Saxon frankpledge, a joining together of the community with all its members bound by social obligation to keep the peace. One supporter of a professional constabulary wrote that:

> the old system might have worked well in the past when it took two days to travel from Bristol to London, but it is inadequate for a time when a traveller can be whirled from one end of the kingdom to the other at the rapid rate of 40 mph. The whole basis was faulty when persons were drawn from their trades to execute warrants and perform the duties of an office for which they were not trained.

But there was also considerable opposition to such a change, one of the many that reduced the responsibilities of the parish, with some feeling that 'the aim should be to uphold local self-government, not to destroy it by centralisation'. Certain people also felt that a new uniformed force could become a tool for government; arresting opponents, stopping protests and destroying free speech. Many local landowners were against it on expense grounds too.

In 1853 there were riots in several northern towns at a time when much of the army had been sent overseas for the Crimean War. This terrible vulnerability decided Parliament and, following an enquiry, a new County and Borough Police Act became law in 1856 making professional policing compulsory. In that same year the Berkshire Constabulary was established. The Act provided for a maximum of one constable per thousand head of population, and Cholsey was assigned its own constable. It was part of the Wallingford district, which itself was a subpart of the northern or Abingdon district. Wallingford was initially allocated a sergeant and single constable, but, soon after, the borough force of three policemen established by the Watch Committee in 1836 was dissolved on condition that there were at least three officers in the town.

The new chief constable of Berkshire, Col Fraser, was inundated with applications for jobs and held interviews in February 1856. There followed a period of training for the new recruits, including military exercises organised by Sgt Major Phillips, before the new constables dispersed to their stations in April. Cholsey's constable was allocated a uniform consisting of two pairs of trousers, a coat with badge, stock[1], boots, top hat, a cape with badge, and a greatcoat. He also received a staff and handcuffs, and some officers were allocated a cutlass where it was 'necessary for his personal protection in the performance of his duty'. The hours of service were often long and constables patrolled a beat of up to twelve miles, with a series of checkpoints where they might be met at appointed times by their superior officers or other constables. However, the rate of pay from 17s to 21s compared favourably with other jobs available to a labouring man.

For some time to come parish constables continued to be appointed in Cholsey, although it was made clear that the county constable was in charge. Policing was now directed from Reading, Abingdon and Wallingford, not from the parish vestry. Also still used occasionally was the small lockup on The Forty, known locally as the Round House, which had been employed by the parish constables since the eighteenth century. When it was occupied, leering village children would peer through the bars on the door at the prisoner or prisoners, adding to their discomfort.

However, the effectiveness of the building was doubtful, as the previous year a prisoner, Robert Bosher, had found it all too easy to escape. He had joined the Royal Welsh Fusiliers during the recruitment excitement of the Crimean War, but then deserted. Returning to Cholsey to visit his mother, he was caught in the village on Sunday 28 July 1855, two years after he ran away. The constable put him in the lockup for the night. But when the police came the next morning to take him to Wallingford, the door was

---

[1] A stock is a cravat.

open and he had vanished. Someone had passed him a screwdriver through the bars and he had taken the door off its hinges. The constables suspected his 67-year-old mother, Sally Bosher, a harmless lady who lived on The Forty, and they took her, only half dressed, and locked her up instead. However, when she was taken to see the JP he immediately dismissed the case. One of the constables was a blacksmith, and a local wag, a ploughman at Hithercroft Farm, made up a skit on the event which included the chorus (to be sung with a Berkshire accent):

> Who took the woman instead of the man?
> The man with the leather apron ahn.

Robert Bosher, however, was soon recaptured and committed to Reading gaol to await the pleasure of the army authorities. At the court martial in Winchester on 5 September he was sentenced to 112 days' imprisonment with hard labour.

Ten years later Revd Lloyd, vicar of Cholsey, wrote to the magistrates requesting the removal of the village lockup. The chief constable agreed that the bridewell was now useless and the magistrates ordered that it should be pulled down and the materials sold.

* * *

The new county constables for Cholsey often came from other parts of the country and, in contrast to the local parish constables and tithingmen, seldom stayed long. One reason was that in its first ten years, the Berkshire Constabulary, which consisted of 100 or so officers, dismissed 83 men for drunkenness and 81 for failing to appear at their checkpoints.

Despite these shortcomings, the new method of policing was judged a success and gradually additional responsibilities were given to the force. In 1857 superintendents were appointed as Inspectors of Weights and Measures, and in 1860 constables became Assistant Relieving Officers. The latter duty mainly involved rounding up vagrants and taking them to the workhouse, which was a major task, with nearly 3,000 per annum reported a few years later in Wallingford district alone. In 1863 yet another task was added, that of keeping order at the assizes, making the so-called 'Javelin Men' redundant. Nevertheless, the number of officers in the constabulary grew only slowly through the century.

One of the first county constables in Cholsey was Alfred Miller. Alfred was in his late twenties and came from Hampshire and Dorset, and quarters were found for him and his family in Ilges Lane. Like many of his colleagues, he had previously been a general labourer, although all were required to have a certain standard of education and to be able to read and write. Constables had to be tough, as violence against officers was commonplace, often treated as of little consequence by the courts. But during Alfred's tenure in Cholsey it was in fact his parish colleague, Matthew Baldwin[1], who was badly assaulted.

Matthew was a sawyer by trade, and was 50 years old when he was attacked in the course of his duty. It was around midnight on Thursday 28 May 1863 when he was called to a fight outside the Brentford Tailor involving James White, a hawker from Wallingford. Matthew said "Peace!", raising his staff, but White responded with foul language. Alfred Cloudsley, a Wallingford groom aged nineteen, hit the constable with his fist from behind, sending him off balance. White grabbed the staff and hit him violently, knocking him down. Cloudsley then took the staff and struck Matthew on the head, rendering him unconscious.

By now others had gathered at the scene, and William Strange raised Matthew up as Cloudsley threw the staff away into Mrs Gammon's garden. Others helped the constable into the public house, whilst Cloudsley became belligerent with Strange. At that point PC Miller arrived and the troublemakers dispersed. Matthew was taken to Dr Barrett in Wallingford and a nasty gash to his head that exposed the skull was dressed.

Alfred Cloudsley and James White were brought before the magistrates a week later. White pleaded not guilty and claimed that he had been dancing in the Brentford Tailor and only came out to help a boy called George Turner who had been knocked about by some older men. After the ensuing fight, he said, it was he who was hit by the staff and not the other way round. Cloudsley pleaded guilty, but said in mitigation that he indeed saw the constable hit White with the staff and that it was only when Baldwin aimed a blow at him that he grabbed it and hit back. He also claimed that the constable was very drunk. PC Miller responded that his colleague did not seem that way.

The court was cleared while the magistrates deliberated and then reconvened to hear the chairman announce that the case had been clearly proved. However, he said they wished to deal leniently with the offenders, who were each fined £1 with additional costs of around another £1 each. In default they would serve a month in prison, but they were able to pay and left as free men.

Some years later in 1872 there was a much worse assault, and this time it was the county constable John Glass who suffered. It started one Saturday

---

[1] Matthew Baldwin was mentioned in Chapter 3 as the man who married Joseph Ilsley's first wife.

Fig. 6.1 The Swan Inn in the 1930s

evening in August with an altercation a little after midnight between James Hopkins and Charles Kearsey outside the Swan Inn. The latter was very drunk and violent, and PC Glass took him home to the Beehive public house, which was run by his mother, where he had to hold him down until Charles' brother came. During this time a great deal of noise could be heard outside, and when the policeman emerged he found Matthew and Philip Higgs, plus a crowd of other labourers.

"Now my lads," said the constable, "it's time you were away from here; you had better go home, or you'll get into a bother."

Philip Higgs said, "I'll see you —— first; the road is as much to me as it is to you!"

When the policeman threatened to lock him up, Philip grabbed him by the legs and brought him to the ground. He struggled up and got his handcuffs out, but was then struck on the ear and thrown onto his back. Several bystanders joined the affray, and George Clifford grabbed hold of John's collar and began punching him in the head and face, while Frederick Norfolk started kicking him as he lay on the ground. PC Glass tried to get hold of his leg, but then Clifford's wife Mary grabbed him round the face and pulled him down again. He lost his senses briefly, and when he later tried to get up again, Clifford struck him in the face again.

"You ——," he said, "you made me pay 15s once; now I shan't get above a month!"

"Let the —— have it," said Matthew Higgs, "kick his —— guts out!"

At this point the parish constable, Frederick Kearsey, another of Charles' brothers, arrived. Before he could intervene, Matthew Higgs grabbed hold of him, and another bystander, David Rumble, hit him in the mouth. He called to the Beehive for help from his brother, but was again knocked down and assaulted by Mary Clifford.

Finally the crowd, which had grown to about 30 people, left them alone and PC Glass was able to get away and send for assistance. Three constables came from Wallingford and Frederick Norfolk and George Clifford were arrested, while Mary Clifford had to be dragged down the stairs. PC Glass then went with Frederick Kearsey to arrest the Higgs brothers, and another constable apprehended David Rumble. Finally PC Glass was driven by a neighbour to see Dr Barrett in Wallingford. His mouth and tongue were cut, both eyes were effused with blood and blackened, and he was covered with bruises on his face and side. The case of his watch had been bent by a kick and had stopped at 12.30 a.m.

All six arrested were held in custody until their trial the following Thursday before Wallingford magistrates. After hearing the evidence all the defendants were found guilty. George Clifford was sentenced to six months, Philip Higgs to three months, and the other four to one month each, all with hard labour.

* * *

Although policing changed with the creation of Berkshire Constabulary, the courts did not, with the same petty and quarter sessions held by magistrates, and the assizes conducted by judges. The levels of punishment also continued as before, with larceny and robbery dealt with much more severely than simple violence. For example, when James Hopkins of Cholsey was caught on Gatehampton Farm in 1858 with a net in his possession, he was convicted of poaching and sentenced to three months' imprisonment. However, the previous year when Robert Wyatt attacked Elisha Stevens, a land agent, with a hammer and caused some considerable wounds, he was just bound over to keep the peace in the sum of £50.

Assaults on women and sex-related crimes were also often treated leniently. A particularly disgraceful case concerned Henry Cox, who was accused of killing his wife in 1865. They were a couple in their early thirties and had been married for seven years, but had no surviving children. Elizabeth was a quiet and industrious woman who never uttered a cross word, even though her husband would sometimes take off his belt and beat her, or otherwise cause her injury. She was also not a well woman, with a weak constitution and disease in her lungs. They lived with Henry's widowed mother Mary and one other lodger in a cottage on The Forty, just twenty yards from the Brentford Tailor public house.

On Friday 8 December 1865 Henry, a labourer with the Great Western Railway, received his pay for the previous fortnight and went straight to the pub, where he sat down in the tap room to drink beer and play dominoes with three friends. A while later, at about quarter to seven, Elizabeth came looking for her husband, begging him to come home for his supper. Henry followed her out but was not pleased, grabbing her by the shoulder, knocking her bonnet off and dragging her along the ground with one hand while he hit her about the head with his fist. With each blow Elizabeth let out a pathetic squeal. Near to the cottage she was sent sprawling on the ground. It was very dark and Henry's mother came to the door with a light and ushered them in.

Henry ate his tea and grudgingly laid down a sovereign to cover the housekeeping, plus two shillings for his wife to buy a piece of pork. Immediately afterwards he rose and went back to the pub. At this point Mary noticed the large bruise on her daughter-in-law's face. Elizabeth said she had run into the gatepost. She asked what she might put on the injury, as she didn't want to go to church on Sunday with a black eye. Mary mixed some salt butter with vinegar, and Elizabeth rubbed it in.

Several beers later across at the pub, Elizabeth's brother Thomas Garlick came in, and Henry asked him over.

"I won't drink with you," said Thomas, "I'll drink with a man. You have been beating my sister. You can't stand up before a man, but you can hit a poor harmless woman!"

A fight ensued, with Henry coming off worst thanks to the drink. Every time he got up, Thomas knocked him down again. The commotion could be heard outside, and after a few minutes Henry's wife and mother came in and brought the scuffle to an end. Elizabeth looked sick and frightened, and crossed the room to vomit. She left soon after, followed by her mother-in-law. Henry went home later, and his mother had to help him into bed.

The following morning Elizabeth did not get up and Mary took some tea and toast up to her. At about nine o'clock Elizabeth brought up some blood, and Mary sent for Elizabeth's mother. When Hannah Garlick arrived she found her daughter very ill. Elizabeth whispered, "It's all over now, it's over now." Hannah went for Dr Breach of Aston, but by the time he arrived her daughter had passed away. John Spokes, who ran Greenhill Farm and was a man of authority in the village, came to the house on the Saturday afternoon to talk to Henry.

"This is a very serious matter, Cox," Mr Spokes said.

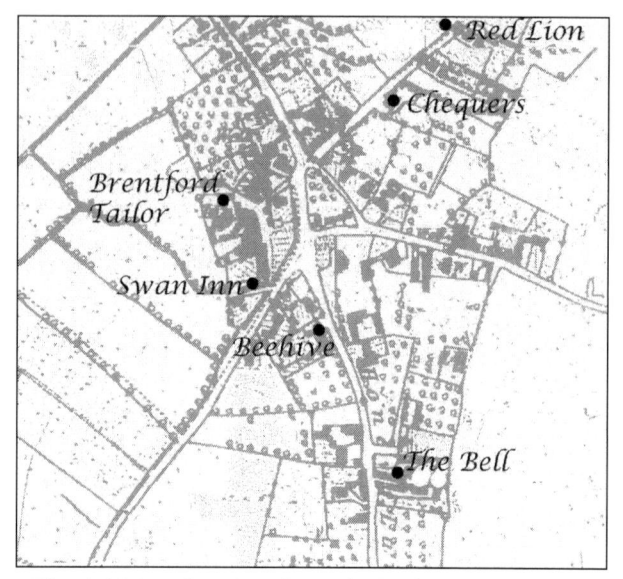

Fig. 6.2 Map showing the pubs in the village centre

"Yes, it is a very unkid[1] affair indeed," replied Henry. "I am sorry for it."

"I saw her going into Wallingford yesterday."

"Yes, she was going into the doctor's. She hadn't been well for some time."

"Of course you will remain and see the end of it."

"Certainly, I'll stand my ground like a man. I'm very sorry for what has happened. I must take what the law gives me."

Just to be sure, the farmer waited until the constable arrived.

The events caused quite a stir in the village and interest was high when the inquest opened on the Monday morning in the Brentford Tailor. The first witness was John Brown, who had seen the attack on the deceased outside the pub, followed by Dr Breach, who had also performed the post mortem. When the doctor said that in his opinion the injuries sustained were the cause of death, the coroner adjourned proceedings for further enquiries.

The inquest resumed on the Thursday. Further evidence was given by friends and relations of the deceased, the landlord of the Brentford Tailor, the Cox's lodger and Mr Spokes. Dr Breach was called again, giving the cause of death as concussion of the brain in somebody of low vital force. He felt that one or more blows had brought about the concussion. The

---

[1] 'Unkid' means troublesome or strange.

coroner asked Henry Cox whether he wished to say anything, but he just replied that he had been the worse for drink and had no knowledge of the accusations. The coroner then summed up and gave directions to the jury. He ruled out accidental death and said the verdict should be either manslaughter or murder. Only if they felt that Cox had killed his wife out of malice aforethought was it to be the latter.

The jury retired for only a few minutes before bringing in a verdict of manslaughter against Henry Cox. The coroner then committed him to the Lent Assizes on that charge.

The trial was held on Tuesday 27 February 1866 in Reading. Mr Williams appeared for the prosecution and Mr Griffits for the defence. Henry denied that he had ill-treated his wife in the early part of the evening, contradicting the evidence of John Brown. His mother and the landlord of the pub painted a rosier picture of the relations between man and wife, and Mr Griffits underlined the fact that she was a sick woman. He also said that the evidence of the principal witness for the prosecution, John Brown, could not be relied upon. He had described in detail the attack on Elizabeth in their passage from the public house to the cottage, and yet he said and did nothing at the time. Mr Griffits suggested instead that the cause of death occurred as she intervened in the brawl in the pub, when she might have received the fatal blow by accident.

Nevertheless the jury found Henry guilty of the charge. The judge, however, felt that a sentence of eight months' imprisonment was sufficient, a large part of which the prisoner had already served.

A couple of years later there was another crime which received a similarly modest sentence for the accused, Joseph Rumble, who was 52 at the time of the incident. The surname Rumble was common in the village, with at least four large families, all descended from Henry and Anne Rumbold, who married in 1776. The men were all agricultural labourers and mostly illiterate, with several different spellings of the surname used over the years.

Joseph Rumble married his wife Fanny in 1840, and a succession of babies followed. At the time of their wedding Fanny was only eighteen, and by the time she died 25 years later she had produced four boys and six girls. Joseph was left with four school-age children, the eldest of which was Harriet. Three years after his wife's death, on 18 April 1868, when Harriet was fifteen, Joseph allegedly indecently assaulted her. Who knows if this was the first occasion, but a few weeks later the local magistrates committed him on this charge for trial at the assizes. At the hearing on 29 June in Reading, the jury had no hesitation in bringing in a verdict of guilty, having heard evidence which the local paper deemed unsuitable for publication. Joseph was sentenced to just eight months' imprisonment.

In the case of suspicious deaths, prosecutions were often brought at the instigation of the county coroner. Established in the eleventh century, coroners had wide powers and could decide, with or without a jury, whether a suspect should stand trial or not. Such a case occurred in 1855 following the death of Bethia Wells, which many villagers suspected was caused by her husband, based on the frequent arguments seen between the couple.

Bethia was 29 years old and pregnant with her first child as a married woman, although she had already borne at least two children out of wedlock. Her daughter Harriet was seven years old, born to a different father when she was known as Bethia Lowe. Margaret Ann, just one, did belong to her husband James, whom she married in September 1853. He was an agricultural labourer, working long hours on a farm some distance from where they lived.

It was the middle of June, a busy time, when she became sick in the stomach and felt poorly through the night, but didn't like to wake her irascible husband. He rose early as usual and went off to work, unaware of her condition. When he came back for breakfast, he found his wife ill, but felt he had to start back for the farm almost immediately, else he would be late. On the way he alerted Bethia's sister, Eliza, an unmarried mother who said she would go round as soon as she had dressed her own children.

But it was some time before she did so, and when she got there she found her sister almost unconscious. She sent for the doctor, but when he arrived he found her already dead. Also in the bed was a lifeless new-born baby. Neighbours were incensed by the uncaring attitude of the family and the coroner ordered a post-mortem. However, no signs of violence were found and the inquest jury returned a verdict for both mother and child of death through a lack of attention and nourishment. In this case the coroner decided that nobody should be prosecuted.

It was a different decision about ten years later in the case of the death of Maria Clifford's baby. She was in fact related to Bethia by marriage, and had already suffered another recent tragedy when her first husband died a few months after their wedding. A widow at 23, she became engaged to be married shortly afterwards. In fact the banns were called just six months after her first husband was buried, but for some reason the marriage was postponed, perhaps because it would have flouted the conventions on mourning. A year later, on 26 August 1866, she finally married James Clifford (the brother of George Clifford, who would later be sent to prison for assaulting PC Glass).

About nine months or so after Maria's second marriage she reached the final stages of her first pregnancy and called for her mother Susanna to help with the lying-in period. Her mother visited several times, but said she had not the time to stay for long. The young woman gave birth in late June and Susanna, who was in her sixties, helped, taking the baby girl away and washing the blood-stained clothing. But the child was not healthy and she promised to take it to the doctor.

Shortly afterwards, when a neighbour went to the privy shared between the five or six cottages in the row, he found a dead newborn infant. He immediately informed the police. The constable made enquiries and discovered Maria with all the signs of having recently had a child. The inquest was held on Friday 28 June 1867 when the coroner returned an open verdict of 'found dead', but Maria's arrest was ordered for concealing the birth. The Offences Against the Person Act of 1861 made it illegal to secretly dispose of the dead body of a recently delivered child, punishable by up to two years' imprisonment, with or without hard labour. When Maria was taken into custody she asked after her baby, still not aware that it was dead. At the magistrates' hearing on 5 July she was committed to the Summer Assizes, but the Grand Jury later dismissed the accusation without a trial. The judge said that the evidence was not conclusive and that there was little motive for a married woman to conceal a birth. But more misery was to follow, as Maria died just over a year later, possibly during the birth of another offspring.

As evidenced by these women, childbirth was often a dangerous and fearful time, especially for those with neglectful husbands and relations. But if the mother was single and alone, it was even worse. A horrific episode happened a few years later at the newly opened lunatic asylum[1] and resulted in a charge of murder.

In November 1870, a month after it opened, Hannah Mulcay or Mulcahy joined the asylum as a laundry maid. She was 26 years old, tall and thin, originally from Ireland, and arrived with good references. It was steady employment and quite good pay at £16 per annum, all found[2]. However, despite being a plain-looking girl, she must have had relations with a man that summer, as the asylum head female attendant, Hannah Horton, noticed in the spring of 1871 that she was becoming rather stout. But she said nothing of her suspicions. As time progressed Hannah would have found

---

[1] The Lunatic Asylum is described in detail in Chapter 8.

[2] 'All found' meant that a servant's accommodation and meals were provided free of charge.

Fig. 6.3 An artist's impression of the County Lunatic Asylum

her job all the harder; it was heavy work six long days each week, and the other two laundry maids were unaware of her condition.

In May Hannah gave in her notice intending to leave in early June, before the confinement. She shared a room with a housemaid, but a few days later the latter left, so Hannah was alone in her bedroom when the contractions started ahead of schedule. As second laundry maid she was in charge of lighting the fires in the laundry room at 6 a.m., but stayed in her room. When Harriett Boulter, the third laundry maid, came to find her at 6.30 a.m., Hannah only opened the door a crack and said she had a headache. Harriett noticed she still had her nightdress on and thought her confused and pale.

At about 7 a.m. Hannah Mulcay found the charge attendant, Martha Attwell, and asked for her pass key, something that servants needed from time to time to carry out their duties. But Martha must have realised something was amiss, for a few minutes later she went to Hannah's room to find her. On the floor she saw a red-stained shawl lying in a fresh pool of blood. Martha ran to fetch the head attendant, who in turn locked the door and went for the medical superintendent, Dr Gilland.

When they returned they found Hannah sitting on a chair outside the door. She followed them inside and, after an examination, Dr Gilland announced that she must have just given birth. Hannah denied it, but Dr Gilland ordered her to be put to bed and sent to Wallingford for Dr Barrett. He arrived at 10 a.m. and conducted another examination, confirming that a child had just been born. Meanwhile Dr Gilland had ordered a search of the water closets and drains for the baby, but none was found. He questioned Hannah again as to the location of the child, and she finally admitted that they were right about the birth. She said her trouble had come upon her prematurely and unexpectedly, and that she had been "out of her mind".

Hannah told them that she had hidden the baby in the drying closet of the foul laundry.

Walter Clayton was dispatched in search. He was the resident engineer, responsible for lighting the engine boiler at 6.30 a.m. for the steam power, which heated the pipes in the various drying closets. Each closet was 8 feet square and contained wooden horses that could be pulled out for ease of access to hang the clothes. When pushed in, the closet door closed. In one such closet, empty of laundry, Walter saw a bundle lying at the back. Crawling on his hands and knees, he lifted the cotton print material off the searingly hot pipes. Inside was a dead little girl.

The inquest was opened two days later at the asylum, but after the initial post-mortem evidence on the child, who was frizzled from the heat, the coroner adjourned the hearing until the Saturday for further medical reports. On Saturday 27 May Charles Barrett and John Hedges Marshall, the two surgeons from Wallingford, were agreed in declaring that the baby had been born alive. Dr Gilland told the coroner that Mulcay was showing symptoms of mental delusion, and should not be asked to give evidence. She did not understand the serious nature of the affair and was not fit to take care of her own interests. The coroner nevertheless ordered that she should be brought in to listen to the hearing.

The proceedings began with evidence from the charge attendant, the third laundry maid and the engineer. Dr Gilland then described his role in the affair and how he had found the blood and accused Hannah of having a baby. At this point Mulcay became hysterical and had to be taken from the room. Dr Gilland ordered a hot wine for her and, after a brief delay, she returned. The medical superintendent continued his evidence, but stated that he had been directed by the Committee of Visitors not to become involved in ascertaining the cause of death of the child. The coroner interrupted that they had no right to place such a restriction. Dr Gilland persisted that he had therefore not attended the post mortem and could make no comment.

Dr Barrett then gave details of the post mortem and confirmed that he believed the child was born alive, but died from the heat. Hannah interrupted proceedings to say that wasn't true; the cause of death was the fall the baby met at birth. Dr Marshall spoke next and said he was of the same opinion as Dr Barrett. The coroner then addressed the jury and said that as the medical evidence was that the baby had been alive and did not die from natural causes, then the verdict must be murder or nothing. After a brief retirement, the foreman announced that they found that the child was wilfully murdered by Hannah Mulcay. She was taken to Wallingford police station and two days later the magistrates committed her to Reading gaol to await trial at the Berkshire Assizes on the capital charge of murder.

Her trial opened on 10 July 1871 in Reading, with Mr Sawyer and Mr Bros for the prosecution. The judge assigned Mr Gough to act for the defence. The evidence given at the inquest was gone through and Dr Barrett gave full and graphic details of the post mortem, detailing the burns and blisters caused by the heat found on the body. He also described a wound to the head, which he said might have stunned the baby, but would not be enough to cause death. It was his opinion that the child might have seemed dead to a confused mother, but that perhaps the little girl regained consciousness in the drying closet, where she cried out the rest of her short life.

Mr Gough concluded with a telling speech for the defence full of pathos, saying that there was no evidence that Mulcay knew that her baby was alive, and therefore she could not be convicted of murder. The jury agreed and acquitted her, but found her guilty of concealment of birth. The judge took into account her state of mind, noting that one of her relations had also been treated at Westminster Hospital in London for a mental condition. He sentenced her to six months' imprisonment with hard labour. The prisoner, who seemed full of anguish through the proceedings, came close to fainting. The father of the child that was Hannah's downfall was neither sought nor found.

Chapter 7 The Growth of the Railway

In 1865 the navvies returned, when work began on the branch line to Wallingford. It was a much smaller undertaking than during the great construction of the main line more than 25 years earlier, and the workmen were correspondingly fewer. But the new junction and link to the market town would provide another boost to the economy and status of Cholsey.

Wallingford had been hurt through a loss of trade, and pressure had been building for some time to do something about it. All the traffic between the town and the railway went by omnibus and cart along the turnpike, which had become highly profitable for the owners. But little was spent on its upkeep, and by 1861 it was in such a terrible state that it was scarcely passable and many preferred to take the detour through Cholsey village instead. In 1862 firm proposals for a branch line were aired and two years later a bill was passed in Parliament.

It was only to be a single track line and the need for embankments, cuttings and bridges was undemanding, at least at the outset. The Wallingford and Watlington Railway Company planned to extend the line across the Thames to Bensington and Watlington once the first section was completed. In Cholsey the platforms at Wallingford Road station would be extended westwards to the turnpike bridge, where a new footbridge would allow passengers to cross to the down line easily. The platform on the up line would extend further under the bridge and into the cutting, which would be stripped back on the north side. A track from a bay near the bridge would run parallel to the GWR lines for a half mile before curving away on an embankment in the direction of Wallingford. It was decided to install only narrow gauge rails, as the GWR was now mixed gauge and the cost would be less.

Much of the route passed over land belonging to Charles Morrison, the eldest son of James Morrison, who had died in 1857. Funding for the new venture as far as Wallingford was assured when he agreed to take the purchase price as shares in the new company. In May 1864 a contract for the construction was agreed with Mr Thomas White and work to set out the line commenced. But progress was slow, and serious excavations at Cholsey only began in 1865. Mr White then undertook to complete the work by 1 October, but this deadline passed with much left to do. By that date the widening of the cutting either side of Silly Bridge in Cholsey was largely complete, and it now presented a near vertical sixty-foot drop on the north side.

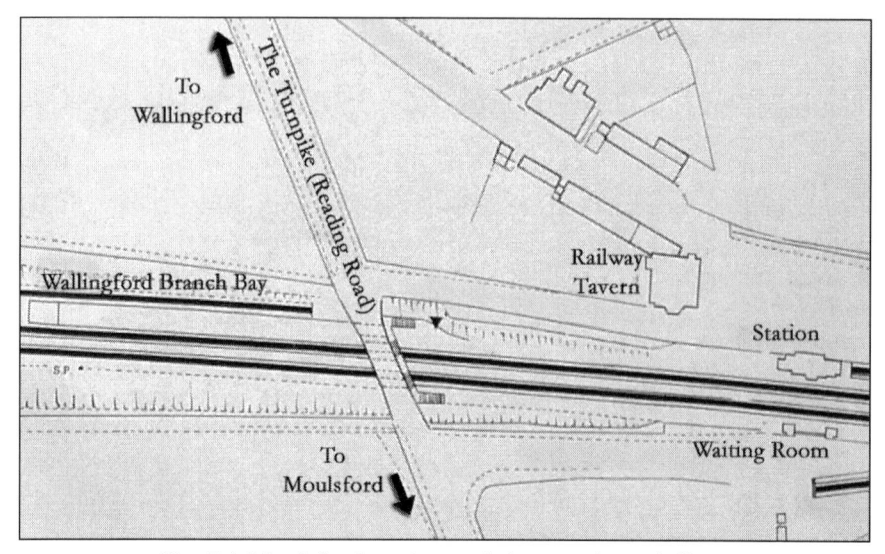

Fig. 7.1 Moulsford station and the new branch line

Progress was slowed again in November when two walls of the new Wallingford station by the Wantage Road were blown down in a gale. In June 1866 a Board of Trade inspection finally passed the line for public use, subject to certain remedial works, including easement of the dangerous slope on the Cholsey cutting. The Great Western Railway had agreed to operate the branch line for a share of the income and they began the service with little fanfare. On Monday 7 July, two days before the Wallingford Regatta, the first train left the town at 7.50 a.m., the engine gaily decorated with flags. Sixty passengers were transported smoothly to the main line and into the new bay at Wallingford Road station, which henceforth was to be known as Moulsford to avoid confusion. GWR subsequently operated a timetable of nine trains per day in each direction.

* * *

Minor crimes associated with the railway continued to be a talking point in the village through the 1860s. Early in the decade, local people were amazed to see a remarkable new contraption installed by the track which allowed mail to be collected and delivered without the train needing to stop. The post was placed in sealed bags which were then secured aloft in a sort of gantry, where they could be collected by a special net scoop held out on a passing mail carriage. At the same time, staff on the train threw out a bag containing the post for Cholsey and Wallingford.

It wasn't long before somebody spotted an opportunity. On 23 March 1862, according to the Wallingford postmaster, Thomas Jenkins, the bags contained about 100 letters destined for London. Very early that Sunday morning a youth, claiming to be called John Smith, found himself in the vicinity. Smith came from Birmingham and was only eighteen years old, but he was already well schooled in criminal acts through his association with James Hardwicke, a swindler and counterfeiter of Bank of England notes. Seeing the bags waiting for the next up train at about 3 a.m. and nobody seemingly about, Smith began to climb the iron ladder fixed to the gantry. Unfortunately for Smith, the mail driver, Benjamin Bartlett, was not far away taking his horse to the stables, and he spotted Smith as he ascended. Benjamin ran towards the young man, demanding to know what he was about, and grabbed the bag which the youth carried. Getting no satisfactory answer, he secured the man and called for help.

James Costiff, a wheelwright, opened the window of his house, which was about eighty yards away down Drove Lane, to see what the disturbance was. As soon as he reached the spot, Bartlett explained the situation, although Smith denied any wrongdoing. Costiff asked him how he came to be on the line, and he replied that he was on his way to Birmingham, but had missed his train at a nearby station.

"Where?" asked Costiff.

"I have forgotten the name of the station, but it began with a 'G'," replied Smith.

"Goring?"

"Yes," Smith replied.

At that point he offered the two men 2s apiece if they would let him go, but instead they took him to Wallingford police station.

Inspector Robert Johnson searched the culprit, finding a considerable sum of money – six half sovereigns, four shillings and a florin – plus, in his carpetbag, housebreaking equipment, including a chisel and a pocket knife. Smith claimed to have been staying at Goring with a female friend, a Miss Hannen, and was walking along the railway as he had missed his train. When the inspector later checked, he found no Miss Hannen in the town. He also found that the sentry box near to the mail gantry had been forced, and the marks corresponded to the shape of the chisel. The magistrates committed Smith to the assizes.

Meanwhile, Smith's accomplice, James Hardwicke, also known as John Jackson, had already been apprehended the previous evening in Reading. Hardwicke had passed off forged £5 and £10 Bank of England notes at a tailor's and a shoemaker's, but the owners had become suspicious and quickly had the notes checked by a banker. The police were alerted and later Sgt Herniman spotted the culprit with a younger man at the Royal Oak. Seeing the blue uniformed officer making his way towards him, Hardwicke took to his heels, followed by the policeman shouting, "Stop thief!" A chase through the streets of Reading ensued, during which one daring citizen was knocked unconscious while trying to stop the fleeing man, until Hardwicke was brought down by Inspector Townsend and others at the railway station.

Two weeks later John Smith was tried for attempted robbery at the assizes. During the interrogation of witnesses, a moment of humour occurred while Benjamin Bartlett was giving his evidence. When asked how he had managed to secure the man until help arrived, he explained that the prisoner had put his hand in his breast as if to pull something out.

"I said to him: 'If you pull anything out I'll put a bullet through your head'."

"Had you any firearms?" asked counsel for the prosecution.

"I had not," replied Bartlett, to laughter. "I told him if he attempted to run away I would put a bullet through his head."

Despite a stout speech by the defence counsel that his client Smith was only standing beside the gantry and had no criminal intentions, the jury were not sufficiently amused to let him off. They found him guilty and the judge sentenced him to six months' imprisonment.

But far worse was to come for the young man. The forgery trial of James Hardwicke was delayed until the next assizes three months later, and after John Smith had been identified as his accomplice, the young man in the Royal Oak, he was brought back to court again. Both were found guilty, with Hardwicke sentenced to five years and Smith to four.

Two years after the attempted mailbag robbery, another minor crime resulted in the same sentence, but with more devastating consequences. Harriett Ann Sawyer was the 15-year-old daughter of William Sawyer, a railway labourer living in Cholsey. One day in February 1864 Harriett was caught throwing a stone at a guard's van on the railway at Cholsey. She was bailed to appear at the Summer Assizes where, five months later, despite saying she only did it for a frolic and never meant to harm anyone, she was sentenced to six months' imprisonment in Abingdon gaol with hard labour.

Harriett returned to Cholsey after she had served her time, but the experience must have been awful and probably caused what happened next. Towards the end of 1865, while still only seventeen, she left home and found lodgings in Aldershot, where she lived a dissolute life. One day, after she had been there a couple of months or so, two soldiers entered her room, and one of them subsequently gave her a severe beating. She returned home on Wednesday 3 January, soon after the incident, complaining of a severe pain in the bowels. On the Friday her mother went to Dr Breach in Aston to get some medicine, and on the following day the surgeon attended the very sick woman. Dr Breach ordered that leeches be applied, but Harriett continued to deteriorate, and on the Monday she died.

Much to the excitement of local people, who felt it was a case of murder, an inquest was held on Wednesday 10 January at the Brentford Tailor. John Breach gave evidence from his subsequent post mortem, saying that the cause of death was severe inflammation of the bowels. But he had found no signs of violence, and Inspector Johnson of the Berkshire Constabulary had little more to add connecting the death to the assault. The jury returned an open verdict, adding that nevertheless they found it a very suspicious case. For his assault on the girl, the soldier had been court-martialled and sentenced to four weeks' imprisonment, subsequently increased to six months for breaking out of his confinement, but he escaped any more serious accusations.

* * *

Railway accidents were unfortunately commonplace on the Cholsey stretch of line, with the consequent damage to equipment and tragic loss of life. Dozens occurred over the remaining years of the century, but here are seven of the most notable.

At around five o'clock on one Saturday morning in July 1863, Thomas Bosher[1] left for work. He was a bricklayer, and the railway track provided the most direct route between his home in West End and the site in North Moreton where he was currently employed. As he walked on the down line, a goods train came towards him on the up line heading for Cholsey. But the noise of the engine and wagons hid another sound, that of a down train. Thomas was struck from behind with great violence.

Fortunately his plight was spotted and he was taken to the Radcliffe Infirmary in Oxford. In immense pain he hung on until the following Tuesday, before dying from his injuries. He was 48 years old and left a wife of the same age and four children. A subscription was started for his widow, who would otherwise have been destitute.

Just seven months later there was another accident in almost the same place. On Wednesday 10 February 1864 John Dowsell, an agricultural labourer aged 67, was walking in the opposite direction, from the Moretons towards Cholsey. It was evening and dark, and John was walking just a little too close to the rails as a train passed. One of the carriage steps clipped his leg, fracturing the limb and sending him tumbling down the embankment.

---

[1] Thomas was the brother of the deserter Robert Bosher mentioned in Chapter 6.

The engine driver, seeing the accident, stopped at Wallingford Road station, and several men walked back down the track to search for the victim. But it took over an hour before they located him in the gloom and could carry him away. He was conveyed to the Royal Berkshire Hospital in Reading, where he recovered slowly from his injuries.

John Dowsell's accident on the railway was not the first misfortune to befall his family. Many years earlier his father, who was a respected horse dealer in North Moreton, was riding from his home to Reading when he fell into the mill stream at Cholsey and was drowned. Then, in 1849, John's brother William was the author of a terrible tragedy in Towcester, Northamptonshire.

William Dowsell was a traveller and clerk for a firm of wine merchants in the town, earning a respectable wage, when he became sweet on Frances Powell, a servant at the Talbot Inn. He was recognised as her suitor but, to their shame, Frances became pregnant in 1847. She asserted that William was the father, but he denied it vehemently, threatening her in a bid to persuade her to withdraw the claim. But she did not and he was recognised as the father after the birth. A few months later they married, but William's affections had now drifted elsewhere, and he was often violent to his wife.

On Friday 30 November 1849 the shutters of their house were closed all morning, and the neighbours became worried when they heard the crying of the baby from within. A ladder was procured and a local surgeon managed to gain access through an upstairs window. After making his way downstairs he found the couple in the back parlour, lying in a pool of blood. One discharged pistol lay on the table and another by the hand of William. The inquest returned a verdict of murder for Frances and suicide for William, and that he had taken his own life after putting an end to his wife's. The baby was taken to be looked after by William and John's married sister.

Fifteen years later the baby's uncle, John Dowsell, recovered from his train injuries – he was lucky to have escaped with just a fractured thigh and a bruise on his arm. Afterwards he was more careful when walking by the railway and lived on to the grand age of 81, finally dying in the Wallingford workhouse in 1879.

Five months after the injury to John Dowsell, there was another railway accident in Cholsey. It was on the day of the Great Western Railway's annual fete in aid of the GWR widows and orphans fund. The event was eagerly awaited each year and thousands converged on Aldermaston Park, conveyed by special trains from the four corners of the company's railway network. One of the revellers was Thomas Morse, a journeyman wheelwright aged 22 who worked for a railway carrier firm in Stroud. The special train from Cheltenham passed through Wallingford Road station, where the platform was crammed with people waiting for the excursion special from Oxford.

The trains were much delayed, but it was a gloriously sunny day and eventually Thomas reached the fete. The park extended over a thousand acres and as *Jackson's Oxford Journal* put it: 'It was a treat, after exposure to clouds of dust and the unclouded rays of a July sun, at length to enter the Park and tread its soft mossy turf, or "rest and be thankful" under its umbrageous trees.' Being a young man, Thomas was probably more interested in the entertainments: shooting galleries, archery, wheels of fortune, music and dancing. On stage there were humorous recitations, comic songs, clowns, feats of the trapeze, and Professor Logrenia's performing cat, birds and mice from the Crystal Palace. Several marquees offered food and refreshment, and perhaps Thomas imbibed a little too much.

The return Cheltenham excursion train left Reading about 8 p.m., but due to the heavy traffic was delayed at Wallingford Road station. Several people alighted to take refreshment at the Station Hotel[1], and after a pause, Thomas decided to join them. To get from a down line train to the hotel, it was necessary to walk to the western end of the platform and cross the lines using the pedestrian bridge, and then walk back along the up line platform.

Fig. 7.2 The Railway Tavern, now private flats

---

[1] The Station Hotel was more commonly known as the Railway Tavern.

Thomas knew a quicker way. He got out of the other side of the carriage and crossed the track. In fact several people had taken the same shortcut, and one or two were wandering about on the up line waiting for the departure of the excursion train to be signalled. Thomas made it to the other side but, perhaps after another drink or two, his attention was distracted on his return. As he stepped onto the rails the Birmingham Express swept through the station at 50 mph, killing him instantly.

It was left to the railway employees to gather together what remained of the young man; splatters of blood marking the passage of the body to its resting place 40 yards down the line. His boots had been thrown off, the legs mutilated, and the skull so shattered that no brains remained within the cavity. The mangled remnants were taken to the hotel to await an inquest, while another day-tripper was treated for leg injuries, having been clipped by the passing express. It was fortunate that nobody else was killed, but for Thomas' young widow, waiting anxiously in Stroud for her husband's return, the news would be devastating enough.

The following year another accident caused spectacular damage but, luckily, no injuries. In March 1865 three wagons were shunted into a siding at Wallingford Road station and insufficient attention was paid to pinning down the brakes securely. A ferocious gale sprang up and, unbeknown to the policeman on duty, George Danford, the trucks started to move. To save money, where the siding joined the main track, the railway company used a small cast-iron block clamped to one rail rather than proper catch points. The trucks had such momentum that they jumped the little block and pushed through onto the main line. Moments later, to the astonishment of George Danford, he saw them reduced to matchwood by a passing goods train.

Like all others in his position, George was summoned to appear before a disciplinary committee in the magnificent boardroom at Paddington. Behind the seated judges hung a large portrait of Charles Russell, eminent chairman of the company from 1839 to 1855, which seemed to stare mockingly at the unfortunate before the panel. Such summonses were known colloquially as 'going to see the picture'. Luckily George was able to convince them of his innocence and departed with his wages intact.

Eight years later another more serious accident occurred at the station. At 7 p.m. on Thursday 11 December 1873, Charles Shepherd, the signalman at Moulsford cabin, just to the east of the station, came on duty. It was a twelve-hour shift, but he was used to it, having been a signalman with the company for many years. The safety of trains was protected by a block system, introduced the previous May, whereby only one train was allowed on each section of track, and the Moulsford cabin was responsible for the Didcot to Moulsford and Moulsford to Goring sections. Communication with neighbouring signal boxes was by way of the Spagnoletti telegraph system, also a recent innovation.

It was a foggy night, but sometime before dawn, the air began to clear. At 6.48 a.m. Shepherd received a signal from Didcot of an approaching broad gauge Bristol goods train, and pinned the block marker disc over to 'train on line'. The next section to Goring was also busy, so the Moulsford signal was set to stop when the Bristol train arrived at 7.05. The driver called up to Shepherd, while the engine was still in motion, "Shall I draw forward to the advance signal?" But by the time the signalman had opened his window to reply, the locomotive was out of earshot, proceeding to the next signal just the other side of the bridge over the Thames. Shepherd signalled back to Didcot, 'line clear', but did not yet mark the logbook to show that the Bristol train had cleared Moulsford.

A moment later the day signalman, Arthur Ward, arrived. A rather nervous and excitable man, he was immediately occupied with complications on the down line involving approaching goods trains and some shunting in the Moulsford sidings. At 7.19 a.m. he received a line clear from Goring and assumed that this was the Bristol train that he had seen pass the station as he had come on shift. Without consulting the logbook, he lowered the semaphore arm on the up line at Moulsford station, unaware that the goods train was actually still sitting a few hundred yards beyond.

At 7.10 a.m. a narrow gauge coal train of seventeen wagons coming from the north passed through Didcot heading for London. They were running an hour and thirty-five minutes late, but made good progress as they steamed through Cholsey cutting heading for London. As the train passed through Moulsford station, the driver suddenly saw the tail lights of the stationary train ahead and realised what was about to happen. He shouted a warning to his mate to apply the tender brake, shut off the steam and reversed the engine wheels, but he had no time to sound the whistle. In the brake-van of the train ahead the guard and under-guard were sitting down when the latter suddenly heard the sound of an approaching engine. He jumped up and peered through the window, before shouting a warning and leaping from the van. The locomotive crashed into the guards van of the Bristol train, turned onto its side and careered onto the down line, scattering trucks and debris from the broad gauge train.

The huge bang must have brought those villagers in the neighbourhood hurrying to see what had happened. The engine driver had leapt clear moments before the impact and landed in the six-foot space between the up and down lines, injuring his ankle but otherwise safe. The fireman intended to stay on the engine but was thrown off onto the bridge parapet, cutting his hand. The head guard was trapped in the mangled remains of the brake-van

Fig. 7.3 The railway bridge at Moulsford

and had to be cut free, but miraculously also survived the crash, albeit with a serious leg injury.

Whilst the injured were taken off for treatment, work began quickly to clear the line. Accidents were all too common, so the response was practised, and by the middle of the afternoon the lines were again working normally. Soon afterwards an enquiry was held, which reported to the Board of Trade a month later. Although the findings were critical of the actions of, in particular, the day signalman, the main cause was put down to inadequate systems at a time of changing shifts. It is just fortunate that nobody lost their life in the ensuing disaster.

Four years later, the stationmaster at Moulsford was less lucky. He died from injuries sustained in his duties, but not caused by a train, rather by a sheep. On Friday 21 February 1878, sometime after four o'clock, Alfred Shaw was helping to drive some sheep into a truck that would be part of a train bound for the market in London. One of them tried to bolt past him, and he grabbed hold of the wool on its back. As it struggled it fell on the flap of the truck, and the stationmaster on top of it. Philip Pugh, a policeman at the station, asked him if he was hurt, and he said laughing, "No – I saved myself by falling on the sheep." He continued with the task and helped drive another fifteen animals into the trucks.

Alfred returned home for his tea at six o'clock, some bread and cheese together with an egg as an extra treat, and then went back on duty an hour later. He told his wife that he had had a hard day and some trouble with a sheep. The animal had jumped at him and he had been bruised in the stomach, although he joked that he had got his own back by tweaking its ear until it cracked. After the last train around 9 p.m. the stationmaster returned home and they went to bed together, talking amiably. His wife slept with her head on his shoulder, but at half-past three in the morning she woke when her husband made a snorting noise. She said to him, "Oh my dear, don't frighten me so," and gave him a slap on the shoulder. But there followed an awful rattle in his throat, and she took him in her arms, calling out for the servant. She came and struck a light, and her mistress sent her next door for assistance. Mary Allnut came quickly and another neighbour, Charles Lewis, was sent for the doctor. But when Mr Horne arrived from Wallingford at 4.50 a.m., he found Alfred Shaw quite dead.

The inquest was held the next day at the Swan Inn and the doctor put the death down to an internal injury resulting from the encounter with the sheep, perhaps to the stomach or maybe the heart. The jury returned a verdict of death by accident and misadventure. After Mrs Shaw had given her evidence she collapsed in a dead faint. Her husband had been just 29, and she was now a widow at the age of 26, with two young children to support.

Most of the railway accidents that affected the locality were, unsurprisingly, on the main line, but occasionally there were also problems on the branch line to Wallingford. One such incident occurred in 1899. On Tuesday 24 January the 11.02 a.m. from Cholsey was ready to leave on time. The crew consisted of Thomas Henry Hine, a young man who usually worked as a fireman but was on this occasion acting engine driver, George Bryden Church, the acting fireman who had just a month's experience, and the guard, Mark Pope, who had been with GWR for over 46 years and had worked the Wallingford line ever since it opened 33 years earlier. It was customary for the locomotive to draw the train from Wallingford into the station and then run round the loop so that it could pull the coaches backwards on the return journey. The porter, George Butler, who had worked at Cholsey for a year, was responsible for re-coupling the train. Perhaps, on this occasion, his mind was elsewhere.

They departed and steamed along the line at their usual clip, and as they approached Wallingford station, young driver Hine applied the steam brake. Nothing happened. As he reversed the drive he sounded the brake signal and shouted to the stoker, who applied the screw brake with all his strength. A few moments later they hit the buffers at speed, the station echoing to the sound of splintering wood and metal against metal.

Passengers were hurled the length of the carriages. One gentleman found himself on the floor alongside another traveller, covered in cushions. The most seriously injured was a Mr Squarey from Salisbury, a land agent, who bled profusely from a wound on his forehead. Charles Morrell, the chairman of the county magistrates who was travelling with him, was badly bruised and shaken, as was Charles Hunt, the 68-year-old farmer from The Elms in Cholsey. In total ten passengers and the guard were injured, although none seriously.

The accident inquiry reported two months later, and found that the porter George Butler had failed to connect the vacuum pipe correctly at Cholsey; the guard had failed to test the brake, as he should, before signalling the departure; the driver had failed to test it as he passed the distant signal on the approach to Wallingford, and he had far exceeded the speed limit running into the station, which should have been at 'hand-brake speed'. In addition these breaches of the rule appeared to be commonplace, and the stationmaster at Wallingford was castigated for not reporting the matter.

* * *

In the early 1890s the population of the village swelled again as labourers arrived to work on alterations to the railway. In a spasmodic progression from London, the main line was being augmented by a further pair of tracks, making four in all. In addition, the station at Cholsey was being moved from the Reading Road[1] to Drove Lane, just before the point where the line to Wallingford diverged.

The new station opened on Monday 29 February 1892 and was a vast improvement on the previous building. It was approached by a capacious yard and the front of the building had a pleasing appearance with a broad pavement and sheltering veranda. A splendid subway made from Staffordshire brick, which was lighted by a large glass roof during the day and by bright lamps at night, gave access to the three platforms. Each had general and ladies' waiting rooms with lavatories, which were supplied with water through the use of a powerful manual pump in the yard. The new junction was also equipped with two signal cabins, four refuge sidings to allow goods trains to be overtaken by expresses, a goods yard, a horse box siding with a carriage dock, cattle pens and the associated water troughs. Because the new station was three-quarters of a mile further west, fares to Wallingford dropped by a penny, from 3½d to 2½d, while fares in the London direction increased by a penny.

---

[1] The old turnpike from Wallingford to Moulsford had been taken over by the local Highways Board and become known as the Reading Road.

Fig. 7.4 Cholsey station c1935

The station opening was greeted with much enthusiasm by villagers. A peal was rung on the church bells, the village anvils were fired[1], and a grand invitation dinner was held at the Swan Inn. There were many songs, toasts to the prosperity of the village and general merriment, ending with a verse of the national anthem. The *Berks & Oxon Advertiser*, in its extensive coverage of the event, said about Cholsey:

> The place will grow, and grow rapidly too, there can be no manner of doubt, for few localities possess such a variety of advantages. There are the glorious Berkshire Downs on one side, quaint villages on the other, the river on the east, the interesting town of Wallingford to the north, and Reading and Oxford both within easy reach, while Cholsey is a pleasant, healthy spot, destined, we believe, to come into prominent note as a very favourite residential neighbourhood.

The old Moulsford station was demolished and the Reading Road bridge blown up using dynamite, prior to the building of a wider construction spanning all four tracks. The last vestiges of broad gauge disappeared from the GWR network in May 1892 and the widening to four tracks was completed through to Didcot by the end of the year. Many of those involved in all this work lodged in the village, and one in particular was the target of a serious accusation.

---

[1] This noisy pastime involved turning one anvil upside down, filling the opening at the base with gunpowder, then placing a second anvil on top. Lighting it with a long red-hot rod caused an almighty bang that sent the upper anvil into the air.

William Whittard, colloquially known as 'Curly', was a builder working on the construction, who came from Stonehouse in Gloucestershire. He was in his forties, a short man with dark brown hair and blue eyes, whose face was marred by a scar on his left cheek and a boil on the other. William came to the village at the beginning of 1891 and spent two years in Cholsey, lodging in the Wallingford Road house of Richard Smith, a retired postman. In that year there were six other lodgers in his house, two stonemasons and four navvies, all probably working on the railway.

Although William had been married for many years and had a wife and two children living back in Stonehouse, he had a chequered past. Going back over 30 years he had convictions for wilful damage and burglary, and in 1885 he was sentenced to seven years' imprisonment for receiving stolen goods. He had been sent to Worcester gaol, but was released early provided he reported regularly to the Wallingford police until the expiry of his term in April 1892. William contended that the cause of his misbehaviour stemmed from an occasion when he had fallen off some scaffolding. Ever afterwards, he said, drink sent him out of his head. As Christmas 1892 approached, the work for William in Cholsey came to an end, and on Christmas Eve he went into Wallingford to do some shopping, prior to catching the train back to his home in Gloucestershire. The holiday was coming up, the mood was festive, and several people treated William to a drink. He took several glasses of wine and some bitters[1] in Wallingford, and then stopped at the Nag's Head in Winterbrook on the way back to Cholsey.

Jane Rumble was fourteen years old and a new servant in the Smiths' household. William Whittard had recently moved out to lodge with Mrs Read in the village, so Jane only knew William by sight. At half-past-three on the afternoon of Christmas Eve, she was working in the house when she heard someone coming down the passage from the back door. She went to see who it was, and William asked her whether Mrs Smith was at home. When she said no, she was alone, William quickly took hold of her arm and forced her down onto the linoleum floor. Jane screamed and fought against the man, but the house was somewhat isolated and nobody was about. A little later, after he had let her go, William assured her that he would certainly buy her a present for Christmas.

A short while afterwards, Jane's sister Alice was passing the house where she found Jane crying at the gate. After she had related her story, Alice took her home and then went to the police. PC Maunders went with Alice and found her sister tear-stained and with dishevelled hair, but could see no sign of any disarranged clothing. It wasn't until the following afternoon on Christmas Day that Jane was taken before Dr Nelson in Wallingford, but he

---

[1] Probably one of the various bitter liquors usually drunk as a digestif.

could find no external marks of violence. Although some of her undergarments were torn, the girl admitted that this had happened before the alleged offence.

By then William was no longer in the locality, and the police were unsure where he might be. But after some detective work, they found where he came from and telegraphed the Gloucestershire police to take him into custody. PC Maunders journeyed to Stonehouse on 12 January 1893 and presented the warrant for his arrest. On the way back to Wallingford William admitted to the policeman that he had been drinking that day, but honestly could not remember anything that had happened. He said, "If I get out of this I won't have another drop of drink as long as I live."

William was brought before the magistrates the following day, charged with having carnal knowledge of a girl aged over thirteen and less than sixteen. He claimed that he could remember nothing of the incident, only leaving the Nag's Head and then being at Cholsey station, where the stationmaster reprimanded him for being the worse for drink. At that point he noticed, by the light of the gas, that he was cut in several places, and assumed that he must have fallen down. During the trial, while Jane's sister was giving evidence, William fell asleep while standing in the dock. On being asked by the magistrate's clerk in a loud voice whether he had any questions for the witness, he awoke with a start, looking dazed. He replied that he hadn't heard, and the deposition had to be read to him before he answered in the negative. She was more or less the last witness, and the magistrates then remanded William in custody to the assizes.

A month later, at the court in Reading, William Whittard pleaded not guilty, but had no counsel to help in his defence. Nevertheless, after they had heard the evidence, the jury decided that there was some doubt, and he was acquitted. Gratefully, William returned to Stonehouse, but whether he kept to his promise and joined a temperance society is not known. In fact nothing can be found in the records about his subsequent life, although by the time of the next census in 1901, his wife was describing herself as a widow. Either he had indeed died, or she had decided to disown him. After the attack Jane Rumble went into service in London, and in the same census is recorded as a general servant to a mechanical engineer.

By then the new station and railway junction that William had helped to build were well established. They had further enhanced the importance of the village and brought more employment, as had another institution established in the latter half of the nineteenth century. But it was with decidedly mixed feelings that villagers greeted the arrival of the County Lunatic Asylum.

Chapter 8 The County Lunatic Asylum

In 1867 it was announced that a new lunatic asylum for the county of Berkshire was to be built in Cholsey. The reactions of local people must have been mixed: on the one hand it would provide a great deal of employment, but on the other, the parish would become home for a considerable population of deranged and possibly dangerous inmates. A large site was earmarked close to both the Thames and Moulsford railway station.

At the beginning of the nineteenth century, the mentally ill were treated as objects of fun or scorn, and Bethlem Hospital in London paraded its patients for public amusement. But as the century progressed, attitudes changed and medical knowledge advanced. In 1845 the County Asylums Act made it compulsory for all parts of the country to provide care, and the Berkshire justices made an agreement with Oxfordshire to use the asylum at Littlemore. By 1867 the facility was full and Berkshire had to provide its own institution.

Seventy-nine acres of land was purchased at Cholsey and work began on building a self-sufficient community, at a total cost of £68,000. The institution would have its own water supply, farm, bakery, laundry and chapel, with both skilled and unskilled staff to ensure its smooth running. Not only would the infrastructure satisfy most of the needs of the asylum, but it would also provide opportunities for therapy through work for the patients. Accommodation for 500 patients was to be built, together with offices and houses for the superintendent, engineer and bailiff.

The buildings were designed by Charles Henry Howell, the consulting architect to the Commissioners in Lunacy, and the main contractor was Mansfield, Price and Company of London. The man in charge on site was Mr Rolph, who had a reputation for looking after his men and completing jobs on time. A well was dug early in 1868 and in May a tramway was constructed from a spot near Little Stoke ferry to the site. The ferry was located at the point where the towpath switched sides and the horses drawing the barges had to be taken across the Thames. As well as heavy material brought by horse-drawn barge, other building materials started to arrive at Moulsford station. An influx of labourers and tradesmen came to join local workers to carry out the construction. Although less numerous than the railway navvies, they nevertheless caused some upsets within the community.

Fig. 8.1 Little Stoke ferry and the asylum c1908

On 11 January 1869 William Vinden, landlord of the Swan Inn, had an altercation with one of the workers. Robert Ridley, also known as Beesley, had caused trouble before, and when he called for some rum and gin on that Monday, Vinden refused to serve him. Robert became very abusive and threatened to "let him have it", raising his fist to strike Vinden. He was prevented from carrying out his threat and taken into custody by a police constable. At the Wallingford Petty Sessions he was sentenced to a £5 fine or 21 days in gaol.

Another crime occurred in March when two wives of labourers from the asylum were charged with stealing two ducks from Thomas Evans of the Waterloo Tavern[1]. Mary Ann Cox was 41 and Harriet Stokes was 48. At the Quarter Sessions the following month they were each sentenced to three months' imprisonment for receiving stolen goods.

By April 1869 the building was well advanced, with much of the brickwork done and a considerable portion of the roof in place. But on Saturday 25 April a serious accident was suffered by a local man. John Bosher, 18, was working as a bricklayer's labourer when he stumbled high up on the scaffolding and fell 32 feet to the ground. He was taken up unconscious and conveyed to the Royal Berkshire Hospital, where he was found to have a broken arm and several other serious injuries. He

---

[1] The Waterloo Hotel or Tavern was the public house near Wallingford Road station that was built earlier in 1816 to serve the turnpike. More recently it was the Railway Children nursery.

recovered, but decided that he would not follow his late father Thomas[1], a bricklayer, into the construction industry. He moved to London and joined the Metropolitan Police, and subsequently settled in Kent.

Another worker on the site was William Young, a carpenter and joiner. In August 1869 he was so savagely attacked that his life was in peril. William, whose father had been the district surveyor for the Watlington Highways Board, was living in Wallingford for the duration of the works. On Saturday 7 August, after entertaining a fellow workman at his lodgings in Oxford House[2] on the Market Place, he left sometime after 11 p.m. to accompany his friend back to where he lived in Winterbrook.

Meanwhile three young men dressed in white smocks, James Durbridge, William Barrett (known as 'Redneck') and John Chesterman, were already the worse for drink at the Town Arms in the High Street. Emerging out into the fine summer night, James started to goad William Barrett, looking for a fight. But William would not, knowing that Durbridge was very drunk and would probably resort to using his knife. The group staggered off across town with two young women in tow, Jane Tomlin and Mary Ann Pratt, a well-known prostitute. Later, however, a fight did break out and Durbridge was thrown to the ground. Mary Ann Pratt started kicking him, but he soon got up and began taking his revenge.

Returning to the town from Winterbrook at about 12.30 a.m., William Young met Elizabeth Peedle at the junction of St Mary's Street and St John's Road, by Lower Green. They were standing by Mr Wilder's House when they heard a great commotion from St John's Road. It was dark and there were no lights, but William clearly saw Durbridge hitting Miss Pratt. He walked up to him and said, "You are no man to strike a woman!" The other man made no reply, but pushed him up against the wall and plunged a knife repeatedly into his stomach. William cried out, "Bessy!"

Holding his stomach he at first seemed too shocked to move, but then staggered off along St Mary's Street and rang the bell at Dr Charles Barrett's surgery. Luckily the doctor was still up and took him into his consulting room. As the surgeon was lighting the gas, William collapsed. When the doctor had lain him on the couch and removed his clothes, he was horrified by what he saw. A mass of intestine was protruding from the lower part of

---

[1] This is the Thomas Bosher who was killed on the railway in 1863, as described in Chapter 7.

[2] Oxford House was at the time a public house, but is now a block of residential flats at 12 St Martin's Street.

the abdomen. The main cut was about 2½ inches long and around 15 inches of bowel, itself punctured in four places, had escaped. Another 3 inch slash was close to the first. Dr Barrett sought help from a fellow surgeon, Dr Marshall, and sent for the police. Together the two doctors did what they could and then, with the help of three police constables, conveyed the young man back to the Oxford House, hoping against the odds that he would recover.

Inspector Mansell took charge of the case and the three men involved were apprehended. PC James Webb found Durbridge at his father's house, where his mother was in the process of washing blood from his face. He was still very drunk. When asked, Barrett and Chesterman showed their knives, but Durbridge could not produce his. A search of the scene of the crime soon revealed the weapon, a large clasp knife, lying beside a pool of blood. The handle was bloodied and some hairs were removed from the blade, which the doctor later said matched the injured man's pubic hair. Durbridge admitted that the knife was his.

The three men were brought up before the magistrates on the following Monday. Long before the hearing at noon, Wallingford Market Place filled with townsfolk anxious to see the culprits in the drama, which could yet turn into a murder charge carrying the death penalty. Chesterman was discharged as not directly involved, while Barrett was found guilty of committing a breach of the peace and bound over in the sum of £10 with two sureties of £5 each, and in default one month's prison. Durbridge was remanded in custody. William Young was too ill to give evidence at the hearing, and was still in a grievous condition when Durbridge was brought up again on the 13, 20 and 28 August. On the evidence of the other witnesses, he was remanded to appear at the Epiphany Assizes.

When the court met on 1 January 1870, William was at last sufficiently recovered to give evidence, although he was still unable to work. Durbridge pleaded not guilty to the charge of wounding with intent to do grievous bodily harm. He had nobody to defend him, and in answer to a question from the judge, he just said that he was very sorry, but he could not remember whether he had committed the crime or not. He was found guilty and sentenced to eighteen months. As for William Young, nothing more is known, but it appears that he made a full recovery.

* * *

Meanwhile, Moulsford Lunatic Asylum[1], as it was to be known after the name of the nearby station, was completed and the first patients arrived on

---

[1] The asylum was also known as Berkshire County Lunatic Asylum and subsequently changed its name several times to end up as Fair Mile Hospital.

Fig. 8.2 The County Lunatic Asylum

30 September 1870. It was a luxurious establishment, at least compared to the workhouse, with gas lighting, heating via hot air ducts and coal fires, bathrooms with hot and cold running water and flushing toilets. The walls were painted in light colours and hung with pictures to provide an environment to help heal the minds of the patients.

Dr Robert Gilland was the Medical Superintendent, both chief medical officer and chief executive. Over the first month and a half a total of fifty men and sixty-one women arrived, largely transferred from Littlemore. But it soon became apparent that some of the ceilings were faulty, and the contractors were called back in. So the furniture, staff and patients were crammed into a limited part of the building whilst workmen replaced the ceilings in the affected rooms. Admissions were halted, and it was only during 1871 that the occupancy gradually rose towards an initial complement of about 280 patients. Staff had been hired to cope with this number much earlier, so there was an overcapacity in the early days.

On Christmas Day 1870 the large dining hall was decorated with festoons[1] and wreaths of evergreens and all the patients enjoyed a meal of roast beef and plum duff. In the afternoon two segregated walking parties set out on routes around the grounds. Four days later, on Thursday 29 December, a temporary platform was erected at one end of the hall. On the stage was a piano and seats for several guests, including the local vicars: Revd Lloyd from Cholsey, Revd Dr Morrell from Moulsford, and Revd W. G. Oliver, the asylum chaplain. The entertainment consisted of songs performed by various members of staff, which alternated with country

---

[1] A festoon is an ornamental chain of ribbons hung in an arc.

dancing in which the patients joined with gusto. It must have been a sight. During an interval, cake and hot spiced beer were served, and the evening ended at 10 p.m. with the national anthem.

The aim of the asylum was to try to cure patients through fresh air, exercise and a nourishing diet away from the stresses that might have caused the illness. The mentally ill were treated with sympathy by most outsiders too, as in, for example, the *Berkshire Chronicle's* welcoming of the Christmas entertainments:

> There can be no class of person more deserving of sympathy and kindness than the insane poor, who having had the misfortune to become afflicted with mental disease, have in consequence been removed from their home and separated from their dearest friends, and who, from the nature of their malady, are incapable of understanding the reasons which have rendered such a proceeding an absolute necessity.

Patients were kept occupied as much as possible, with work on the farm, in the gardens, the workshops and the laundry, or assisting with household tasks such as cleaning and sewing. As well as the better environment, the nutrition was also far superior to the workhouse and much more than many could expect at home, with the daily ration for men being 20 oz bread, 2-3 oz butter, 7 oz meat and vegetables, plus 3 pints of tea. The ratio of patients to staff was held at around 10:1, although in the early days, because of the ceiling problem, it was much lower. The hours were protracted for the staff and many did not stay long. Some were also to prove unreliable.

On the day of the first Christmas entertainment, the steward at the asylum, Edwin Stott, gave the hall porter £5 and asked him to go to Wallingford to change it into silver. Joseph Castell, the 28-year-old porter, left, but he did not return. Instead of visiting the bank, he frequented the hostelries and became roaring drunk. He later claimed not to remember anything subsequently until later in the day when he awoke to find himself in a railway carriage heading for London. A warrant for his arrest was issued and he was apprehended a week after his departure at Fenchurch Street station in London. He had twelve shillings and a farthing left. What was really stupid about the escapade was that the miscreant had left his belongings behind in the asylum and was due a month's wages that very day, viz. £1 13s 4d. In his drunken state he had bought a return ticket, and at least part of his brain planned to come back. Because of his previously good character, including eight years as a soldier in the 11th Regiment of Foot, he was sentenced to only two months' imprisonment with hard labour.

However, indictments against the staff were comparatively rare, and the asylum had to deal with the justice system much more frequently because of violent deaths amongst the patients. Suicidal tendencies were common with certain mental conditions and, despite the vigilance of the staff, many found the means to end their lives. Here are the first five cases, from the asylum's first decade, which show the resourcefulness of the deranged mind.

* * *

Robert Warren was a tailor, born in Chard in Somerset in 1820, who moved to London after the death of his first wife. He was married again in Reading in 1854, to a woman six years his junior, Mary Ann Costiff, the daughter of an agricultural labourer in the village of Moulsford. Together they had five children, but Robert began to complain of pains in his head, started talking incoherently, and became increasingly depressed. He would go down to the meadow in Reading, take his coat off and walk up and down beside the river in an excited fashion. His wife was greatly alarmed at what he might do, and in 1870 he was committed to the lunatic asylum in Littlemore.

When Robert was transferred to Moulsford Lunatic Asylum in May the following year, it became much easier for his wife to visit him. But he was

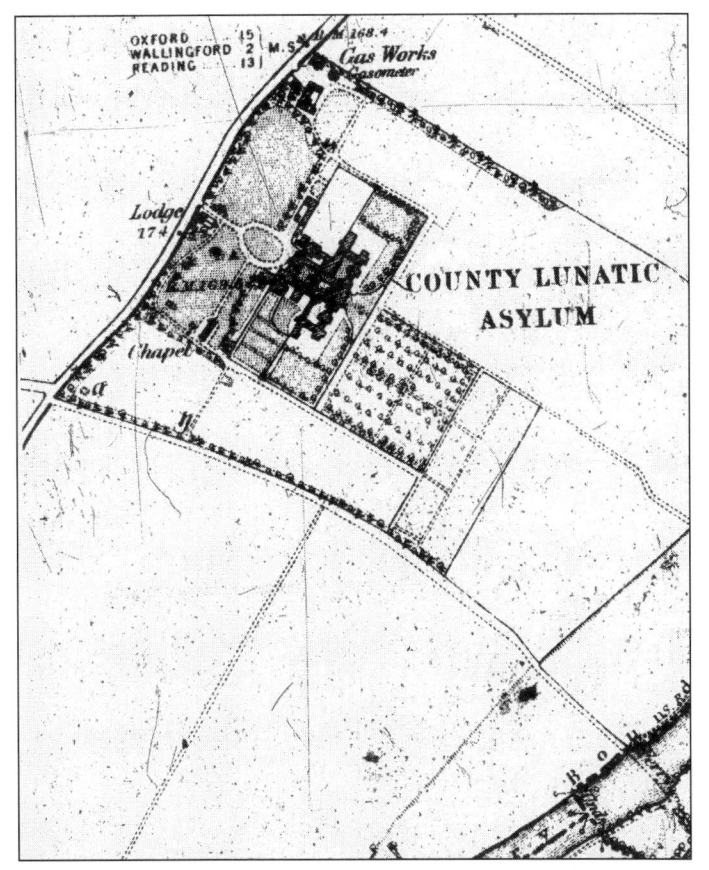

Fig. 8.3 Map of the asylum, roads and Little Stoke ferry in 1883

still in a poor state, feeling miserable, sleeping badly and complaining of a crawling sensation in his scalp. He had a bad tremor in his hands and would walk up and down the gallery moaning. He gradually improved under the new regime and became much happier after he started working in the tailor's shop. In February 1872 his wife asked the medical superintendent whether he could be discharged back to his family, given his improvement. Dr Gillard said that it was too soon, but hoped he could be released on trial in the not too distant future.

His wife also asked the head attendant, Henry Wormley Cater, if her husband could be allowed out on the Sunday afternoon walks that many of the patients were permitted to take under supervision. But Robert did not want to walk along the road, the usual route, because he knew many of his wife's relations from Moulsford and was ashamed to be recognised. On Sunday 14 April an alternative opportunity arose.

On that day Henry Cater had arranged to take two private patients (as opposed to pauper patients) on a walk in the field, and he asked Dr Gillard whether he might take Robert too. The superintendent agreed, but emphasised that he must be carefully supervised and not allowed to go near the river. The head attendant thought it unlikely that he would want to, as he seemed afraid of the water, complaining during the recent floods that the water would reach the asylum and he would be drowned.

For his walk Robert was dressed in his Sunday best, although as usual he had failed to attend divine service in the chapel. The four set off just after 3 p.m., accompanied by another patient, an old man by the name of John Joseph. Beyond the asylum boundary to the east was an arable field, with a garden in the centre, and Robert expressed a desire to see the plants. He talked coherently on several subjects as they walked and commented on the quality of the vegetables. At the edge of the field they came to a fence three or four feet high and they all climbed over into the water meadow beyond. They walked alongside the fence until they reached the spot where the walkway came from the asylum on the way to the river. All of them sat down on a pile of wood beside the gateway, except for Robert. The Thames was about 150-200 yards distant.

While the others rested, Robert began pacing up and down. Gradually he drew away from the group, and the head attendant asked him to come back. Robert took no notice, but continued to distance himself. Henry Cater stood up and walked towards him. Robert moved more quickly. Henry broke into a run and Robert took to his heels. At first he headed straight for the river, but then branched off to follow a footpath. By about halfway to the river the attendant had nearly reached his quarry when they came across a drainage ditch. Robert leapt over it, but Henry fell in. He climbed out again quickly, but Robert had gained vital seconds. By the time they reached the river, Robert was five or six yards ahead. He launched

Fig. 8.4 Star Terrace, Papist Way

himself from the bank and landed with an enormous splash. Neither man could swim.

At first Robert drifted, floating in the current, with Henry Cater following on the bank in alarm. About 200 yards from where he had left the bank, Robert slowly sank beneath the rippling water and did not resurface. William Walters, a tailor from Cholsey, saw the whole episode as he walked from his home in Star Terrace[1] down Ferry Lane towards the Little Stoke ferry. He agreed to look after the other patients while Henry went to seek help from the ferryman. John Joseph was sent back to the asylum to raise the alarm. The ferry punt was quickly on the spot but they could find no trace of the man. They dragged the river until it was dark, and began again at first light. Robert Warren's body was finally recovered at noon.

The inquest was held in the asylum on the following morning. After hearing the evidence, the jury returned a verdict of suicide whilst in an unsound state of mind, criticising the decision to go into the meadow and the insubstantial nature of the fence. Robert's widow, Mary Ann, when asked if she had any questions for the medical superintendent, said, "My husband was put there to be taken care of, and it seems to me that I could have taken more care of him myself." He was just the first of many to meet a similar fate.

---

[1] Star Terrace is the group of nine three-storey houses on Papist Way, next to the Morning Star, which were bought by the asylum in 1872.

* * *

The next suicide was six months later, although this time the authorities could not be held directly responsible. Jane Tinson was born in 1822 and lived all her life in Sutton Courtenay, near Abingdon. Her father was an agricultural labourer, dying in 1849 at the age of 53. When she was old enough, Jane was employed as a slop worker[1] and, following her father's death, she continued to live with her mother and many siblings. The youngest, Benjamin, was then only four, and all the family worked to earn enough to live: her mother and two of her brothers as agricultural labourers and the three girls as slop workers.

In August 1858 Jane was finally married to an older widower named Thomas Harding, a railway labourer. Jane was 36 and her new husband 47. Her mental problems started over a decade later, when she was four years into the menopause, and began with a physical symptom. She started to whistle whenever she breathed. She later described the onset as being "struck in the chest by God Almighty" and that from then on she had had "a whistling breath which she could not stop". She had difficulty sleeping, became miserable, and in spring 1872 started to become delusional. She thought that she was immortal, unless she was put into the water. Soon after, she tried to drown herself in the nearby Thames.

Jane Harding was admitted to Moulsford Lunatic Asylum on 15 July 1872 and was diagnosed as melancholic. The medical superintendent prescribed a daily draught of medicine, which included Tincture Opii, otherwise known as laudanum[2]. She soon became more cheerful and began to sleep much better, although the delusions continued. She imagined she would not die unless someone killed her, and night-time sounds often made her think that a porter was coming to shoot her. But by the end of September these fantasies had all gone and she was working well and talking coherently. On Tuesday 22 October she was allowed to return home to Sutton Courtney on a trial basis.

On the Thursday evening at about 7 p.m. her younger brother Thomas Tinson, who lived nearby, called round. He found his sister seemingly content, with Jane's husband full of kindness towards his wife. A little bit later Thomas Harding went out to get some tobacco from the shop. Shortly afterwards Jane went out the back door, telling her brother that she was going to look for the cat. She did not return.

---

[1] A slop worker made cheap ready-made clothes.

[2] Laudanum was a popular remedy made from opium.

A search was organised, but no trace of her could be found that evening or the next day. On the Saturday evening at about 5 p.m. George Allen, the lock keeper at Culham, was clearing weed from the middle lock at the Sutton ponds. Suddenly he came across a body, the legs entangled in the uprights, preventing it from being carried further along the river by the current. It was Jane Harding.

The inquest was held the following Monday and the verdict was an open one: 'found drowned'. But it was clear to the medical superintendent and all in the village that it had been suicide. Away from the closed environment of the asylum and the calming medicine, her old symptoms had returned.

* * *

It wasn't long before a patient thought of a way to end their life without recourse to the Thames. Hester Turrill was about the same age as Jane Harding when she came to the asylum and was also roughly four years into the menopause. She was born Hester (or Esther) Cox in 1822 in Keevil, Wiltshire, a parish of 500 souls midway between Devizes and Trowbridge. Her father was a farmer who moved farms to better himself from time to time. When she was a teenager they were in Teffont Magna in the south of the county, and there she met Thomas Best, a young farmer of the same age. They married in 1839 when Hester was just seventeen and heavily pregnant.

They christened their daughter Emily Selina, but she never reached adulthood, dying when she was twelve. Their second child died when still a baby, and after that they had no further offspring. The couple moved repeatedly, for example in 1851 they were to be found at Holbrook Farm, Trowbridge, where Thomas worked as a farm bailiff and Hester as a dairymaid. Hester's father had also moved, to a village a few miles away, where he now farmed 50 acres and employed a boy as well as his eldest son Abraham. In the 1850s they moved together to Garlands Farm at Sparsholt, a Berkshire village three miles west of Wantage. William Cox now farmed 140 acres and employed three labourers, while his son-in-law Thomas acted as the farm bailiff.

But Hester and Thomas were having marital problems. In 1863, with no children to constrain her, she left him, claiming that he had ill-treated her, although it is not clear that this was actually the case. She also said she was fed up with having to repeatedly set up a new home, after moving fourteen times during their 23-year marriage. Later that same year Hester's father died. The farm passed to Abraham and, after provision for his wife, the remainder of William Cox's estate was divided up amongst his several children. However, Hester was specifically excluded from receiving any capital under his will, just the income from her share of the inheritance during her lifetime. This may have been to ensure that her husband did not get his hands on the money[1], or perhaps he no longer trusted his daughter.

Two years later her mother also died. This time a legacy of £70 was due to Hester, but she could not claim it without her husband's signature. However, she had lost contact with Thomas and, despite contacting the police and advertising for him, he was not to be found. Perhaps he was dead, and in 1867 she adopted that stance when she moved in with James Reuben Turrill, a slightly younger unmarried carver, becoming both his housekeeper and his mistress.

They lived in Reading and that was where, one day early in 1868, Hester's husband suddenly reappeared. They were reconciled and James moved out to make way for Thomas. They went to Wantage to collect the money owing to her. But the reconciliation only lasted three weeks, and in March they split up again, with Thomas moving out to lodgings in the Builder's Arms in the next street and James returning to the house in Stanshawe Road.

Despite the £70 collected in Wantage, which Hester claimed he had pocketed, Thomas was destitute once again. Although he had once been a farmer and dealer, now he could only get labouring jobs, and that rarely. But the landlord of the public house was kindly and let him stay on rent free until he had the means to reimburse him. On Saturday 18 April Thomas and his landlord went down to the market together, parting at around 1 p.m., the latter lending his tenant some money for dinner. Thomas returned for his tea that evening and drank a beer before going out again at 10 p.m. He didn't return. On the Sunday morning the publican was out walking towards Caversham Bridge when he was alerted by a fisherman to the discovery of a body in the Thames. It was Thomas.

At the inquest on the Monday, the evidence of Thomas' landlord and Hester diverged significantly. Hester said that Thomas had taken the £70 and spent it all on drink, threatening to murder her and then do away with himself. The publican said that Thomas was a sober and quiet man who, depressed by his wife's adultery, had frequently threatened suicide. Under questioning from the coroner, Hester grew extremely agitated and left the room as soon as she was released. The jury returned an open verdict.

Now unencumbered, Hester married James Turrill a few years later. But, soon after the marriage, Hester's health began to suffer. After developing an ulcerated bowel and passing blood, she started taking draughts to help

---

[1] Until the Married Woman's Property Act of 1882, a wife's money and possessions would normally actually belong to her husband

her sleep. She refused food, ceased caring about her appearance and became depressed, fearful and delusional. Hester gradually became emaciated and anaemic, and after a month and a half her husband took her to the Union workhouse, the cheapest way to access medical care. By then she was dirty and her thick grey hair was densely matted. She told the doctor that she shouldn't be in the workhouse but at the police station, as she had been robbing everybody. Her husband said that she had done no such thing, but also mentioned that she had accused him of being the cause of the recent railway accident at Shipton-on-Cherwell. The Great Western Railway disaster of Christmas Eve 1874 just north of Oxford had killed 34 and injured over a hundred.

Hester, now clean but in poor health, was admitted to the Moulsford Lunatic Asylum on 23 February 1875, a week after being taken to the workhouse. She was diagnosed as being suicidal, as well as melancholic and delusional, but soon settled in and was otherwise quiet and orderly. Her husband visited her fortnightly and Hester began to make herself useful cleaning the dormitories. Both of them declared that they were well satisfied with the care.

Thursday 1 July 1875 was a day like any other. Hester was employed in scrubbing the number one dormitories, and then a little before ten o'clock she went down to the scullery. She asked the charge attendant, Ellen Blunson, whether she might have two pieces of bread for lunch, and was given the bread with some cheese and her ration of beer. At about this time the dormitories were cleared of patients and attendants, the former going to

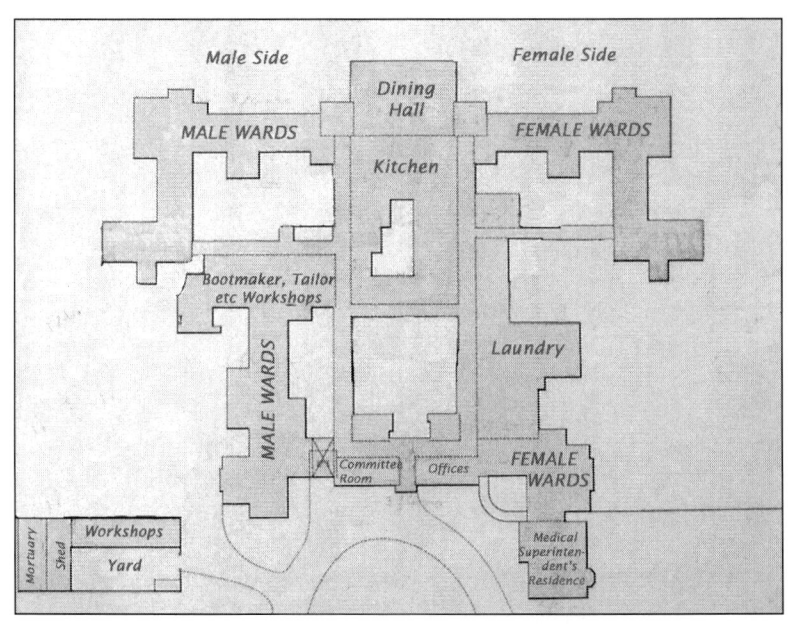

Fig. 8.5 Plan of the asylum in the 1870s

the scullery to get their lunch which they then took into the day room. Hester would normally have followed the others, but the staircase and lavatory doors, which were normally locked unless in use, had been left open. Hester slipped into the lavatory, took a round towel, then went quietly upstairs.

It was visiting day, and Hester's husband presented himself soon after ten. At 10.15 the head attendant, Alfred Lockie, went to look for Hester in the day room, and it was only then that she was missed. He immediately sounded the alarm and a search was instituted. Attendant Steele was the one to search the dormitories on the third floor, and it was in the far room that he found her. Over the door was a bracket for the gas fitting and suspended from it, the towel tied in a running noose, hung Hester. A chair lay upended on the floor nearby. Steele called for help and she was taken down and artificial respiration attempted, but all in vain. It was twenty-five minutes since she had been last seen in the scullery. Close by on the floor was the half-eaten bread and cheese and the remains of the beer.

The inquest was held the next day in the asylum and a verdict of suicide whilst in an unsound state of mind was returned. Hester's husband did not make a fuss. He had only been married for a few months, and he never married again.

* * *

Hester Turrill had shown the inmates a different method of suicide, but it was nearly four years before there was another such death. Susan Jones was 52 and another woman going through the menopause, a period which often seemed to cause depression. She had been born at Ufton, a hamlet southwest of Reading, and had spent all her life in the vicinity up until her admission. She was sent into service at a young age, first to Padworth House and then to Mortimer Hill House, the home of Sir Claudius Stephen Hunter, a London alderman. Susan lived in the imposing main house with three or four other female servants, while five other servants lived in an outbuilding. One of them, a coachman, was Augustus Charles Jones, and they married in 1858, when Susan was 34. She gave birth to three sons over the next six years.

Susan was a tall woman and quite cheerful, and they lived in comparatively comfortable circumstances, but things started to go wrong after she turned 50. Her hair turned grey and thinned, and she became depressed. She would not go out beyond the garden gate and shunned visitors. She stopped doing the housework and cooking meals for the family, and would spend hours just staring at her hands, weeping for no reason. Her son Frederick, who by then was eighteen, wanted to leave home to be apprenticed (he later became a commercial clerk), but Susan wouldn't countenance his departure. She started to have delusions, believing that the possessions they had obtained were gained unfairly, and that the family were destined for utter ruin and destruction. She lost weight and developed spots on her face and back, which she then picked at.

In October 1877 she was persuaded to see a doctor, and was committed to Moulsford Lunatic Asylum. She was not classed as particularly suicidal, nor in any way a danger to others; rather she would just sit alone, still and sullen, refusing to talk. Under the asylum's regime, her weight and bodily condition improved, but there was little change in her depression and taciturnity. Through 1878 she returned to full health and became more industrious, helping with the needlework. At that point there was no indication of what would happen in early 1879.

On Sunday 12 January the evening service was held in the dining hall rather than the chapel, and Susan Jones was in attendance. At 6.10 p.m. she left with the other patients to return to number three ward. The attendant in charge, Mary Addison, began giving out the new dresses for the coming week, calling each patient's name in turn. Part way through the process, the housekeeper came in to talk to Mary, and she paused in the activity. After a while she resumed and nothing was amiss until she took out Susan's dress. She called out her name, but there was no reply. Mary had noticed her earlier, but now could not see her. It was not unusual for her not to respond when called, and in any case she might be in the water closet or along the gallery, so Mary put her dress to one side and continued with the remainder. But she did not finish as then the bell for teatime sounded. She put the dresses away and led the patients to the dining room. Before locking the ward door, she checked that nobody was left behind in the day room or the closets. Once everyone was seated, grace was said, and it was at this point that Mary noticed with surprise that Susan Jones' place was still vacant.

With the help of another attendant, Mrs Barron, she went off to search. They checked the number three ward, the single rooms, the water closets and the scullery without success. Finally they climbed the stairs from the day room up to the dormitory. It was dark in the long room and Mrs Barron carried a candle to light the way. She bent down and lowered the flame to check under each of the beds, gradually moving further from the door. As she stood up partway along the dormitory, the flickering candle illuminated a shape in the middle of the room. It was Susan Jones, suspended by a round towel from the gas bracket in the centre of the room.

The medical assistant was called and he stood on the settee that was underneath the woman, lifting her up so that the towel could be unhooked. They lowered her to the floor, tore her clothes off and made every attempt to resuscitate her. But her face and hands were already cold, and after twenty minutes Dr John Barron gave up. It was 6.45 p.m.

The inquest was held on the Tuesday evening, and the jury returned a verdict of suicide while in an unsound state of mind. It was believed that the ill-fated woman had taken the towel from the store when Mary Addison was distracted and then hidden it under the shawl that she carried over one arm. In the confusion of the departure at teatime, she had slipped away. The coroner declared that no blame should be assigned to the attendants and the body was released for burial. She was interred back in her home town of Stratfield Mortimer four days later.

* * *

Towards the end of the 1870s, work was begun to extend the asylum and by 1880 it accommodated around 600 beds. During the construction, the village again saw an influx of workers. As always that was good for business, but George Horne, the landlord of the Morning Star, was over-helpful. The public house was only a short walk from the asylum down Papist Way, but the workmen were forbidden to leave their post. George decided to provide a delivery service by taking the beer to the men each day and collecting their tabs weekly. In September 1878 he was summonsed for selling beer on unlicensed premises and fined 4s 6d plus costs.

The final untimely death of the decade happened to the asylum's very first patient. Admitted on 30 September 1870 and number one in the

Fig. 8.6 The Morning Star c1914

register was William Goodyear, a poor fifteen-year-old boy born an idiot[1]. He came from Windsor and was the third eldest of a family of eleven children. His father was a farm labourer and his mother would have had little time to deal with his difficult upbringing. He suffered from epileptic seizures and at school he was extremely violent, frequently biting other boys, knocking their heads against the wall and throwing them to the ground. Later he would say he could not remember what he had done.

Matters came to a head in June 1869 when William bit a George Clarke on the wrist so severely that the latter was taken into the Union workhouse infirmary for a week. William was subsequently certified and taken into Littlemore Lunatic Asylum on 8 July. Fifteen months later he was one of the first batch of 40 patients transferred to Moulsford. He was assessed as in good bodily health, but mentally very weak, talking in a childish manner and when questioned given to outbursts of laughter without cause.

During his time at Moulsford his mood fluctuated. Sometimes he was docile and willing to work in the tailor's shop; at others he was very irritable and occasionally violent. For example, he once struck an attendant and then threw a chair at another. In particular he could not brook interference and was often sulky. From time to time he suffered attacks of 'le petit mal', the less severe form of epilepsy, which nevertheless could include fainting, vomiting, delusions and memory loss. He was also known to masturbate frequently, an established cause of insanity, according to the medical experts of the time.

Gradually the quieter interludes became more common and his convulsions less frequent, so nobody was prepared for the events of Saturday 31 May 1879, almost a decade after he was first certified. On that day George Bunce, one of the attendants, took six patients for a walk along the turnpike in the direction of Wallingford. They were all dressed in blue pilot suits[2] and quite distinctive, but nevertheless, at Bow Bridge William managed to slip away whilst George's attention was distracted. He was spotted going through the gate beside the brook by the head laundress, Louisa Langford, who happened to be walking along the road at that moment. She watched him run along by the brook until he reached the river, turn left to cross the brook on the small bridge that carried the towpath, and then start to return towards the turnpike on the other bank before sitting down in the long grass. When she reached the walking party

---

[1] Idiot was the Victorian term for what we would now call somebody with severe learning difficulties.

[2] A pilot suit was, it is thought, a sort of boiler suit.

she asked George whether he had lost a man, and it was only then that he realised that William was missing.

Whilst Louisa stayed with the patients, George took the path to the river until he was opposite the man and about 40 yards distant. He came back to the road, however, telling Louisa that it was not the right man, although he later admitted that his eyesight was rather poor. George set off to take the other five patients back to the asylum and to raise the alarm. But Louisa was not sure that George was right and waited and watched. Presently she saw the man get up from the grass, run towards the river and disappear amongst the bushes on the bank. When help arrived they searched the area, but now there really was no sign of William Goodyear.

James Whiting was a 37-year-old labourer living in Harts Lock in Whitchurch, down river from the asylum. On Saturday 7 June he was working with several other men in the reed bed near the Grotto[1], south of Streatley, when he came across the floating body of a man. It was a week since William Goodyear had disappeared. With the help of a boat they drew the body to the nearby island and went off in search of PC Marshall, stationed at Streatley. They moved the body to the granary where the policeman searched it, finding in the trouser pockets a hymn book, snuff box, handkerchief, cap and a purse containing 6d.

The body was still in the same building when the inquest jury came to inspect it two days later. In court George Bunce and Louisa Langford were interviewed as to how William Goodyear came to escape, but in the end an open verdict was recorded. A note was added stating that: 'sending out a party of patients with only one attendant is very improper and should be discontinued'. But William Goodyear was far from the last suicide at the asylum, only the last of the first decade. Patients continued to find inventive ways to end their lives, with the express train playing a significant role in subsequent years. The closeness of the river and the railway, which had proved so useful during the asylum's construction, were not perhaps such a good idea from a patient safety point of view.

---

[1] Grotto House is now occupied by the Institute of Sports, Parks and Leisure and lies on the west bank of the river near Lower Basildon.

Chapter 9 The Philandering Curate

Just after Christmas 1883 a new curate started work in Cholsey, a handsome cleric by the name of Friedrich Wilhelm James Albert Agassiz. Since the retirement in 1873 of Revd Henry William Lloyd, who had arrived as a young man of 28 just before the construction of the railway and served the parish for 36 years, there had been two changes of vicar. The current incumbent was Revd Richard William Perry Circuitt, a keen cricketer, who felt that he needed an assistant to help with his ministry.

Friedrich was 39 years old and accompanied by his wife Jessie and their six children. They settled in a house in Horn Lane and his strange name and unusual past soon excited the interest of villagers. Most of the clerics who had served in the parish came from wealthy country families who sent their sons to be educated in divinity at Oxford or Cambridge University. Friedrich was born in Honef on the Rhine, the son of a Royal Marine who had fought in the Anglo-American War of 1812-15, qualified as a priest in Nova Scotia, and claimed to be the godson of the King of Prussia. As an army chaplain he had served in Malta and been present at the renowned battle of Tel el-Kebir less than two years earlier, when British forces defeated the Egyptian army under Col Ahmed Orabi.

In their tight corsets and bustles, several ladies of the parish were drawn to Friedrich, with his good looks and charm. One of those attracted to him was a schoolmistress, Annie Bower, who was only 22 years old. She was the daughter of William Bower, who had been the headmaster in Cholsey for 25 years, going back to the days when it was in the single-storey building beside the church. That school opened in 1838, using land bestowed by James Morrison, the Lord of the Manor, and was one of the many National Schools managed by the Church of England that were set up around that time. Over the next 38 years all age groups were taught together in its two schoolrooms. Following the Education Act of 1870, these facilities were deemed inadequate, and William Bower oversaw the construction and fitting out of a new building[1] on The Causeway under the aegis of an elected School Board. Classes began in this fine new Board School in January 1876, and the Bower family moved from Honey Lane into the new house built alongside for the master.

---

[1] Closed in 1983 and now known as the 'Old School', this building currently houses the Day Centre.

Fig. 9.1 The new Board School and master's house

At the beginning of 1880 William sent his young daughter Annie to attend the Diocesan Training College for Mistresses at Felstead House in Oxford. The college had been built four years earlier in the fields bordering the Banbury Road beyond the church at the end of St Giles. Under the leadership of the Yorkshire-born Lady Superintendent, Selina Simplon, Annie did well, graduating two years later as a Certified Teacher first class. Back home in Cholsey she was put in charge of the Cholsey school infants department, with assistance from the pupil teacher, Bessie Willmott. Once every year they received a visit from one of Her Majesty's Inspectors for Schools, and just four months later their report found the department in 'excellent order', although they were less complimentary about Bessie. The reports in later years were also fulsome, for example: 'This school is most ably conducted by Miss Bower. The children are animated, happy and intelligent.'

The school year ran from 1 April with breaks for haymaking, harvest, Christmas and Easter. Annie supplemented the core curriculum of reading, writing and arithmetic with special lessons of her own devising. In Natural History she devoted a lesson in turn to each of 31 animals, from the cow to the camel by way of the spider, while 32 Common Objects embraced such things as coal, salt and soap. Natural Phenomena included another 32 items, such as rain, frost and the stars, while other lessons covered the trades, from the carpenter to the draper, form and colour, and moral instruction in topics such as honesty.

The vicar visited the school at least once a week to help guide the development of the children, particularly with the moral and religious curriculum, and occasionally he was accompanied by the handsome curate. However, it was with the choir, which Friedrich led, that Annie saw the latter most often, and where she perhaps should have paid more attention to her own moral instruction. Through 1884 the curate and his family became established in the village, and it was the following year that events took a more reprehensible turn.

At choir practice Friedrich and Annie began to behave in a manner inappropriate for a curate and a single parishioner, and soon his wife Jessie became too embarrassed to continue attending the rehearsals. Jessie had also become pregnant once again, and in January she gave birth to another daughter, their fourth. It was later that spring, while Jessie was still occupied with the new baby, that her husband's unseemly relationship with the young woman developed further. No doubt he flattered her and talked of the poor state of his own marriage. Then, one evening after choir practice in May, in the old school rooms so close to the church, the curate and the schoolmistress broke the seventh commandment[1].

* * *

Of course Jessie had also been charmed by Friedrich once, back in Devon over ten years earlier. As a young woman she could boast an exotic past too, having been born in India. Her father, Joseph Garnault, was a member of the Indian Army in the Madras Presidency[2], where he had risen from a humble ensign to become a lieutenant-colonel. He had enlisted with the Honourable East India Company[3] at the age of sixteen, arriving in Madras in July 1811. First joining the 25th Native Infantry regiment, he was promoted to lieutenant three years later and then moved to the 24th. The promotions continued every few years, to captain in 1824, major in 1834 and finally lieutenant-colonel in 1839, moving regiment occasionally, but spending most time in the 47th, where he became the commanding officer. In 1826 he married Emma Carruthers White, and a couple of years later came the first of a succession of annual or biennial babies. Their birthplaces formed a gazetteer of British army stations: Kamptee, Masulipatum, Rajahmundry, Cuddapah, Dharwar, Kulladghee and Cuttack. The Madras army saw no major action during this time, although Lt-Col Garnault's time spent in Dharwar and Kulladghee, in the Bombay Presidency, was to replace units sent to fight in the first Afghan War.

---

[1] Thou shalt not commit adultery.

[2] India was divided into three administrative provinces known as Presidencies: Bengal (in the north), Bombay (in the west) and Madras (in the east).

[3] The East India Company managed trade with India from 1600, and later ruled the country through its private army until the Crown took control in 1858, following the Indian Mutiny.

Most of the children survived, with five daughters and three sons growing to adulthood. Jessie was the tenth child, born on 15 July 1844 in Cuttack, situated in the province of Orissa, just south of Bengal. In fact she was the last live birth, because two years later the next was stillborn, and her mother, exhausted, died the following day. Lt-Col Garnault was devastated, and was granted furlough to return to England; eleven months later he sailed for London. It is believed that he left Jessie and several of his other offspring behind, all those that had not already been sent to England for schooling. In fact Jessie's father never returned and, at the age of two, she would have effectively become an orphan. From then on she would have been raised by Indian ayahs[1] and servants under the watchful eye of her mother's relations.

Jessie would have grown up accustomed to the life of privilege that prevailed for the English in India, and become used to the extreme climate, with the raging heat of the summer broken by the arrival of the monsoon from the Bay of Bengal in June. Cuttack was the most northerly outpost of the Madras Presidency, about 200 miles southwest of Calcutta. A narrow isthmus of land projecting into the wide river Mahanadi, it was protected on three sides by water. The fortifications would have seemed a blessing when, in 1857, a couple of months before Jessie's thirteenth birthday, the Indian Mutiny broke out at Meerut in the upper Ganges plain. Most of the fighting was far away to the north, but it must have been a worrying time.

Jessie's father settled in Withycombe, near to Exmouth in Devon, where he lived out most of the rest of his life with one or two of his daughters and a few servants. He remained officially on furlough, and in 1854 was promoted to major-general, allowing a further increase in pay. It is not known exactly when Jessie came to England, but in March 1871 Joseph's five surviving daughters were gathered at his house, Post View Villa, in Withycombe Raleigh. His three sons had long since returned to India after their English education and become officers in different regiments of the Indian Army. The gathering of the daughters was perhaps because their father, at the age of 76, was suffering from ill health. A year later he passed away. His estate was valued at nearly £14,000, and he left each of his daughters an annuity, plus up to £200 to be spent before their wedding day.

A few months after her father's death, Jessie's eldest sister, Julia Mary, became the first of the five spinsters to marry, very belatedly at the age of 41. Jessie was the youngest of the five, but she was already 28, and it was with delight that she also became betrothed, to a dashing young man by the name of Friedrich Agassiz. The prospective groom also came from a large family, with around a dozen brothers and sisters, and he did indeed have a

---

[1] An ayah was a nanny.

Fig. 9.2 The burning of Washington in 1814

royal godfather. His connection with the King of Prussia came about through his illustrious ancestors.

Friedrich's father, Lewis Agassiz, joined the forces even earlier than Jessie's father, at the age of thirteen, when he became a midshipman on *HMS Rattler*. This sloop was commanded by his father, Friedrich's grandfather, and mainly protected convoys travelling between England and Newfoundland. Two years later, in 1809, he became a 2nd lieutenant in the Royal Marines, the soldiers carried by Royal Navy warships. He was initially involved in operations during the Napoleonic Wars at Cadiz, Malaga and Toulon, but was then sent to America. The war between British/Canadian forces and the United States of America raged between 1812 and 1815. The conflict see-sawed, with victories on both sides, but Lewis was part of the task force that defeated the U.S. Chesapeake Bay flotilla in the summer of 1814. In August they captured Washington DC and Lewis Agassiz led one of the parties that set fire to several public buildings, including the White House and the U.S. Capitol.

Friedrich's father retired from the Royal Marines on half pay in 1817, settling in Bradfield in Essex near the river Stour, and he married the same year. His first wife gave him a son and a daughter before dying in 1825, and two years later Lewis remarried. His second wife bore fourteen children, most of whom survived to adulthood. In 1829, hankering after more adventures, Lewis took his family to visit the country of his ancestors, Switzerland. He arranged transport to Lausanne by coach for himself, his wife, his eldest daughter, a governess, two infants and two servants, at a cost of £95. They left on 6 April for the sixteen-day journey.

Having installed his family in Lausanne, Lewis went on his first long walk that took him a hundred leagues[1] through the mountains and valleys of the Bernese Oberland. During the twenty months of their stay, he took two further long hikes through the Alps and the Jura. On one occasion he passed close to the hamlet of Agiez, near Lake Neuchâtel, the original home of his ancestors and the surname, which in the local dialect meant 'magpie'. Neuchâtel was both a canton of Switzerland and a principality headed by the King of Prussia, who nominated the governor, the Council of State and most of the Grand Council, but was not allowed to change the laws or raise taxes. On his accession the sovereign would swear to protect the rights and liberties of his Swiss subjects, and was in fact often a major benefactor.

It was Lewis' grandfather who left Switzerland for England in the eighteenth century, where he amassed a fortune in the City of London. He was a close friend of Jacques-Louis de Portalès, a wealthy merchant and the benefactor of the hospital in Neuchâtel that bears his name, who became godfather to Lewis' father. Through Jacques-Louis' sons, who had become counts in Prussia, the Agassiz family had links to the Prussian court.

During their stay in Switzerland Lewis' wife gave birth to another daughter, and a few years later several children were born in Prussia during two extended stays in the Rhineland. In 1834 a daughter was born in Mannheim, and between 1841 and 1844 two sons and a daughter were born in Cologne and in the wine-growing town of Honef, situated on the banks of the Rhine 25 miles south of Cologne[2]. The last of these sons was Friedrich.

Fig. 9.3 Friedrich Wilhelm IV

By then Lewis had used his connections to the Prussian court and become a friend to the current sovereign, Friedrich Wilhelm IV, who had acceded to the throne in

---

[1] A league is about three miles.

[2] Honef was situated just south of Bonn and was renamed Bad Honnef after the discovery of a mineral spring in 1897.

1840. The king had already given major sums of money to Lewis' second cousin, the soon-to-be-famous naturalist Professor Louis Agassiz, for the establishment of the Academy of Neuchâtel and his work on glaciers. The king now agreed to be the godfather to Lewis' latest son, who was given the same Christian names, with the addition of James, after his grandfather, and Albert, after the German prince consort of Queen Victoria. On 14 May 1845, when he was ten months old, the child was baptised in Honef, Lewis' ninth son, with the King represented by Herr von Bethmann Hollweg, the Principal of the University of Bonn.

Friedrich did not stay long in Germany but spent most of his formative years in England, in either Bradfield or Exeter, where Lewis had been born. His father died in 1866 of apoplexy and, not long after, his mother moved to Louisa Terrace, just up from the beach in Exmouth. It was less than a mile from Withycombe Raleigh, and it was while staying with his mother that Friedrich met Jessie. How they were introduced is not known. Perhaps it was at one of the balls at the Imperial Hotel, or maybe the families already knew each other; the society was small and two or more of the many daughters might already have been friends.

In any case the couple were married on 12 August 1873 in the church of St John in the Wilderness in Withycombe Raleigh. They did not stay long in the area, as Friedrich had decided to enter the church. He did not go to either of the major English universities, perhaps because he did not have the right connections, or sufficient money, or maybe he just wanted to travel. Not long after their marriage they embarked for Nova Scotia, where Friedrich enrolled at King's College in Windsor, a small town on the Bay of Fundy 40 miles across the peninsula from the capital Halifax. Perhaps Friedrich just remembered the stories that his father had told him of his journeys to Newfoundland as a young midshipman, and he wanted to see what the Canadian eastern seaboard was like. His eldest surviving brother had also gone to Canada following a military career and married in Ontario before settling in British Columbia[1].

After growing up in India, Jessie must have found the weather in Devon a shock, but Nova Scotia was far worse. The climate was said to be similar to Scotland, its namesake, and indeed there was a lot of rain, but much worse was the fog that seeped in from the ocean for much of the year. Jessie had to live for the next three years in a very different society from the one she had experienced in India and Devon. During this time Friedrich studied for his vocation at King's College, which was the first university in

---

[1] The town of Agassiz in British Columbia is named after him.

Canada, having received its charter in 1802. He graduated in 1876 and, not long after, was appointed vicar of Seaforth, an isolated rural parish surrounded by water about twenty miles along the coast from Halifax.

Jessie gave birth to three children while they lived in Nova Scotia, the first exactly nine months after they had married. She was baptised Vaudine Jessie Garnault Agassiz, the first name being a favourite amongst the English Agassiz family as a reminder of the original village in Switzerland, which was in the canton of Vaud. All of the children were baptised with Garnault as their third Christian name. Vaudine was followed at two year intervals by Maude Clemence Garnault and Henry Roland Garnault, who was the last born on Canadian soil.

In 1878 the family returned to England and in September Friedrich joined the army, becoming a Chaplain to the Forces fourth class, the equivalent rank to a Captain. They spent over two years based at Dover, and would have enjoyed the life of an officer's family. During this time Jessie gave birth to another daughter and another son. Early in 1881 Friedrich was sent with his family to Malta, where he spent more than a year, and Jessie had yet another son.

In July 1882 Friedrich and the military garrison on the island were told to prepare for war. In Egypt the Suez Canal, built by the French but now largely owned by British interests, was the main shipping route to Britain's Indian domains. The two European powers had ensured that the Khedive of Egypt was sympathetic to their interests, but he lost power in 1882 through the rise of Orabi Pasha, an army officer. In June rioting in the streets of Alexandria resulted in perhaps a hundred Europeans losing their lives, and the British consul was pulled from his carriage. The British fleet had already arrived and began bombarding Alexandria on 11 July, and two days later a large naval force took the city. British troops were halted in their progress south to Cairo, however, and it was not until the Suez Canal was taken by a flotilla of 40 warships that a larger force was able to approach the capital from the east. On 12 September the army under General Wolseley crept up under cover of darkness to the main defences at Tel el-Kebir and overwhelmed Orabi Pasha. The retreating Egyptians were pursued by the cavalry back to Cairo, where the Khedive was reinstated as a British puppet ruler.

During the battle, 57 British troops were killed (compared to around 2,000 Egyptians), and Friedrich Agassiz was there to help with the men's spiritual needs. Following the British victory, as part of the army of occupation, he and his family were stationed with the 1st Battalion of the Gordon Highlanders, who had been at the forefront of the attack at Tel el-Kebir. For his work, he was promoted to Chaplain third class, the equivalent rank to major, and awarded the Egypt 1882 medal with clasp for Tel el-Kebir, and the Khedive's Bronze Star.

Fig. 9.4 The battle of Tel el-Kebir

Friedrich and his family stayed in Egypt for about a year altogether, before returning to England and resigning from the Chaplain's Department. He looked for openings in the Church of England, and came across an opportunity for a curacy in a Berkshire village where his father's cousin, Revd Robert Agassiz, had once owned property. He secured the position and around Christmas 1883 moved with his family into the very house once owned by his relation, known as 'The Chestnuts'[1], on Horn Lane in the Parish of Cholsey.

* * *

It was not long before Jessie found out about Friedrich's affair with the schoolmistress. One day he said that he had to go away to Uxbridge for a few days, and it wasn't difficult to discover that Annie Bower was away at

---

[1] The Chestnuts is now 26 and 28 Wallingford Road.

the same time. In July 1885 she discovered a letter from Annie to Friedrich that started 'My darling' and finished 'With fondest love, believe me, your loving Annie'. Jessie confronted her husband, who admitted that they had stayed in Uxbridge as man and wife.

This wasn't the first time he had been unfaithful, and indeed their relationship had become very difficult only a few years after their marriage. He seemed unable to hold onto money. When his father died in 1866, Friedrich came into property, but he later sold it to his mother to help clear his debts. By 1884 when his mother died, he again owed her money, which fortunately she cleared in her will, as well as leaving him £300. In addition to being a spendthrift, he was also sometimes violent to his wife. One time when they were living in Dover he had struck her in the street with a walking stick, and later with his fists at the Halmer Palace Hotel in Deal. By 1883 she had had enough and left him, but he later sought her out and begged her to return. Jessie could be a forceful woman, and she only agreed on certain conditions, arranging for a solicitor to draw up a memorandum containing a code of conduct for him to sign.

Jessie was also practical, and after this his latest affair, she decided to stay. She now had seven children aged from six months to eleven and alone she would only have her father's annuity of £70 per annum to live on. Perhaps a labourer could survive happily on that sum, but she was a gentlewoman without any means of income, and wanted to bring her children up without always being in a state of want. As a wife Jessie also had limited legal rights. Indeed up until the Married Women's Property Act of three years earlier, she was not a recognisable separate legal entity and all her property would have belonged to her husband. The situation was now somewhat improved, but women separated from their husbands usually found themselves impoverished.

Jessie also knew her husband. Not long after the affair was discovered, he finished with Annie and began a liaison with another woman. What had happened earlier must have been guessed at by others in the village; if Jessie had noticed Friedrich and Annie's behaviour at choir, others probably had too. But however widespread the gossip was, it did not become a public scandal, and both of those involved were allowed to continue with their respective jobs. Friedrich continued to preach, warning of the perils of a sinful life, while Annie continued to run the infants school and win favourable comment from Her Majesty's Inspectorate. Presumably she was initially distraught at what had happened, but eventually she must have got over it. Four years later she married George Albert Jones, a schoolteacher, and went with him to run the village school in Peasemore, about ten miles away. Her father remained headmaster at Cholsey school until his death in 1896.

Friedrich changed jobs two years after his affair with Annie. Revd Circuitt left the parish in June 1887 and his successor was Revd Augustine David Crake, who had previously been chaplain at the lunatic asylum. He had wanted to hold down both jobs, but the diocese ruled that he was 'unequal to the continuation of duties as vicar of Cholsey and chaplain of this large asylum'. Friedrich, who from time to time had worked at the asylum, applied for the job and was accepted. The vicar graciously wrote in the Chaplain's Journal that he happily yielded the post to his colleague whom 'I truly believe well qualified in the post, as a younger and stronger man'. No mention of piety, and in fact Friedrich was only seven years younger, although perhaps Revd Crake was already in poor health; he died three years later. For Friedrich the change meant an increase in pay, as the salary was £200 per annum, paid each quarter day, as opposed to the curate's stipend of £120. He and his family moved from The Chestnuts on Horn Lane to another house on Wallingford Road, and he officially started in his new job on Friday 24 June, Midsummer Day 1887.

It had been a week of celebrations for the Queen Victoria's Golden Jubilee, with three days earlier an awe-inspiring royal procession in London watched joyfully by over a million of her subjects. Cholsey decided to hold its own celebration on the Thursday, with a thanksgiving service in the church at noon, followed by a dinner at one o'clock to which the entire parish was invited. The sum of £90 had been raised to fund the event and about 400 sat down in two separate barns at Manor Farm, with the food provided by Mrs Powell from the Chequers. The health of the Queen was toasted and Revd Agassiz was thanked, amongst others, for the help he had rendered. Later that afternoon, another 300 or so children, together with the women who were unable to attend the dinner, sat down to a first class tea. Afterwards, in fine weather, the populace danced to Cholsey brass band and sports events were held in the meadow beside the church until 9 p.m., when the vicar awarded prizes.

Friedrich began work in his new post, but not for long. On 9 July he went on leave for two weeks, and the Revd Crake was forced to deputise. Nevertheless he was assiduous enough on his return, persuading the management to invest in a new altar cloth and hangings to brighten up the chancel of the large chapel. The chaplain held three services on a

Fig. 9.5 Queen Victoria

Sunday and regularly attracted well over 200 attendees. At the Harvest Festival on 25 September Friedrich noted how much the singing had improved thanks to the training of the choir organised by the medical superintendent. Friedrich worked through the winter, holding regular services and visiting the patients in the wards, until he went away again towards the end of July 1888. This time he was absent for a month, and when he finally returned, it was not for long, although not even his wife was aware of the shocking event to come.

On Tuesday 16 October Friedrich suddenly announced that he was going to London to see a friend and would be away for a while. The asylum also had no notice of his forthcoming absence. He said goodbye to his wife and seven children, who expected to see him again before long. But the following day Jessie received a letter through the post from her husband. In it he broke the news that he did not intend to return. He explained that he had fallen heavily into debt through gambling, and the previous day he had backed a horse to recoup some of his losses, but it did not win. To escape his creditors, he was leaving immediately for Montevideo in South America. Jessie and the children never saw him again.

* * *

Jessie was left alone to look after her seven children, now aged from three to thirteen, and she had no choice but to try and exist on her annuity of £70, perhaps with some assistance from her family. Her brother Alfred had, like his father, become a colonel in the Indian Army, while her three unmarried sisters were still single; indeed they remained spinsters for the rest of their lives. Friedrich had left so precipitously that some of his salary remained unclaimed, and Jessie collected £11 10s from the asylum to cover the period since Michaelmas. Soon afterwards she and her children left Cholsey, and at the time of the census in 1891 they were to be found in Bedford. Money might have been tight, but they still existed as gentlefolk, with one live-in general servant and the eldest child still at school. Later they moved to Leyton in Essex and, as the children left home, Jessie had to relinquish the live-in servant. Her two sons emigrated to Canada where they married two sisters, but three of her daughters remained single, and from time to time lived with their mother.

When Friedrich left her he wrote in his letter that Jessie was entitled to a divorce, but he hoped she would avoid the scandal for the sake of the children. Before 1857 divorce was only possible by Act of Parliament, but subsequently it was in theory open to anyone to pursue through the Court of Divorce, provided the grounds were adultery and there was no collusion between the two parties in seeking the divorce. However, it was expensive and one-sided. A husband only had to show that his wife had committed adultery; a wife had to show causes in addition to adultery, such as cruelty or incest.

Towards the end of the century Jessie received a legacy of £150 following the death of one of her sisters and she decided to sue for divorce. By then there were around 700 divorces each year, but it was still a costly and embarrassing procedure. In 1900 she instructed Charles Wilkinson, solicitor of Martins Lane, London, who arranged for the required affidavits to be sworn and in December filed the petition.

The hearing was on 4 March 1901 at the Royal Courts of Justice before Sir John Gorrell Barnes, Justice of the High Court. Jessie travelled to these imposing buildings in the Strand, designed to strike awe into litigants, to give evidence in open court, which must have been a daunting affair, even though the suit was undefended. Mr Inderwick, King's Counsel, appeared for the petitioner and summarised the case before leading her through the events and causes. The judge, who must have heard no end of such stories before, nevertheless seemed appalled when he heard about her husband's gambling losses and subsequent flight. "Was he acting as a clergyman at this time?" he enquired, and counsel replied in the affirmative. He also asked about the identity of the co-respondent in the affair, but Mr Inderwick explained that she was now a respectable married woman and he preferred not to mention her name in open court, asking the judge if he would mind referring to the petition papers instead.

Further evidence was then given in support of the case. At the end of the hearing Mr Justice Barnes said that he was satisfied as to the facts and did not feel that there had been undue delay in bringing the suit. He awarded a *decree nisi* on the grounds of adultery augmented by cruelty, and gave to Jessie custody of her four remaining children who were still minors. Although the decree was made absolute the following September, Jessie

Fig. 9.6 The Royal Courts of Justice

never married again.

During all this period Jessie was ignorant of Friedrich's whereabouts. He may well have gone to Uruguay as he claimed, but in 1892 he returned to England. His name was included on the passenger list for the Cunard liner *Gallia*, which docked in Liverpool from New York on 1 February. Two years later he returned to the United States, and in 1898 he apparently remarried, bigamously. His new bride, Catherine, was twenty years his junior and came from New York. Together they had at least one child and in 1910 they were to be found in Worcester Square, Boston, a pleasant development of five-storey terraced houses about three miles from the downtown area. At the age of 65, Friedrich no longer called himself a cleric, but earned a living as a salesman in the publishing industry.

Friedrich is believed to have died a couple of years later, although his new wife probably lived much longer. His first wife also considerably outlasted her former husband, dying in 1929 at the grand age of 84. Jessie had certainly lived an exciting life during her early years, full of travel and interest, and it was her misfortune to fall for a handsome man who turned out to be a cad and a bounder.

Chapter 10 The Rise of Democracy

During the last third of the nineteenth century, the number of men who had the vote rose by a factor of five. At the same time there were major changes in local government. What had started with a move of both relief for the poor and policing away from the parish to a district and county level, continued with the Public Health Acts of 1873 and 1875, which created the Wallingford Sanitary District. The existing Guardians of the Poor were given the responsibility for water supply, sewerage and health in the area covered by the Wallingford Poor Law Union, which included Cholsey.

But the Wallingford Rural Sanitation Authority had few powers and little funding, so little changed in the village. Only the better off used flushing water closets, while most relied on bucket toilets or a shared privy, a small outhouse with a toilet built over a cesspit used by several cottages. Cesspools worked by allowing liquid waste to drain away, whilst solids collected and were emptied from time to time and used as manure. Unfortunately the often poorly-built cesspits were frequently sited close to the well, and waste could seep across through the soil[1]. Water samples taken at the time were often 'foul, yellow in colour (especially after rain), with a most disagreeable and unsatisfactory smell, quite unfit for drinking purposes'. In addition the low-lying central part of the village often flooded, the rain run-off swirling with sewage. The stagnant water would only subside slowly due to the lack of any effective drains.

It is not surprising that disease and death were never far away. In the 1860s there were two severe outbreaks of cholera in Cholsey, and then in September 1893, long after the sanitation authority had been set up, there was a typhoid outbreak. It had been a dry summer and the wells were low, but whether the lack of rain exacerbated the problem was not clear. By 15 September there were fourteen cases in eight families, and the old schoolhouse by the church was turned into a temporary isolation hospital. The Wallingford Rural Sanitation Authority hired three professional nurses to attend to them, but on 21 September Lucy Sawyer, an elderly woman of 66 who lived in a cottage near the school, died[2]. The symptoms took three or four weeks to reach their peak, by which time the sufferer was typically prostrate and suffering from extreme muscular debility and delirium.

---

[1] There was no mains water in the village until the 1930s, and no mains sewerage until the 1950s.

[2] Lucy Sawyer was the mother of Harriett Ann Sawyer, whose tragic death was described in Chapter 7.

Fig. 10.1 The old schoolhouse by the church

Although it was explained that the disease was not particularly contagious, few would attend to the sick and most of the village kept to their homes and work, scared as to where the horror might next strike. The authority distributed a circular to the whole village entitled 'Plain Words about Cholera and Typhoid Fever', and use of the suspect wells was suspended, the locals being told to use water from a nearby stream instead. In due course deep tube wells would be sunk, which drew water from a much lower and safer level.

However, the authorities' actions failed to lessen fears following the appearance of another nine cases and the need for an extra cottage, lent by the vicar, to hold the sick. There was another death on 5 October, Ellen Ford, whose husband John and three small children were also languishing in the temporary wards. They survived, and John Ford, a gardener and groom, was left with three children under seven to look after, with only the help of his mother-in-law. The sanitation authority hired three more nurses, and gradually through October and November the other patients passed the worst and the situation slowly improved. No further deaths occurred, but the authority had to raise an additional rate to pay for the £375 cost of the outbreak, which included staff, the temporary hospital equipment, and fumigation after the outbreak.

Cholera and typhoid were not the only dangers lurking in the waters, and the following year a particularly horrible death showed up the risks. Edith Kate was a small baby, but healthy, the daughter of Mary Ann and George Cottrell, who was a beerhouse keeper living in Horn Lane. On Wednesday 19 December 1894, when she was 2½ years old, Edith appeared to have a cold. Her mother gave her a warm bath, and the next day she seemed recovered, but she became unwell again in the evening. She had a restless night, but, after some teething powder and another bath, seemed easier on the Friday. Then at 9 p.m. she suffered some convulsions, which then ceased. Her father went for the doctor in Wallingford, asking if he could come on the Saturday morning. But at midnight the convulsions came again and this time did not stop. She passed away at 3.30 a.m.

The doctor, William Bremmer Nelson, was asked by the coroner to carry out a post mortem. At the inquest, held on Christmas Eve in the Red Lion, he revealed that in the stomach he had found a large round worm, ten inches long. The great intestine contained another, and in his opinion they were the cause of death. Such worms typically grow from eggs ingested in infected and uncooked food or water, another whole class of hazard well beyond the capabilities of the sanitation authority.

Childhood diseases and epidemics were an accepted part of life, having a major impact on village schooling. For example, 1904/5 was a particularly bad year for illness amongst the children. On 3 June 1904 the first case of whooping cough was reported in the village, and four days later 42 children were affected. In many families the persistent coughing, which could last for a hundred days, echoed around the cottage, with mothers most concerned for the lives of their babies. At the school the headmaster watched the daily attendance drop by a half, and on 15 June the medical officer ordered the school closed. It remained closed all summer, and only reopened after the harvest holiday on 5 September.

Fig. 10.2 The Red Lion

The following February it was the turn of measles and the school was again ordered closed. Measles was not a notifiable infection and did not normally require isolation, so when eight-year-old Bessie Howse caught it, her father John, landlord of the Chequers, let her brothers and sisters visit her in bed and then go out to play with their friends. A week after Bessie became ill, her sister Ida Mary, ten, also fell sick. This time a doctor was consulted, and he had no hesitation in declaring, from the peeling of her skin, that it was scarlet fever, a much more serious infection. Although those affected were taken to the isolation hospital, by then it was too late and the epidemic spread through the village. By 5 May 1905 the number from Cholsey so confined had risen to 36. The school was again closed when the epidemic was declared, and stayed shut for nearly two months. In the course of a year the pupils had missed nearly half of their schooling.

* * *

The work of the local authority may have made little impact on the health of the population of Cholsey, but it did cost money. Farmers and landowners had been having a tougher time since about 1875, when an agricultural depression set in. The price of corn and other imported foodstuffs began to fall, as railways and steamships lowered the cost and speed of transportation from more productive lands in North America and elsewhere. A succession of wet, cold summers and harsh winters led to poor harvests over much of the next twenty years, lowering incomes and forcing economies. For some labourers still in work, life actually improved, as the cost of food staples fell, while those younger and more adaptable acquired new skills or moved to the towns and cities. Already by 1881 the railway employed around 30 men in Cholsey, the lunatic asylum was another big employer, and less than half the men now worked on the land, a number that declined year by year. Some farmers went bankrupt, whilst others survived by changing from arable to dairy and livestock farming, supplying the need for fresh milk and meat in the burgeoning cities.

However, it was not a good time to increase taxation, and ratepayers were worried about further changes established in the Local Government Acts of 1888 and 1894. The first of these established county councils, which would take over the administrative responsibilities of the Justices of the Peace that were previously dealt with at the Quarter Sessions. These included the management of court houses, police stations and lunatic asylums; the appointment of Medical Officers of Health and control of contagious animal diseases; weights and measures; and the maintenance of major roads and bridges.

Elections for councillors were held on 22 January 1889, but about half the seats were uncontested as the political parties and local interests had already agreed who would be nominated for each ward. For the Wallingford rural constituency, Mr Stephen Willesley Cozens, owner of Blackall's Farm, was returned unopposed. The first meeting was held at the Assize Courts on 31 January.

The next two levels of local government were established in 1894. For the rural area covered by the Poor Law Union, Wallingford Rural District Council took over the responsibilities of the Sanitation Authority and those highways not covered by the county. Fourteen parishes were included, with Cholsey by far the largest, having a rateable value twice that of the next two parishes, South Moreton and Didcot, and a population three times that of those two other places combined.

But by far the most exciting change for local people was the establishment of an elected parish council to take over the non-ecclesiastical responsibilities of the vestry. After centuries of being ruled by the local elite, villagers were free to choose who should represent them. A Fabian Society tract for the working man put it this way: 'Hitherto nearly all the public business of the villages and country parishes has been done by the squire and the parson and farmers, just as they thought best. In future the people themselves can do it as they like.' It urged all who could to vote for the best people for the job, 'not the wealthiest man in the parish, not the parson, unless he is a specially good man, not the man who talks most nor the man who employs most labour, but let them elect the man who will do most work of the right kind in the right spirit'.

On 4 December 1894 at 6.30 p.m., according to statute, a parish meeting was held in the Board School to accept and consider nomination papers for parish councillors. The number of nominations was large and the meeting packed. William Bower, the headmaster and assistant overseer, was elected to chair the meeting, and then proceeded to describe the reason for the assembly and to explain that they were bidden to elect eleven councillors from their midst. All classes and interests should be represented on the council; no one should be elected because he was a Conservative or Liberal, nor a dissenter or a churchman, but because he showed moral conduct and business capacity such that he could be trusted to act for the common good of all. The headmaster warned that the new system "would not alleviate or end the present depression in agriculture, nor keep our most intelligent young men from migration to the towns," but nevertheless extolled its importance as part of "the grandest empire on this earth".

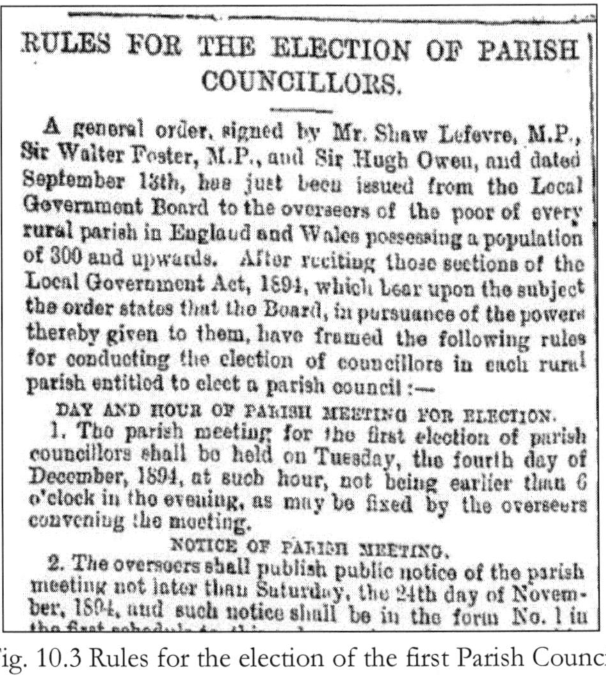

RULES FOR THE ELECTION OF PARISH COUNCILLORS.

A general order, signed by Mr. Shaw Lefevre, M.P., Sir Walter Foster, M.P., and Sir Hugh Owen, and dated September 13th, has just been issued from the Local Government Board to the overseers of the poor of every rural parish in England and Wales possessing a population of 300 and upwards. After reciting those sections of the Local Government Act, 1894, which bear upon the subject the order states that the Board, in pursuance of the powers thereby given to them, have framed the following rules for conducting the election of councillors in each rural parish entitled to elect a parish council:—

DAY AND HOUR OF PARISH MEETING FOR ELECTION.

1. The parish meeting for the first election of parish councillors shall be held on Tuesday, the fourth day of December, 1894, at such hour, not being earlier than 6 o'clock in the evening, as may be fixed by the overseers convening the meeting.

NOTICE OF PARISH MEETING.

2. The overseers shall publish public notice of the parish meeting not later than Saturday, the 24th day of November, 1894, and such notice shall be in the form No. 1 in

Fig. 10.3 Rules for the election of the first Parish Council

This speech was greeted with cheers and afterwards the chairman accepted the nomination papers, which were twenty in number, the names being written up on the blackboard. As that was more than the number of seats, the meeting moved to attempt an election by a show of hands. An opportunity was first given for a statement by each candidate and for electors to question them, but as everybody thought they knew what each man stood for, nobody said anything. Taking each candidate in turn, the vote was then held. A total of 762 hands were raised, with Thomas Lawrence, a platelayer[1], in the lead with 60 votes and Anthony Buckell, a Winterbrook farmer, last with 22. Any elector could demand that a proper poll should be conducted instead, and this is what happened in Cholsey, it being remarked that often the outcome of a secret managed ballot was quite different to that of a show of hands. No control was exercised on how many times an elector put up his hand, nor indeed on how many hands he raised. The final task of the meeting was to choose a Rural District councillor, and this time Mr Buckell was returned unopposed.

The election was scheduled for Monday 17 December between noon and 8 p.m. at the Board school. In the meantime five candidates took out adverts in the local paper extolling their virtues as a representative. On the day there was a strong turnout, and it must have been a novel experience for many new electors faced with the foolscap voting slip containing the twenty names. Out of the 265 registered in the parish, 192 voted, including fifteen who confessed they couldn't read and one who was physically incapacitated and couldn't write, who were all helped by the Presiding Officer, Mr Bower.

The total number of candidate votes cast was 1,492, and the tellers worked late into the evening so that the headmaster could post the results outside the school for the waiting crowds. Revd Augustus Farrar, the chaplain of the lunatic asylum, topped the poll with 122 votes, with Henry Watkin Wells, the famous Wallingford brewer who lived in Winterbrook, second. But there was a good mixture of classes elected alongside these two, including a gardener, a GWR signalman and three platelayers, including Thomas Lawrence. Of the more well-to-do, Anthony Buckell was in fact elected, together with George Norcutt, the grocer, and Stephen W. Cozens, farmer at Blackall's, who would later be a long-standing council chairman. Those who failed to gain enough votes were Edward Hearmon, landlord of the Swan Inn; Charles Hewitt Hunt, farmer at Barn Elms; Thomas Webb, magistrate's clerk; plus another platelayer, a bricklayer, a florist, two basket makers and a labourer.

Late in the evening festivities broke out at the return of so many working class men, with the station bell rung in honour of the election of four out of

---

[1] A platelayer worked on maintenance of the railway track.

the five railway candidates. Although the contest was not supposed to be political, nevertheless many looked on it as a battle of Conservatives and churchmen versus Liberals and non-conformists. In Cholsey, six of the eleven elected were Liberals, who were jubilant about their gains around the county. But as the new guardians of village life got down to business over the next weeks and years, it was not as expected. Many of the responsibilities that were remembered from earlier times had moved to the district or county level, and the parish was left to look after the graveyard, the recreation ground, the allotments and some footpaths, appointing the overseers to work with the Poor Law Union, and not much else. A year later there were sixteen candidates for the eleven seats; the following year fourteen; and thereafter no elections were necessary as the number of would-be councillors never exceeded eleven.

* * *

More important matters tended to be handled at a county or district level, where the parish was only entitled to one or two councillors. Vested interests could manage to sideline those representatives, as happened in 1902. In July of that year, Stephen W. Cozens, chairman of the Parish Council and now also a Councillor for the Rural District, got a shock. He had been pushing for more attention to be paid to Cholsey's needs, and no doubt the question of sanitation and health was high up on his agenda. A new isolation hospital for the district was planned and Mr Morrison had offered a site in Clapcot, just opposite Rush Court on the Shillingford Road, where Mr George Dennison Faber lived, an influential banker. On 3 July Mr Cozens learned by chance from Mr Morrison's agent that the site was no longer needed as another had been selected. At the Rural District Council meeting the following day it emerged that the isolation hospital planned for the district would be located in Cholsey.

The decision had been taken by the Hospital Board at a meeting when his fellow District Councillor (Cholsey now had two), Anthony Buckell, who sat on the committee, was ill in bed. Further more they had already purchased the land, which was situated on the Wallingford Road in Larkcom's meadow, very close to Mr Cozen's farm. He was outraged, suspecting foul play. Another attempt, he said, was being made to foist an undesirable institution on the parish as a *fait accompli*, something that would lower the attractiveness of the village and the value of housing, just as the asylum had done many years before.

A meeting was called at the Board School in the village for 7 p.m. on Monday 14 July 1902, at which the following resolution was passed:

That we the parishioners of Cholsey in public meeting protest most earnestly against an Isolation Hospital being erected on the site selected by the Wallingford Joint Hospital Board, because it is most unsuitable on account of its low-lying position and the non-porous nature of the soil, water standing on the surface for six months in the year. We also protest against the very discourteous behaviour our Representative was subject to by being kept in complete ignorance of the proposal till after the very unsuitable proposed site had been acquired.

The site chosen was where the Cholsey brook had originally run before it was diverted, and was frequently under water. Mr Cozens said it was like putting a hospital in a puddle. The lowness of the site meant that sewage could not be dealt with, and the ground was of black mud of the same type as had been contaminated elsewhere. The meeting also passed a resolution questioning whether a permanent hospital was actually necessary, given its cost.

The campaign must have been effective, because the following March the Local Government Board inspector approved the construction of an isolation hospital on another site close to the workhouse in Wallingford.

The power of the local councillors might have been limited, but it gave many ordinary people a taste of democracy. Suffrage had gradually been extended through the nineteenth century. As *The Graphic* later put it in its review of the nineteenth century: 'Up to 1832 the people had practically no voice in the direction of public affairs; their control rested exclusively in the hands of an aristocratic oligarchy. But when once the floodgates were thrown open, the dammed-up waters poured through in ever-increasing volume, and the "privileged classes", as they used to be called, found themselves more and more disinherited. It is greatly to the credit of the nation that this transformation has been peacefully accomplished.'

The Reform Act of 1832 had lowered the value of property-ownership required to vote, increasing the electorate to about 650,000. In 1867 enfranchisement was extended to all male householders, including those who occupied rather than owned property, tripling the number of voters. Finally in 1884 the right was extended to men other than the head of households, and for the first time the majority of men could vote. But not women, at least not in parliamentary elections. Local elections were slightly different, and women over 21 living in a separate cottage could vote, and indeed could stand as candidates at district and parish level. Nevertheless there were no female representatives on the Cholsey Parish and Wallingford Rural District Councils, indeed of the 265 people on the electoral roll for Cholsey in 1894, few were women.

It took a long time for attitudes to change. The National Union of Women's Suffrage Societies was founded in 1897, and younger women were becoming more independent minded. One factor behind this change was, surprisingly, the bicycle, which gained great popularity in the 1890s and allowed more women to get about without their menfolk. It was also a focus of concern: the ability to meet up with young men away from the eye of a chaperone; the daring frivolity of bloomers as an alternative to corsets and crinoline, which had rendered cycling virtually impossible. As well as worrying about the threat to a lady's morals, some were anxious about the huge popularity of cycling for other reasons. Professor Jung of the University of Geneva predicted that natural evolution would result in human feet becoming stunted through a lack of use for walking, while in perhaps a thousand years men and women would have only short and slender legs, and their arms would be lengthened and strengthened, the better to manipulate the handlebars.

The Women's Social and Political Union was founded in 1903 by Emmeline Pankhurst, and in a few years more militant action by the Suffragettes began to fill the newspapers. In 1908 they began a series of 'caravan tours' in the south of England, to educate the public about their cause. They were often greeted by jeers and sometimes pelted with rotten eggs, but usually talked the crowd round and certainly drew more women to the movement. One particular tour through rural Berkshire was made by Anna Munro, a striking single woman in her mid-twenties who had been imprisoned for six weeks in January 1908. She travelled the countryside in a horse-drawn caravan, speaking passionately at crowded meetings from the tailboard. It all caught the imagination of the girls at Cholsey school, who put on a play about the suffragettes in that year. Nobody guessed, however,

Fig. 10.4 A school play about the suffragettes in 1908

how long the fight for equality would take, with female suffrage for those over 30 finally arriving only in 1918. The age limit was reduced to 21 to match that of men ten years later.

Chapter 11 The New Century

As the last day of December 1899 approached, the country hotly debated whether the next day would herald the start of the twentieth century. The Registrar General said that it would not, and most agreed that it would be another year before the new era began, as the first year of the Christian calendar was year one, not nought[1]. Not that there was much in the way of celebration on the night of 31 December 1900; the religious festival of Christmas was far more important. But it was a chance for newspapers to dwell on the changes over the previous hundred years and look forward to life in the twentieth century.

The new era was less than a month old when there was also a change of monarch. Queen Victoria died on 22 January 1901, aged 81, and was succeeded by her eldest son, Edward VII. The Edwardian Age would bring many changes, including further improvements in democracy, such as the limitation of the power of the House of Lords in 1911. But at a local level life went on largely as before, with mutual support most important, the community working together to avert disaster and celebrate good fortune.

In Cholsey, on Sunday 19 May 1901, in the middle of divine service, one of the workers from Manor Farm rushed into the church shouting, "Fire!" A large straw stack by the roadway was alight, and the farmer, Mr Stephen Cozens[2], had sent to the church for aid. The fear was that the flames would spread to the great barn, which, as well as being an important building, contained 25 tons of wheat and other stock. The congregation poured out to help. By then the upper doorway to the barn had caught and all the efforts of the villagers were put into stopping it from spreading. The Wallingford Corporation fire engine arrived soon after one o'clock, but proved of little use as there was no suitable source of water. However, the fire gradually burnt itself out with no further damage, a total of 27 tons of hay having been destroyed.

It did not take long to discover the cause of the fire. It was arson, and the culprit was Isaac William Lay, a boy of eight years who was the son of the shepherd on the farm. The lad was brought before the magistrates five days later, when several witnesses reported seeing him in the vicinity, and a

---

[1] So according to the popular consensus on its beginning and end, the twentieth century only lasted 99 years.

[2] Stephen Cozens junior, the tenant of Manor Farm, was the son of Stephen W. Cozens of Blackall's Farm.

little girl of the same age, Maud Colin, gave some damning testimony. She lived at Manor Farm Cottages and was out with her younger brother on the morning of the fire when they met Isaac. He pulled out a box of matches and said, "Let's set the rick on fire." She demurred, but apparently her little brother, aged four, joined in as they struck a match. The bench sentenced Isaac to four strokes of the birch.

Some older members of the congregation might have recalled how the fire had a strange symmetry with that of another Sunday, 40 years previously. On that occasion it was Benjamin Baldwin, also a shepherd, who noticed smoke issuing from the church roof. As with the later event, the service was suspended and the churchwarden, Job Pocock, and many of the congregation rushed outside to help. Ladders were procured from the farm and Job climbed up and began hurling hot slates off the roof to reveal the cause of the conflagration. The pipe from the stove in the church ran too close to the rafters, which had caught fire, but thanks to the timely action, serious damage was avoided.

The year after the later fire, on a happier note, plans were made to celebrate the coronation of the new king, Edward VII, in a similar manner to the late Queen's Jubilee. But on Tuesday 24 June 1902 word came through that the King was critically ill with appendicitis and that the coronation had been postponed. Many towns and villages cancelled all their planned festivities, and some experienced outbursts of riotous behaviour as workers expressed their disgruntlement at having their holiday stolen. Cholsey, however, decided not to miss out on a spot of fun, and proceedings went ahead. A church service was held at 11 a.m. on the Thursday morning, and afterwards Mrs Faulkner presented the choir, bell-ringers and Board School children with a Coronation cup and saucer or

Fig. 11.1 An invitation to the Cholsey coronation festivities

plate. A dinner was provided at one o'clock in Mr Stephen Cozens' large barn at Manor Farm for all the adults of the parish able to come, around 400 people. The feast featured local beef and mutton and was followed at 4.30 p.m. by a tea for all the children and their mothers, another 500 parishioners. As a mark of respect, the sports were cancelled and the prize money of £20 held over until the real coronation. This turned out to be a shame as 26 June was sunny and warm, whereas when Edward VII was finally crowned on 9 August, the day was rather grey and cool.

* * *

Of course, during this time, there were also many personal disasters where the community was unable to help. For example, in 1900 another local man died from drowning.

Enoch Bailey was an attendant at the asylum and often lived in, but his family occupied one of the asylum houses in Star Terrace on Papist Way. Enoch came from Gloucestershire, which was where his son Walter had been born, but they had now lived in Cholsey for about fifteen years. Walter, seventeen, was a printer by trade and worked at Mr Jenkins' works in Wallingford, but he was not a strong lad and suffered from a weak heart. The third week of July 1900 had been hot, with the temperature reaching 90 degrees, and on the Friday, ignoring his father's warnings, Walter announced that he was going to bathe in the river. He called for Heber Eltham, fifteen, at about 6.30 p.m., and together they collected the two young Bosher boys before walking down to the river at a spot close to the railway bridge. They undressed.

The two Bosher lads swam off under the arches and Heber, who was not a good swimmer, kept close to the bank. Walter, who could not swim at all, walked into the water. None of them knew that at that point the clay river bed sloped gently down at first, but then dropped abruptly several feet. Heber looked on in horror as Walter stepped off this invisible cliff and promptly disappeared beneath the water. Walter rose to the surface and paddled ineffectively, then sank again. He came up once more, then a third time, before vanishing definitively. Heber could do little to help and the Boshers were too far off. Five minutes later the two lads returned and Joe Bosher[1] dived down to try and find Walter, but without success.

---

[1] No Joseph or Joshua Bosher has been found in Cholsey, but Albert John Bosher was one of the sons of Charles W. Bosher, who lived at Thames View on the Reading Road, and was fourteen at the time.

Just then Dr Edwin Dunn, one of the two medical assistants at the asylum, came by in a boat. He could do little himself, but put his back into rowing as fast as he could downstream to summon help at the Beetle and Wedge in Moulsford. Frank Cox, the landlord of the riverside inn, came straight away and after ten minutes or so located Walter's lifeless form and dragged the body to the bank. Dr Dunn tried to resuscitate him, but three-quarters of an hour had passed and nothing could be done.

The inquest was held the following day at the Waterloo Hotel and evidence presented by those involved. The foreman of the jury, Mr Money, returned the jury's only possible verdict: accidental death. The coroner remarked that a string of corks should always be worn by non-swimmers to ensure they kept their heads above water. Walter's parents were non-conformist, and three days later the first part of the funeral service, led by Revd Salt of the Wallingford Thames Street Chapel, was conducted at their house. The second part was held in St Mary's churchyard, where the body was interred and the Revd Salt addressed the mourners, speaking of the sad loss of a young life.

Some years later it was the elder brother of the 'Bosher boys' who was, rather more unfortunately, in the news. The scandal concerned Elizabeth Howse[1] who, in 1897, when she was 40 and still a spinster, met Charles William Bosher, 26, at a school treat. The following year she began walking out with the young man, who worked as assistant to his father, also Charles William, a prosperous builder. In August he proposed, and after she asked him whether she was not too old, he allegedly said, "Oh, no; I don't want a young wife."

Elizabeth accepted him and wore his engagement ring, but no date was set for the marriage as she continued as housekeeper to her aged father at East End Farm, and her fiancé saved up to build them a fine home before the wedding. In 1901 her father died, and she received the following letter from Charles:

Cholsey, [Friday] Aug 2, 1901

My dear Bessie,

My only hope is that you will bear up through all your sad trouble. Dear Bess, take all things quiet, not upset yourself, as there is generally little cross ways at such times instead of being solemn and quiet. Let your brothers and sisters have their own, as my regards to you are keener than they were, and don't be afraid of a home worthy of you

---

[1] Elizabeth Howse was the sister of John Howse, the landlord of the Chequers mentioned in Chapter 10.

(when the time comes). You know, Bessie, that I am not a boy, and what I am writing you is not pen and paper talk, it is from my very heart, and the last few nights I have not had scarcely any rest, being thinking and worrying that your sad bereavement will cut us asunder; but I hope, please God, that it will not be so, as I love you most dearly, and after three years being together… You need not be afraid of having a home; I will make a home for you wherever you, dear, wish for one. Write me as soon as you possibly can. Sunday delivery here will be anxious.

From yours for ever,

C. W. Bosher

From soon after their engagement there had been 'improper relations several times', but still no date was set for the wedding. At Whitsun 1906 she heard rumours that he was going out with Sarah Hearmon, the 26-year-old daughter of an engine driver. When Elizabeth confronted Charles, he denied it and reaffirmed that she was his intended. But on 22 December, away from local people in North Moreton church, Charles married Sarah. Elizabeth, upset and at the age of 49 now unlikely to marry, began proceedings for breach of promise.

The case was heard at the Berkshire Assizes in June 1907, and the whole courtship was made public. Charles in his defence said that Elizabeth had told him that she would only marry if he came to live at East End Farm, which he did not want to do as he did not get on with her brother Thomas, who now ran the enterprise. Elizabeth said that this was not the case, and the court finally found in her favour. Charles was ordered to pay £75 in damages plus the costs of the litigation. It is rumoured that Bessie spent part of the money on a personal luxury to compensate for her misfortune: a fur coat.

* * *

The Edwardian age also saw its fair share of crime, such as the unusual incident that occurred at Cholsey railway station in 1902. William Francis Povey, the signalman, was in charge on the evening of Wednesday 13 August, and after the last train had left at 9.50 p.m., he closed up. He went down to the booking office and let himself in, locking the door from the inside, and then went through the room behind where the parcels were stored and out through the back door, locking it from the outside. He then took himself home to his cottage in West End, to his wife Annie and their delightful first baby daughter, who in a rush of originality they had named Dallas Lorial.

Edwin Thomas Owen, the railway porter, was the first to arrive at the station the next morning, just before six o'clock. He was surprised to find the window in the booking office door smashed in. The booking office was a mess, with books and papers hurled about, the parcels room ransacked, and the cloakroom door open. The porter went straight to the police house in Honey Lane and PC Ernest Spratley came to inspect the damage. The cash drawer had been forced and the ticket case was broken open, while in the parcels office other drawers were pulled out and a tin trunk was wrenched open.

Superintendent Hearnes from Wallingford took charge of the case and it was established that five shillings was missing from the cash drawer. Blood stains were found on the booking office door, so the culprit must have cut himself while removing the glass. The broken-open trunk was found to belong to Matilda Cox, a nurse at the lunatic asylum, who had had clothing and other items sent from Maidenhead. From amongst the dishevelled heap of her belongings she found that a blue serge dress, a pair of glacé kid shoes[1], a blue blouse and a nightdress were missing. Miss Alice Dorothy Saville, a nursemaid in the service of a Mr Cross at Aston Tirrold, had left a cardboard box at the station the previous day, and some of the contents of that had also disappeared.

PC Spratley went off to search the area, and in a bean field alongside the path leading from the current station towards the old Moulsford station, about halfway to Silly Bridge, he found a clutch of discarded items: a Bible and prayer book, a hand mirror, some stationery and photographs, a hat and a cardboard box. Close by in a shock of wheat[2] he found a hat containing some green apricots. Two days later whilst continuing the search, in a hedge at the top of Moulsford Hill he found another green apricot, and a local described how he had seen two people in the vicinity on the morning of the burglary. Superintendent Hearnes circulated the description of the suspects, along with a list of the missing items.

The following Wednesday Deputy Chief Constable Dorrell was on his way to work in Maidenhead, when he spotted a man and a woman fitting the descriptions carrying bundles on the Bath Road. Sergeant Ilott was dispatched to the Model Lodging House in Bridge Street where the suspects were staying, and found them with two packages wrapped in large handkerchiefs. Once the parcels were opened, he recognised several items from the list of stolen goods. The culprits made a half-hearted attempt to

---

[1] Glacé in this context means highly polished.

[2] A shock was a group of twelve sheaves of grain placed on end in a field to dry. The word stook is also used to describe a similar arrangement.

Fig. 11.2 Honey Lane with, probably, PC Ernest Spratley c1906

escape, but with the help of others they were apprehended and taken into custody.

James Bowen, 26, and Fanny Beeson, 22, described as tramps, were brought before the bench the next day. James claimed initially that he had just met the woman and knew nothing of the thefts, while Fanny said that in fact they were married and her surname was Bowen, not Beeson. Both retracted their statements later, and the case was complicated by accusations of a burglary in Knowl Hill and other crimes in Buckinghamshire and Surrey. After further appearances before the magistrates in Maidenhead and Wallingford, the pair were finally tried for the two crimes in Berkshire at the Quarter Sessions in October. They pleaded guilty and James and Fanny were sentenced to six and four months with hard labour respectively. The justices could not say whether they might be rearrested on their release to answer for the crimes in the other counties.

Accidents on the railway also continued, with a particularly mysterious occurrence in 1913 involving a local celebrity, making it the talk of the district for many weeks. It concerned Charles Morrell, the chairman of Wallingford magistrates and a leading light in the county, who had been hurt in the Wallingford branch line accident of 1899. This time it was far worse.

As well as being a magistrate in Berkshire, Charles Morrell was also a Justice of the Peace in Oxfordshire, Buckinghamshire and Worcestershire, a partner in one of the Wallingford banks, and a member of countless committees and boards. He now lived in the Manor House in Dorchester, and drove to Wallingford station whenever he had a need to travel to

London. Early on Tuesday 2 September he was his usual self and during the journey chatted to his coachman, who intended to take the carriage back home later as it was needed during the day. Mr Morrell ordered his return to meet the 5.30 p.m. train back, and went off to London. A tall and quite stout man, he was wearing a blue serge suit, top hat and a light brown mackintosh, and carrying an umbrella.

For some reason Mr Morrell must have missed his intended return train, and caught the 6.10 from Paddington instead. At Cholsey he alighted on the middle platform at 7.24 p.m., and said good evening to the guard of the Wallingford train waiting in the bay. But he did not get into a coach, and instead placed his coat on a bench before entering the lavatory. The engine steamed off without him. The next train was not due until 8.48 p.m., and Mr Morrell went to the Railway Hotel[1] nearby, where he asked for a brandy and water. In the public house he spoke to Gadd Baldwin, a platelayer, who talked about the weather and the state of the crops. Mr Morrell seemed in a hurry and left soon after, walking down the road parallel to the line that led to the bridge under the railway and to Pancroft Farm. It had been raining and the evening was already quite dark.

George Toe was the driver of the 6.50 express from Paddington, which drew into Didcot at 8.08 p.m. Walking round to the front of his engine, he immediately saw the unmistakable signs of flesh and fresh blood. He alerted the authorities and Inspector Ernest Hund quickly ordered up an engine and coach to go back down the line. About half a mile from Cholsey station he saw a mackintosh beside the line, and a broken umbrella beneath the bridge that carries the track from Manor Farm to The Lees. At a spot on the down line where expresses regularly reached 60 mph were the mangled remains of a body, still warm and wearing the remnants of a dark serge suit. The face was unrecognisable, but when PC Spratley inspected the body the next morning he found a knife engraved with the name 'Charles Morrell'.

The inquest was held on the Thursday at the Railway Hotel. The coroner questioned the witnesses as to the events and the deceased's health and state of mind, looking for clues to explain the tragedy. It would seem that he was in good spirits, his usual affable self, and that his health was no different from normal. As a master of fox hounds he had taken a fall on his head sixteen years earlier, and he occasionally suffered from giddy spells. His doctor was also treating him for heart troubles, but there was no evidence in support of a sudden attack.

---

[1] The Railway Hotel was on the corner of Station Road and West End, and was known latterly as the Brentford Tailor (after the pub of the same name on The Forty had closed) and then the Walnut Tree, before closing about 1998.

The most likely conjecture was that he was not feeling completely well, which might explain the visit to the lavatory and the brandy. Subsequently, having an hour to wait, he went for a walk and got up onto the track by the West End bridge. Perhaps he intended to walk down the line to Wallingford, but he must have been seriously disorientated to have mistaken the four lines of the main railway for the single track. All the witnesses discounted the theory that it was suicide resulting from some unknown worry or circumstance. In the end the jury agreed, returning a verdict of 'accidentally killed while trespassing on the line', and asked that their condolences be sent to his relations.

* * *

A great concern during the Edwardian era was the rise in the military might of Germany. The rapid growth of their navy, which might one day equal that of Britain's, was seen as a particular threat. Many feared that the challenge to Britannia's rule over the waves eventually would lead to war. Although the Kaiser was one of Queen Victoria's many grandsons, Germany had already clearly shown its anti-British feelings by supporting the Boers in the South African conflict at the beginning of the 1900s.

The Second Anglo-Boer War had seen the largest British army fielded in any conflict to date. England had not been involved in a major war since the Crimea nearly half a century earlier, when a force of perhaps 30,000 men was fielded. The Boer War saw the deployment of almost half a million soldiers, drawn from all corners of the empire, to overcome a force of fewer than 100,000 Afrikaner farmers and reservists. The conflict had come about mainly through the tensions created by the discovery of diamonds in the Orange Free State, which soon accounted for 90% of the world's production, and the huge gold mines in the Transvaal. When the influx of British settlers threatened to overwhelm the local population, the Transvaal and Orange Free State governments restricted the right to vote and discriminated against the incomers. Britain felt this breached earlier agreements and sent a large body of troops to the Cape Colony. War broke out on 11 October 1899.

Initially it went very badly for the British forces, with three major defeats in what became known as the 'black week' of mid December. The Boers were highly mobile and equipped with the latest Mauser rifles, which through enfilade fire[1] caused great losses amongst the British infantry. The

---

[1] In enfilade fire, riflemen shot at a line of advancing troops from either end, making hits much more likely.

Fig. 11.3 Boer commandoes

cavalry, who had largely relied on swords and lances, also proved surprisingly ineffective. The forces at Kimberley, Ladysmith and Mafeking were besieged and in a perilous state. In the New Year overall command was transferred to Lord Roberts, and reinforcements poured into southern Africa.

Britain was gripped by a wave of patriotic feelings, and many men enlisted to help in the conflict. What the army wanted most, of course, was trained men. In Wallingford and the surrounding area, part of the response came from the Wallingford Volunteer Rifle Corps, established in 1860 and attached to the Berkshire Regiment. At the beginning of March 1900 the first three of their number were escorted to Wallingford station by the town band and a large crowd as they left to join other volunteers heading for the front. More local people were involved in other regiments, but few it would seem from Cholsey. Amongst the casualties, only one born in the parish has been found, Frederick Walters.

Frederick was the sixth son of Arthur Walters, who farmed in Cholsey for more than 30 years from around 1850, running Rectory Farm just off the Westfield Road. They left the parish sometime before 1891 and Frederick enlisted in the 1st Royal Dragoons, a cavalry regiment. He was killed on 19 June 1901 near Lake Chrissie in the Transvaal, during an attempt to capture the Boer commander-in-chief, General Louis Botha[1].

Ten days before Frederick's death, the Wallingford Volunteers returned to a heroes' welcome. During the war they had seen plenty of action as part of the Royal Berks Regiment, marching 780 miles through the Transvaal, suffering casualties in the battle at Zitika's Nek, and having some of their number captured by the Boers for a short time after the enemy had approached the men disguised in the khaki of the British Army. Of the three who had left fifteen months earlier, one had died of enteric fever[2], and

---

[1] Louis Botha was later the first Prime Minister of the Union of South Africa.

[2] Enteric fever was another name for typhoid.

the two who survived were accompanied back to Wallingford by a third from a later contingent.

Their arrival saw such scenes of celebration as had rarely if ever been witnessed before in the borough's history, and no doubt many Cholsey people joined in the festivities. At 7.45 p.m. on that Sunday, when the soldiers' train drew into Wallingford station, more than a thousand people were there to greet them. As the three men emerged, a huge cheer went up and they were taken to a decorated van, part of a long procession led by a local detachment of mounted infantry, escorted by the town band playing Home Sweet Home and by 'M' company of the Wallingford Volunteers, resplendent in red. Followed by a huge crowd, the procession wound its way down Station Road to the Market Place, every window crammed with cheering faces. Outside the Town Hall a service of thanksgiving was held for the three and they were each presented with a silver watch, followed by a reception when they were toasted with champagne.

Whilst there was rejoicing at home, it would be another year before the war finally came to an end. The Boers had invented guerrilla warfare and continued to harry their foe, while the British had conceived the idea of concentration camps to confine anybody that might help the enemy. Before the end, 22,000 British troops had been killed in action or died of wounds and disease; 7,000 Boers died in the fighting, and another 28,000 of infections in the camps. The Transvaal and Orange Free State were annexed, but less than five years later self-government was reinstated.

Subsequently, although the Boer War had demonstrated the killing potential of modern weapons and the limited capability of the British Army, few took that lesson on board. Soldiers and war were still largely remembered for the glory. At the start of the century a review in the *Leeds Mercury* had celebrated the might of Britain and its empire compared to the other nations of Europe following the South African War.

> Before that war, and during its earlier stages, all the Continental Powers, with the exception of Italy, were envious, adverse, and inclined to coalesce against Great Britain and put an end to her superiority. Such a dream of crushing England is dispelled for a century. No European nation would now alone dare to provoke a war with Great Britain, and no two are sufficiently of accord to unite for such a purpose.

How affairs can change in thirteen years. On 28 June 1914 Archduke Franz Ferdinand of Austria was shot by a Yugoslav nationalist in Sarajevo. It was not big news in Cholsey, but the consequences would decimate a generation of its young men.

Chapter 12 The Great War

The assassination of Archduke Franz Ferdinand, heir to the Austrian throne, led to frantic diplomatic exchanges between the European powers that came to be known as the July crisis. Wanting to protect and expand its Balkan lands, Austria (who were allied with Germany) presented its neighbour Serbia with an unacceptable ultimatum and, on 28 July 1914, declared war. Russia mobilised its forces the next day, ready to support its Slav ally. France had an alliance with Russia, and as a consequence the Germans had prepared the 'Schlieffen Plan', which envisioned a quick massive invasion of France to neutralise their army, before turning to face the Russians. The Kaiser ordered mobilisation in the German Empire on 30 July.

It still seemed possible that the expanding conflict would not involve British forces. On 31 July the *Berks & Oxon Advertiser* wrote: 'The greater part of Europe seems to have gone mad on war, and England is almost the only Great Power that retains its sanity.' Nevertheless, the leader writer was worried about government naval preparations, noting that 'the most powerful fleet of battleships the world has ever seen has gone to sea under sealed orders'. The paper continued, 'It is hard to feel any justification for our taking part in the horrible carnage that is going on, but at the present time it is impossible to know what is proceeding behind the scenes.'

Germany invaded Belgium and attacked French forces on 2 August, forcing a reluctant France to declare war. Britain was a guarantor of Belgian neutrality and the German occupation was seen as an unacceptable

Fig. 12.1 The shooting in Sarajevo

threat, so an ultimatum was issued demanding that their forces withdraw. Receiving no satisfactory answer, and in support of the 'Entente Cordiale' with France, Britain declared war on Monday 4 August.

Throughout the land the country rapidly moved to a war footing, which meant immediate mobilisation for the Cholsey reservists and men in the territorial forces. By a quirk of fate, the call to action happened to coincide with the annual camp of the local territorials. Members of the 4th Battalion of the Royal Berks (later renamed the 1/4th) in the Wallingford half-company (which was paired with Wantage) had marched out of the town centre the previous day to the cheering of large crowds. Led by Major Francis Reade Hedges, a solicitor who was born in Winterbrook but now lived in the town, they travelled by train to Bovingdon Camp, near Marlow. Later that Sunday evening they retired to their tents, but in the night were awoken by the sound of a motor car arriving at speed. Soon after the orderly sergeant call sounded out, followed a little later by the order to break camp. The battalion left at 5.30 a.m. and arrived at Reading, the regiment's headquarters, at 6.30 a.m. The Wallingford men were sent back to the borough, with orders to be ready to depart at a moment's notice.

Monday 4 August was a bank holiday and, although still a work day for most, few could bring themselves to carry on as normal. When the special editions of the London papers arrived they were seized upon for the latest news. During Tuesday a steady stream of reservists passed through the town heading for the station, and at 7.20 p.m., after the declaration of war, the order to mobilise was received at the territorials' headquarters. The news was spread through the night by motor car and bicycle, and the following day the 50 or so men of the 4th were assembled in the Market Place. In the pouring rain, they marched out led by Major Hedges and preceded by the Boy Scout band. At Wallingford station a crowd perhaps a thousand strong cheered the departing men, their relatives and friends waving frantically. A thunderstorm was raging as the train steamed out, the reports of fog detonators[1] deliberately set on the line accompanying the crash of the heavens and the diminishing roar of the multitude.

In their sodden khaki uniforms the soldiers were nevertheless in high spirits as they passed through Cholsey station, exchanging banter and singing patriotic songs. They wondered how long they would be away; most thought not for long and the general consensus was that they would definitely be back before Christmas. A more sombre note was struck by some of those present from Cholsey because of one absentee from their ranks. Alfred Abdey, a labourer and territorial man whose parents Edwin

---

[1] Railway detonators were small explosive charges meant only to be set on the track to warn engine drivers of danger in thick fog.

and Susan lived in Station Road, died that same day in Wallingford Hospital of a malignant disease of the lung, aged 20.

At Reading the regiment formed up and in the evening around 800 men left by train for a pre-arranged war station near Portsmouth. Three days of training followed, before they were ordered to move to Swindon to join up with the rest of the division. Surprisingly, they were at this point requested to volunteer for overseas service, even though the extent of the war was still not known and the regular army had yet to engage with the enemy. But it turned out to be premature, and it wasn't until March the following year that the battalion set off for France.

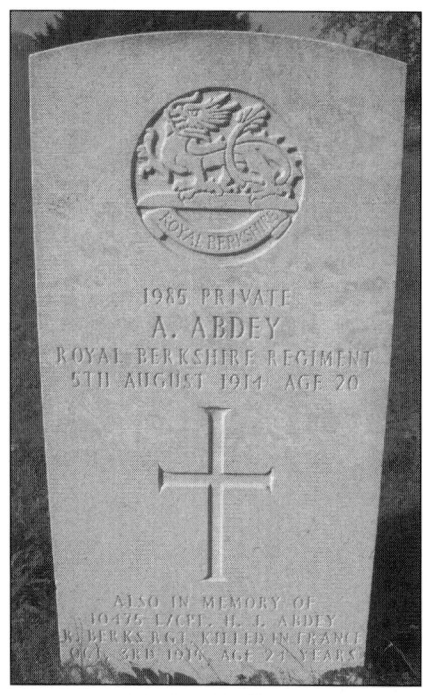

Fig. 12.2 Alfred Abdey's Cholsey gravestone

However, other Cholsey men saw action much sooner, such as Leonard Franklin Gale and his two brothers. Leonard was the son of Joseph John Gale, head of the old established Wallingford firm of Franklin & Gale, the farm and property auctioneer and estate agent. Like his father, Leonard lived in Winterbrook, sharing a house with his elder brother Harold James, the two sons working in the family business. Although both of them were born in Cholsey, along with their younger brothers William Douglas and Ronald, their father came from Oxfordshire. They decided to join a rather different territorial regiment, the Oxfordshire Yeomanry, also known as the Queen's Own Oxfordshire Hussars (QOOH).

Harold enlisted first, when he was eighteen years old, leaving three years later in 1905. Leonard was a keen sportsman and in 1910, after attending Abingdon School and Malvern College, Worcestershire, he joined up, followed by William, a bank clerk, the year after. Harold rejoined at the outbreak of war, waiting in line for the recruitment sergeant just after his cousin from Cholsey, George Shrubb Abbott, the son of an important farmer who lived at 'The Hazells', opposite the church. Leonard was in 'C' Squadron, which was based in Henley-on-Thames and led until the outbreak of war by Major Winston Churchill, who latterly was also First Lord of the Admiralty. The QOOH were a mounted unit armed with swords and rifles, with regular drills and shooting practices conducted through the year and an annual camp in the summer, usually at Blenheim Palace. Leonard was promoted to corporal, and by the outbreak of war had reached 29 years of age, still a bachelor.

Leonard and the others were at work on Tuesday 4 August when the order came through to regimental HQ to mobilise. Over the next few days 'C' squadron, now led by Major C. R. I. Nicholl, gathered in Henley, and on Tuesday 11 August they marched to Reading. Two days later their officers dined with Winston Churchill, whose brother John Strange Spencer-Churchill led 'D' squadron, and Sir Ian Hamilton, Commanding Officer of Home Forces. On the Saturday the brigade was sent in a series of special trains to Bury St Edmunds, where they were expecting to spend six weeks training, but on the 27th they received the startling order to proceed at once for embarkation to Egypt. However, the order was soon rescinded, and instead they were taken by twelve trains back across the country to Churn camp, on the Downs south of Blewbury. It was a hot day and the twelve-hour journey in the stuffy wagons was very distressing for the horses.

Now the QOOH were told that they would remain in England for many months. But Winston had other plans for his brother, and in the early hours of Saturday 19 September the order was received to proceed to Southampton. The regiment embarked the same day on the *Bellerophon*, a cargo steamer of the Blue Funnel Line, and they sailed for France the following morning. On board were 24 officers, 447 men and 455 horses. With no time to prepare, the officers took everything they possessed, around 50-100 pounds of luggage each, and some even loaded the ship with their motor cars. The boat arrived at Dunkirk at one o'clock on Monday morning, but the seas were heavy and the ship was forced to lie at anchor for more than 24 hours before it could dock. A week later they reached Hazebrouck, 25 miles from Dunkirk, but they had barely arrived before they were ordered to retreat towards the coast before the advancing German army. Their encounter with the enemy was sporadic, but they became the first territorial unit to be involved in the fighting.

Of course the QOOH fought alongside units of the regular army, who were mobilised immediately after the declaration of war on 4 August. The 1st Battalion of the Royal Berkshire Regiment were stationed at Aldershot when the order came through that same day at 5.30 p.m. and they left for France a week later, reaching the front on the 23rd. Following on a month later were reinforcements for the battalion, including Pte John Alder, who landed in France on 12 September. He left behind in Cholsey his pregnant wife Lucy, who was the sister of Alfred Abdey, the man who had died of lung disease on the day the war broke out.

The 2nd Battalion of the Royal Berks was in India when war was declared and it was much longer before they saw action. Amongst their number was

Corporal Alfred Alder (no relation to John), the son of William and Harriet Alder of Hithercroft Cottages in Cholsey. William was a farm labourer, but Alfred joined up as soon as he was able and by the outbreak of war had already been in the army for at least four years.

The 2nd Battalion sailed from Bombay on 20 August aboard the transport ship *Dongola*, part of a convoy of 45 troop ships, four warships and three armed auxiliary cruisers. After docking at Liverpool on 22 October, the battalion crossed the country and joined up with other regiments to form the 8th Division, before taking ship and landing at Le Havre on 5 November. Journeying by train and route march they reached the trenches at Fauquissart, about ten miles west of Lille, on 14 November. They had journeyed halfway round the world full of optimism, only worried that the war might be over before they got there. But as they became accustomed to trench life, the mood of Alfred Alder and the others abruptly swung.

The brigade that included the 2nd Battalion held two miles of trench facing an enemy at times only 40 yards away. An ideal slit trench was 3 feet 4 inches wide and 7 feet deep, with a fire step taking up half the width to allow a soldier to rise up above the parapet to shoot. It was difficult to move along the line at the best of times, and usually the construction was far from ideal. The British lines were in low-lying ground and constant pumping was needed to prevent flooding and, to prevent collapse in the rain, the sides had to be shored up with whatever material was available. Mud was everywhere, covering boots and coating clothing, which in any case were often sodden from the rain. 'Frostbite of the feet', later known as trench foot, started to appear, beginning with a numbness, then a foul odour and blisters, until gangrene finally set in. During bombardments the noise from the artillery was deafening, and during battles it became impossible to bury the dead, causing the stench of putrefying decay to spread over the land.

Life for Alfred Alder and the others was a pure test of endurance; boredom separated by bursts of terror. Later the trenches would be better constructed, in a zigzag line to limit damage from direct shell hits, with spurs to latrines and officer shelters, and communication trenches back to the support lines to reduce the danger when moving to or from the front line. But for the moment, they were little more than muddy holes in the ground.

* * *

The lives of those left behind in Cholsey also underwent a major change. Every day when the papers arrived, they were avidly read for the latest news, and more copies were sold each day than ever before. The events were discussed in the streets, the fields and the pubs, and the latest letters sent home from loved ones read and reread. Everywhere servicemen were on the move and the Reading Road was a good location to see the assembling of the army. On the morning of 11 August a company of the QOOH rode by, accompanied by motor vans and camp wagons loaded with luggage. At other times groups of soldiers marched past, heading for Reading and the south. The Middlesex Imperial Yeomanry were holding their annual camp at Moulsford when war was declared, and 'B' Squadron were billeted at Kentwood and Manor Farms in Cholsey.

A few weeks later the Middlesex and other units welcomed an illustrious visitor to Cholsey on an inspection: the King. Thursday 8 October 1914 was a fine autumn day and George V arrived at Goring station by train and then motored up to the Fair Mile, the long stretch of turf leading to the Downs at the southern end of the parish. Buglers sounded the royal salute as the King mounted his charger and walked his horse down the ranks. Thousands of mounted Yeoman stretched in a long khaki line from the Wantage Road and the King saluted as he rode past them up to Lowbury Hill, where he then watched the squadrons execute manoeuvres across the wide Churn basin. Although the visit was only known about a few hours before his arrival, thousands of folk came from Cholsey and district to watch the spectacle and cheer the King.

Less welcome were the army scouts who visited all the farms and stables in the parish, compulsorily purchasing horses suitable for the cavalry, mounted infantry or transports. Many lost their animals at a time when they were most needed for the harvest, and patriotic support for the war effort was tested by the forced enlistment of what were often dear four-legged friends. Another widespread fear was of German spies and sabotage, and from the start the railway was guarded by GWR staff, military and other personnel. Boy Scouts, many of whom were on their summer camps when war was declared, were also mobilised to help in the war effort. As well as carrying out such guard duties, they also acted as messengers, worked on the land and helped at supply depots, and in the first year alone 100,000 were employed in public service. The Girl Guides helped in female occupations, such as nursing and the production of clothing.

The banks did not reopen on the day after the bank holiday, but stayed closed for the first week of the war as gold sovereigns and half-sovereigns were withdrawn from circulation and

Fig. 12.3 George V

replaced by paper one pound and ten shilling notes. On Saturday 8 August Parliament passed the Defence of the Realm Act (DORA) in just five minutes, suspending many civil rights and giving the government virtually unlimited emergency powers. Press censorship followed two days later.

The price of food started to rise immediately as panic buying by those with sufficient money led to shortages. For those with their main wage earner now absent, this was a double blow, supposed as they were to exist on 'separation allowances'. These were initially set at 7s 7d for a soldier's wife plus 1s 2d for each child, while the soldier was expected to contribute to this sum from his weekly pay of 6s 8d. But there were delays in setting up even these meagre payments, and the Rural District Council, responding to a national call, formed a committee to handle any distress, which would work with the National Fund now collecting contributions. Mr Harry Clark Hunt, the well-to-do farmer at 'The Elms', was the Cholsey representative. In other initiatives, spare clothing was requested to furnish the Red Cross with stores, and voluntary groups of women with a little time on their hands gathered to sew garments and knit socks.

A few days after the declaration of war, a call to arms was posted in all the newspapers from Lord Kitchener, asking for 100,000 volunteers for the army. The commander was 'confident that this appeal will be at once responded to by all those who have the safety of our empire at heart'. The request was for able-bodied men aged 19 to 30, although those under 42 with earlier military service were also asked for. A recruiting sergeant was appointed for Cholsey and Wallingford, and Lord Kitchener's assumption was proved correct as hundreds of locals flocked to join up. Everywhere men were excited, eager for adventure as in the stirring tales of derring-do that they had read as boys; the war offered a welcome change from the normal boredom and grind. Stories of German atrocities in Belgium further fuelled the patriotic fervour that was enveloping Britain.

Over the next couple of months a second company of territorials was formed, which became the 2/4th Royal Berks, and four new regular battalions, the 5th, 6th, 7th and 8th were created. Many Cholsey men were amongst their ranks. Recruits first underwent an extended period of training, and none of these units left England until well into 1915. By that

Fig. 12.4 Lord Kitchener

time the regular and territorial troops had already seen plenty of action.

After the Oxfordshire Hussars' withdrawal from the front at the end of September they spent two weeks training in St Omer, learning to use the new regular army rifles and bayonets that were issued. They also practised digging trenches, little knowing that rather than pursuing the enemy on horseback they would spend most of the war in the mud. The regular army referred to the QOOH sarcastically as 'Queer Objects On Horseback', but in fact they saw little of the regiment in the saddle. Instead their mounts were more of an impediment, carted about the country and having to be looked after all the time, but of little use to the war effort. By contrast, the horses used for haulage were vital, with motor transport in short supply and in any case less effective on the poor quality roads.

On 30 October the QOOH left St Omer, proceeding back through Hazebrouck and then taking up positions in the vicinity of Messines, where they came under artillery fire. Cpl Leonard Gale from Winterbrook was in the 3rd troop of 'C' squadron, which was led by Lt Muirhead. On the night of Friday 6 November they were well entrenched, exchanging fire with the Germans only about 200 yards away, but it was difficult to see anything in the fog. In the early hours Cpl Gale spotted an opportunity to take the regiment's first prisoner. With the help of another soldier he captured an officer's cook, lost and stumbling around in the murk looking for his officers and clutching two mess tins containing a vile-looking white mixture.

The next two weeks were spent in and out of various trenches, at times a miserable experience. The three days in the Kemmel trenches were the worst. Wet through from an eight-hour snowstorm, they spent 72 hours motionless in icy-cold flooded holes in the ground, without hot food or drink. Climbing up the muddy side of the trenches was difficult, and once visible to the enemy invited almost instant death. Some men were frostbitten and some died later from gangrene. Thankfully then they were relieved, and as German pressure on that part of the front reduced, they did not see the front line again for another three months.

During this time Leonard learned of the death of his youngest brother, Ronald Gale. Soon after coming down from Oxford he had gone to Bishop's Hostel in Farnham, Surrey to study for the clergy, which was where he died on 12 December following a short illness. Meanwhile their brother Harold Gale had not crossed the Channel with the first contingent, and instead went for officer training and was commissioned into the 2/4th Royal Berkshire Regiment in March 1915. Brother William and cousin George Abbott were both commissioned later in the year as 2nd lieutenants in the regular 2nd Battalion. Leonard might have expected a similar future, but it was not to be.

In March an epidemic of measles swept through 'D' Squadron, and in April Leonard's squadron was afflicted, appropriately enough, by an outbreak of German measles. Despite the disease, on 23 April the regiment was suddenly ordered to move and soon found themselves back in the front line trenches for what became known as the second battle of Ypres. Four days later, on 2 May, the enemy released poison gas[1] and attacked. Fortunately the approaching haze did not reach the QOOH positions, although other units were affected, and the attack was repulsed. After a week's break from the front line the regiment was back in the trenches in the middle of May for seven days, when the rain was so heavy that the sides collapsed in muddy landslides and the parapets had to be repeatedly repaired.

Three days' rest behind the line was granted on 21 May, but on the 24th they moved back, and at 2 a.m. took up positions in open ground in Zouave Wood. Defences were dug and it was a relatively quiet day, with just a few snipers disturbing the relative calm. Unfortunately, on 25 May one of the targets was Cpl Gale, who was hit and died the same day. It fell to his brother William, who had been in action nearby, to write home with the terrible news and offer the comfort that at least Leonard had not suffered. On 10 June a memorial service was held in St Mary's church Wallingford for Leonard and other officers and men of the district who had fallen. The concluding music, Chopin's *Funeral March*, reflected the gloom felt by all the relatives and friends.

The previous year, the 1st Battalion of the Royal Berkshire Regiment had a similar experience to the Oxfordshire Hussars after they reached the front line deep inside Belgium on 23 August. They did not stay long, but were soon retreating, this time without the benefit of horses. Over fifteen days they marched 236 miles in the retreat from Mons, before crossing the Marne, advancing again and finally settling into trench warfare. They were involved in the first battle of Ypres in October/November 1914 and then spent the winter and most of the following year in and out of the trenches. The general rule was for a battalion to spend no more than a few days or a week in the front line trench, the rest of the time in the support line, in reserve or carrying out other duties. Nevertheless the life was hard and the attrition from shelling, sniping or enemy forays was steady. On 5 January 1915 a shell fell directly into the headquarters trench of 'C' company, killing the commander Capt Birt and several others. One of these was Pte John Alder. His 27-year old wife Lucy received the news a few days afterwards, devastated to learn that she would now be a single mother. When the baby

---

[1] The Germans first released chlorine in April 1915, to widespread condemnation. France had used non-fatal tear gas in August 1914.

Fig. 12.5 The wedding of John Alder and Lucy Abdey in 1913

was born two months later, she named him Alfred John Festubert after the Christian names of her dead brother and husband, and the location where her beloved met his end.

By April 1915 the 1st Battalion had lost a large part of their complement, and welcomed a significant batch of replacement soldiers freshly arrived from England. One of these was Stephen Draper, who was 30 years old and came from Enfield in Middlesex. A few years earlier, when he was working as a gardener at a rose nursery in nearby Cheshunt, he met Mary Louisa Wyatt, who was employed as a parlour maid at the Bishop's College in the town, an establishment for the training of Church of England clergy. Mary came from Cholsey, where she had entered service at the vicarage, and after the couple married in 1912, they moved back and lived in Elizabeth Cottages[1], close to Mary's parents Mark and Louisa Wyatt.

Sometime after the declaration of war Stephen volunteered and was later assigned to the 1st Royal Berks. He landed in France on 1 April 1915 and joined his battalion, who were by turns occupying the Cuinchy trenches or in reserve at Béthune. On 15 May an attack on the German positions was successful, but with severe casualties, the Royal Berks suffering 423 men killed, wounded or missing. Through the summer Stephen was not involved in any major attack, but took part in an assault in the early hours of 28 September during the battle of Loos. With unfamiliar terrain and the

---

[1] Elizabeth Cottages are the set of six terraced houses on the east side of Honey Lane close to Buckthorn Lane.

battalion scattered on fatigues[1], they were ill-prepared, but the high command said the attack was imperative. It was bright moonlight, and as the British advanced past some captured German trenches they were spotted, bringing forth a rain of fire illuminated by Very lights[2]. They fought bravely, indeed one lieutenant was posthumously awarded the Victoria Cross, but in the end they had to pull back. More than half of the total of 288 casualties did not live to see another day. One of these was Pte Stephen Draper. Not long afterwards his young wife received the notification in Elizabeth Cottages.

Another Cholsey man killed right at the outset of the battle of Loos was Harry Turner. He was part of the attack by the 8th Battalion on the opening day of hostilities. They had only arrived in France the previous month, and up until that time they were mostly involved in training and preparing for battle. At 6.30 a.m. on 25 September the British began a bombardment of German lines and released poison gas towards the enemy[3]. Unfortunately some of the battalion were immediately incapacitated due to leaks of gas, but, under cover of smoke bombs, they went over the top at 6.30 a.m. They came under heavy fire, and when they reached the enemy's barbed wire defences found that they had been little damaged by the bombardment. As they cut their way through many fell before the relentless machine guns, and to make matters worse a change in the wind drove the gas back towards them. Nevertheless they reached their objective, only to find that most of the German troops had been withdrawn, leaving only the machine gunners. A victory, but nearly half the battalion was lost, including Pte Harry Turner, the son of Isabella and Jasper Turner, a gardener living at The Chestnuts[4] on the Wallingford Road.

A few days later Herbert John Abdey (brother of Alfred) suffered a similar fate just a few miles away. Herbert, who was a gardener by occupation, was with the 5th Battalion of the Royal Berks, which arrived in France on 31 May 1915. During training, likely-looking recruits were chosen for promotion to create an NCO cadre, and Herbert was made a lance-corporal. Through the summer they learned trench warfare and alternated between frontline and reserve duties, without any serious battles. Nevertheless, casualties occurred from a sniper's bullet or a well-directed

---

[1] Fatigues in this context means menial tasks.

[2] Invented in 1877 by Edward Very, a Very light is a flare launched by rocket which then descends slowly on a small parachute.

[3] This was the first use of poison gas (chlorine) by the British.

[4] 'The Chestnuts' was where Friedrich Agassiz had lived, as described in Chapter 9.

Fig. 12.6 Herbert, William, Alfred, Edwin and Susan Abdey c1906

shell. On 5 October Herbert became one of these victims, a minor footnote in the story of the battalion's involvement in the battle of Loos. He was 24 years old, and his parents Edwin and Susan, now living at 7 Star Terrace in Cholsey, must have been devastated when they learned the news that they had now lost three family members: two sons and a son-in-law.

* * *

Christmas 1914 arrived on the home front with no sign of the village women's husbands, brothers and sons returning, as had been widely expected. For those with money, food was still plentiful in the shops and early warnings of severe shortages had not materialised. But prices had risen hugely, with flour up 70 percent and meat costing almost double its pre-war price. An effort was made for a decent Christmas dinner, but the church bells were silenced by DORA as a mark of respect for those who had already lost a loved one. Everywhere were calls to aid the war effort, and Cholsey carol singers managed to raise £12 4s in Christmas week to provide comforts to the troops.

Anti-German feeling and fear of spies continued, and those with any kind of connection to the Central Powers[1] made efforts to hide or sever those links. Cholsey welcomed some refugees from abroad in January 1915, but M and Mme Hoffmann were forced to point out in the local paper that although their surname was of German origin, they themselves were loyal Belgian citizens. Key components of the country's infrastructure, such as bridges, railways and the telegraph, continued to be guarded, something

---

[1] 'Central Powers' was the term used to refer to the German and Austro-Hungarian empires.

which was of great help to Mr Henry Silvester of Kentwood Farm. In February a fire broke out in one of his barns opposite the station, and the military, assisted by villagers, prevented the conflagration from spreading.

In August the Gloucester Territorials were replaced as guardians of the railway by the Oxon and Bucks Light Infantry Reserve. The work was new to them, and one of their number, Edmund Thomas Loft, met an unfortunate end. On Wednesday 18 August he was crossing the line as the Swansea express approached, and took no notice of, or did not hear, his colleague's shouted warning. The impact went unremarked by the engine driver, but death was instantaneous and the mutilation horrible.

In July 1915 Parliament passed the National Registration Act, and everybody between the ages of fifteen and 65 was obliged to carry an identity card giving their name, age, place of residence and employment. Within a year of Kitchener's call to arms, nearly 3 million men had volunteered for the forces, but the army was voracious for more. The government started to become more belligerent with those men who had not volunteered for war service, and most of the public was of a like mind. From around this time, any man not in uniform, regardless of whether he was unfit or in an essential occupation, was liable to be given a white feather as a sign of cowardice.

However, the local paper held up Cholsey as a shining example of patriotism, listing 136 men in the forces and saying: 'If every county did as well as Berkshire, and every parish as well as Cholsey, there would be no lack of recruits and no talk of conscription.' Although most of the roll call were soldiers, one was in the Royal Flying Corps and eight were in the Royal Navy. The attrition rate in the navy was much lower than in the army, although there was one sad case. Edward Ferdinand Green, a signal boy and the son of Emily and James, a labourer living in Honey Lane, was the youngest person in the parish to die on active service. In August 1915 he succumbed to disease in Malta while serving on *HMS Europa*, aged just sixteen.

Support for the war effort by the women of the village continued through 1915, although the army launched an appeal to end the deluge of knitted socks. As more and more men left for the front, the Board of Trade issued an appeal in March for women to take up paid work in trade, commerce or agriculture, saying: 'Any woman who by working helps to release and equip a man for fighting does national war service.' The Register of Women for War Service quickly attracted 124,000 recruits, and no doubt encouraged many Cholsey women to undertake full-time work on the farms, the railway and local businesses. Several were employed by the Army Ordnance Corps established at Didcot in early 1915, while some may have gone further afield to work in the expanding munition factories. Many of the gentry lost their servants forever.

Fund-raising amongst the better off also continued. In December a joint meeting was held at the Baptist Chapel with the Band of Hope and the National Women's Temperance Association, which had provided three fully-equipped motor kitchens for use by the troops at Boulogne, Salisbury Plain and Whitchurch in Shropshire. Light coffee vans, recreational institutes and billets were also planned for France and Flanders. The meeting featured an address and musical selections, including a solo delivered by Mrs Edith Hutt, whose son Edward would later die on the Western Front, serving with the Manchester Regiment.

Around half of all Cholsey men ended up in regiments other than the Royal Berks, and not all of them fought in France. One such was Reginald Montague Griffiths Hearmon, whose father, Edward, had for many years been the landlord of the Swan Inn, but now lived in Ilges Lane and worked as a butcher. Reginald found employment with Mr Dix, the baker and grocer in Cholsey, taking responsibility for the bakehouse. At the outbreak of war he was 21 years old and solidly built; tall at over 5 foot 9 inches and with a chest measuring 36 inches which, when expanded, increased to a massive 49 inches.

When he enlisted on 4 January 1915, the skills from his trade were recognised and he was assigned to the Army Service Corps to work in one of the field bakeries. After spending six months training in Aldershot, he transferred to Devonport and sailed for the Near East in August as part of the 10th Field Bakery. Landing at Alexandria in Egypt on 22 August, he gradually moved closer to the front line of the war with Turkey. On 5 September he arrived at Kephalos on the island of Kos, and a week or so later he sailed for Tenedos, a small island close to the mainland which was the launch point for the attacks on the Gallipoli peninsula.

But by then Reginald was a sick man, with stomach cramps and fever contracted from something he had eaten, and on 15 September he died of enteritis. A week afterwards his father received the letter carrying the worst possible news, and later that autumn his effects arrived: a handkerchief, some letters, a purse and a

Fig. 12.7 Band of Hope medallion

few photographs. It was left to Reginald's sister Violet[1] to acknowledge receipt of the parcel.

Another soldier whose peacetime skills were recognised was Henry Francis Woodward. He was an older man, 34 at the start of the war, but nevertheless volunteered to fight in 1915. A bricklayer by trade, he was assigned to the 250th Tunnelling Company of the Royal Engineers and served on the front south of Ypres. Tunnelling had become a major activity for the British, but it was the Germans who first adopted the strategy.

By the end of 1914 the front line was largely static, a siege between opposing forces stretching from the North Sea to the Swiss border, and old methods of undermining the enemy were recalled. On 20 December ten small mines exploded at Givenchy under British positions, followed immediately by a deadly infantry attack. The military responded quickly by recruiting miners and tunnellers working on the London Underground, and the first British mine exploded on 17 February 1915. It was difficult and dangerous work. The primary technique was 'clay kicking', where the lead man lay at the face with his back on a sloping board and drove a specially shaped spade into the earth. The 'bagger' alongside him filled a sandbag with the spoil, and a 'trammer' loaded a rubber-wheeled trolley which was then pulled back out of the gallery on rails. It would return filled with wood to make props supporting the roof every nine inches. Vertical shafts hidden behind the lines provided access to the galleries via ladders for the men and pulleys for equipment and spoil.

The attrition rate amongst tunnellers was high. Death could come through flooding, entombment when a roof collapsed, the enemy discovered and blew up the workings, or worst and most commonly of all, silently, by carbon monoxide poisoning. Each side developed listening posts to detect excavators at work below, although it was easier for the British as the Germans employed noisier picks against the face. Occasionally opposing tunnellers might meet, resulting in a scrabble of deadly hand-to-hand fighting far underground. As time went on, the tunnels became more extensive, and it could take many months of work to position the high explosive. By mid 1916 there were 25,000 trained tunnellers, supported by almost double that number of unskilled infantry men. Detonation was usually followed immediately by a rush to occupy the crater, in an attempt to break the line of the enemy's defences.

---

[1] Violet Hearmon was by then a teacher at Cholsey school, a post she occupied until 1961.

Henry Woodward landed in France on 16 October 1915 and was assigned to work on a massive excavation near the Messinine ridge, a German strongpoint. They started digging 500 yards behind British lines and constructed a set of deep mines that ended 57 feet below the German positions. It took more than eighteen months, but finally the end points were stuffed with 22 tons of high explosive in nineteen charges. They were detonated at 3.20 a.m. on 7 June 1917, creating huge craters and seriously breaching the enemy line.

But Henry never saw the successful result of his labours, dying on 28 March 1916. It is believed that, unusually, Kate Woodward managed to travel to France to see her husband before his death. Back home in Elizabeth Cottages in Honey Lane, she was left to share her grief with her seven-year-old daughter and their neighbour Mary Draper, whose husband had died six months earlier.

Chapter 13 The Conscientious Objector

Not every young man rushed to join the armed forces during 1914 and 1915, and the supply of new volunteers began to dry up. On 27 January 1916, after great debate, forced conscription became law, requiring all single men and widowers aged between 18 and 41 to enlist. Exceptions were allowed for unfitness, men required for essential occupations, those with dependants, and conscientious objection, and the government set up local tribunals to adjudicate on claims for exemption. Of those giving excuses for not going to war, the most reviled were the conscientious objectors.

One such 'conchie' was Frank Beale, a rather stout mail sorter and telegraphist at Wallingford Post Office. He lived with his widowed 66-year-old mother, Keren, at Mount Pleasant in Honey Lane, Cholsey. Misfortune had dogged Keren's life, and perhaps she was glad that her only child was refusing to fight. She was born in 1849 and named after her paternal grandmother, Kerenhappuch Bosher, one of the many Boshers given unusual biblical names[1]. Keren was the daughter of Emma and George Beal, who was an agricultural labourer and, later in life, the farm bailiff at Hithercroft. She went into service at a young age and worked in households in London and at Wargrave.

She stayed a spinster until late in life, but at the age of 42 she finally married her first cousin Joseph Beale, who was a printer compositor in Reading. Joseph was six years' younger than Keren and the son of Charlotte and Joseph. Joseph senior spent some of his childhood in Wallingford workhouse before becoming a footman and later an innkeeper. Following their nuptials, Keren's married bliss did not last long. Despite his younger age, her husband died less than a year after their wedding day. But he left her pregnant, and her son Frank was born in the summer of 1892.

Keren returned to Cholsey with her baby to live with her mother Emma in Honey Lane. Emma existed on parish relief, while her daughter lived on a small income from her late husband. Frank turned out to be a bright lad and after he left school he secured a position as a learner at the Wallingford Post Office in October 1907. Amongst other tasks he learnt how to transmit telegrams using the telegraph network, which at 6d for twelve words could be sent quickly to anywhere in the country. Although the telephone was growing in importance as a means of communication, few had a receiver, while telegrams could be sent to anybody. While 6d was not

---

[1] Kerenhappuch was the third daughter of Job in the Old Testament.

to be spent by ordinary people except on special occasions, for businesses and those better off they were ideal. Two years after he started, Frank moved to Buckingham to take up an appointment as a sorting clerk and telegraphist, before moving back to Wallingford in July 1911 to do the same job.

Frank was a politically aware youth and became a member of the Independent Labour Party in 1913. The party was strongly anti-war, believing it was wrong to take arms against workers in other countries. Although many changed their view after the start of hostilities, their erstwhile leader, Ramsay MacDonald, was forced to resign after being accused by the popular press of treason because of his objections. Frank also joined the Church of England Socialist League and was secretary of the Workers Joint Committee (presumably a work trade union organisation, the Post Office being a strongly unionised civil service organisation). In November 1914 the No Conscription Fellowship (NCF) was formed and Frank joined as soon as a local group was established. After July 1915 when conscription looked increasingly likely, the highly active organisation fought against the whole idea, with the help of sympathetic Liberal and Labour MPs, then helped ensure conscientious objection was an allowable exception, and finally sought to help those persecuted for their beliefs in prison and elsewhere.

On 2 March 1916, following the Military Service Act, all eligible men were classed as having passed into the army reserve and became liable for call up, and Frank applied to the Wallingford tribunal requesting exemption. On Monday 13 March 1916 he appeared before the committee, which consisted of a board of eight, including the military representative, Lt-Col Hart-Dyke. Frank sought exemption on the grounds of conscientious objection and that he was the only support for his widowed mother. The committee questioned him closely on his beliefs, which were that war was morally indefensible and inconsistent with Christianity. He believed in the 'solidarity of the human race and the common unity between the people of all nations'. He did not believe that any good came from meeting force with force.

The clerk asked him, "Do you think if we laid down our arms at the present moment, the Germans would do the same and retire?"

"Yes, I think so," he replied. "The only way to overcome hatred is by love."

"If you saw your family slaughtered," questioned Mr Wells, "would you stand by and do nothing?"

"I should do my utmost to save them, but I cannot take a life."

The military representative pointed out that a Non-Combatant Corps was being formed for those with such views. Frank responded, "I cannot accept non-combatant service because I can make no distinction between the fighting forces and those forces which are organising and maintaining the military."

Tribunals were not given guidance on what constituted valid conscientious objection and by a vote of five to three the panel rejected his exemption on the evidence given. The military representative said that he believed that Frank's mother did have other means (indeed, she had said as such at the previous census), but he was overruled and the exemption was allowed for him to support his mother. As a declared 'conchie', now well known thanks to the newspaper reports of the hearing, Frank would have been discriminated against at work, insulted, reviled and possibly physically abused in the village. His mother may well also have been despised for providing the excuse for his non-involvement.

As the months and years rolled by and the war continued, the scope of conscription was gradually extended. On 25 May 1916 married men were included, and later the upper age limit was gradually extended to 51. The Quakers and the NCF, who included the distinguished philosopher Bertrand Russell on their national committee, started organising classes for conchies who were ill-equipped for a philosophical discussion before a tribunal, and Frank Beale travelled the country helping other would-be objectors. A two-day emergency national convention was held in Bishopsgate in April 1916 at which 2,000 delegates passed resolutions and promised mutual support. Outside a huge crowd intimidated the 'peace cranks' entering and leaving, while inside the delegates were asked to wave their handkerchiefs rather than cheer, so as not to enrage the mob.

In May a group in the Non-Combatant Corps (NCC) were forcibly sent to France where they came under war zone regulations, and 35 were sentenced to death for disobeying orders. Back home their friends worked on their behalf, and at a secret meeting between the Prime Minister and a delegation that included Bertrand Russell, Asquith agreed that no one would be shot. As a Liberal, Asquith was himself only a reluctant supporter of conscription and sympathised with the plight of the conchies. The death sentences were

Fig. 13.1 Bertrand Russell

commuted to ten years' penal servitude.

In August Frank found himself before the tribunal again in an attempt to preserve his exemption. The Post Office no longer said that he was in an essential occupation and Frank withdrew his claim to be indispensable in supporting his mother, seeking exemption on the grounds of conscientious objection alone. Frank explained his case fluently before the assembled worthies once more. His confidence and self-assurance were not common and some feared appearing before such an august group. In June the body of a sorting clerk from York Post Office was found hanging by his braces from a tree, a notice to appear before the appeal tribunal in his pocket.

Frank re-iterated that he thought war morally indefensible and inconsistent with the teaching of Christianity. He also said that he could make no moral distinction between the fighting forces and those who were engaged in war work such as the making of munitions, road-making, sanitary work etc., which all tended to the increased efficiency of the military organisation whose object was the slaughter of his fellow man. In addition if he helped to restore wounded soldiers to life then he would be helping them to go and fight and kill again. Frank pointed out that his views were not held lightly as they had resulted in conflict with his superiors at work and persecution in the village.

Fig. 13.2 An anti-CO poster

The military representative said that the work he did at the Post Office had some military value. "You must have transmitted an enormous number of letters connected with the war," continued Col Hart-Dyke, "is not that against your conscience?"

"I must object to that," replied Frank. "I know nothing about what is in the letters and by statute I am not allowed to."

"I telegraphed to a man in Abingdon about being called up and I believe it was transmitted by you, but your conscience apparently didn't strike you then."

"I believe you are rather prejudicing your official position. How do you know it was I who sent the telegram in question?"

"By your voice."

"Surely that is rather indefinite evidence to come to such a conclusion, especially as I rarely touch the telephone." Frank then requested of the chairman that he might exercise his right to put questions to the tribunal. He then addressed the colonel, "Is the military representative aware that telegraphists in the army are trained in the use of arms and have on occasions worked in the firing line."

"Yes."

"Will a conscientious objector be called upon to do that work?"

"That is a matter for the tribunal to decide."

"Is it not a fact that one of the principal rules of discipline in the army is that a soldier must obey orders?"

"Certainly."

"If I were in the Army and were taken to a strike area and called upon to shoot strikers, should I have to do so?"

"Yes."

"As a soldier if I were called upon to execute a man whom I knew to be innocent, should I be obliged to do so?"

"Yes."

"Even though shooting the man almost irrevocably settled the question?"

"Oh yes. If he were shot then I suppose it would," replied the colonel, to laughter.

"If I attested as a soldier and we had the enemy in this country who captured my mother and myself and threatened to tear the former to pieces before my eyes unless I divulged plans in my possession, what would be my duty as a soldier?"

"Refuse."

"Then because my pacifist point of view may imperil the lives of others, it is not more absurd than the militarist plan which may do so also."

The general view was that the conchies were not doing their duty to protect the country from foreign aggressors, and Frank felt that he had shown how taking a militaristic stance equally put innocent lives at risk. Col Hart-Dyke didn't respond, so Frank tried a different approach.

"As a military gentleman whose opinion is entitled to respect, can you give me any definition of what you consider Christianity to be?"

"Bishops and Archbishops cannot do that, surely a humble follower cannot be expected to."

"Might I suggest that Christianity is the application of divine love to the progress of human affairs."

"That may be, but it is not my business here; we have leaders in the Church who will see to that."

At this point the chairman called a halt to the cross-examination and the panel retired to consider the application in private. Most hearings by tribunals lasted no more than five minutes, but the group took nearly an hour more to reach a decision. When they returned the chairman announced that the tribunal had agreed to exempt the applicant from combatant service and that they were of the opinion that he would be most usefully employed in his present trade working for the military. This meant that he would have to undertake non-combatant service in the 'army without rifles', a somewhat illogical decision. On the one hand they must have accepted his conscientious objections, but on the other they were ordering him to carry out service which went against those objections. However, other tribunals were making similar decisions up and down the land.

Frank Beale appealed against the ruling. A month later his appeal was rejected and towards the end of October he received his official call up and was posted to No. 5 Southern Company of the Non-Combatant Corps (colloquially known as the No Courage Corps). He was now under military law and when he immediately disobeyed an order, probably refusing to put on a uniform, he was arrested. The court-martial was held on 4 November and he was sentenced to 112 days imprisonment with hard labour. Of the 16,300 conscientious objectors of the Great War, nearly 6,000 suffered a similar fate.

Like others in the same situation, Frank was taken to serve his time in a civilian gaol, the army having no prisons of their own and unwilling to risk the pacifists polluting the minds of serving soldiers consigned to detention barracks. Frank passed through the forbidding gates of Wormwood Scrubs on Wednesday 8 November. It must have been a shock. His clothes were taken away and he donned prison uniform before being locked up in his solitary cell. All alone and enclosed, with no handle on the inside of the door, and just a flat board for a bed, a stool and two buckets: one with water and one for a toilet. Occasionally there would be the sound of a click and an eye would appear at the spy hole in the door before disappearing again.

The bedclothes had to be folded in a certain way to avoid punishment; the floor had to be blackened with lead, which fouled the hands and required some of the precious water. By standing on the stool he could peer out through the bars of the window, but that was forbidden too. The food was inadequate, with skilly[1] for breakfast, perhaps soup for dinner followed by bread with animal fat and a small portion of dessert, and then more bread with cheese for supper. In between he was given mailbags to sew, a tiresome and tedious exercise.

The pernicious silent system was still in operation and Frank was only allowed out of his cell for 45 minutes exercise a day, when it was forbidden to talk to other prisoners. But his profession was of great benefit, as the conchies had learnt to communicate by tapping on the pipes using Morse code: two taps for a dot and one for a dash. Some prisoners even acted as telegraph exchanges, transferring messages from one pipe to another, although of course all of this was forbidden too. The communications were sometimes quite intellectual, for example playing chess; one inmate was even disciplined for transmitting Gray's *Elegy* in Morse.

After two months Frank agreed to take advantage of the Home Office Scheme. Set up later in 1916, it allowed conchies to opt for work in special centres where they would carry out tasks to benefit the nation. Conscientious objectors held a wide range of views, from the 'absolutists' who would do nothing of a conscripted nature, to the 'alternativists' who were willing to work provided it did not benefit the military directly. Frank decided that he was in the latter category and, after being interviewed successfully by the Central Tribunal, he was moved to Army Reserve Class 'W' on 2 January 1917, and a week later released from prison and transferred to Warwick Work Centre. This settlement was based in the old prison, but the locks on the cell doors were no longer used and the warders were renamed 'instructors'. Frank was supposedly a free man, although the place retained its prison atmosphere and he was subject to a set of conditions that if broken would make him liable to be returned to the army. The work involved was deemed of national importance, but would have been simply working on the land or in construction.

During the war the number of criminals in the prisons gradually diminished, and in February 1917 the government decided to close Dartmoor Prison and distribute the remaining inmates to Portland and Parkhurst. The dark grey fortress then reopened in March as the Princetown Work Centre for Conscientious Objectors. Towards the end of that month Frank was transferred along with most of the other Warwick inmates and journeyed across the bleak moor to enter through the grim gates inscribed with the motto *Parce Subjectis* ('Spare the vanquished'). At least one of their number was familiar with the place, remarking that it was

---

[1] Skilly is watery porridge.

strange that while his father-in-law had come here because he had killed a man, the new intake were brought there for being unwilling to do likewise.

The conchies were put to work in domestic duties, on the land and in the quarries. As at Warwick they were not locked into cells and were free to do what they wanted in their spare time, provided they kept to the settlement rules. The food was more substantial than in prison, if a little boring. Breakfast and tea consisted of ½ lb bread with a pint of tea, cocoa or coffee, the latter made from ½ oz coffee, ¼ oz chicory, ¾ oz sugar and 4 oz milk. Dinner consisted of 9 oz each of meat, potatoes and vegetables, and was followed by 4 oz of rice or suet pudding. Lights out was at 10 p.m.

Fig. 13.3 Dartmoor prison gate

From the start local people complained about the nearly a thousand conchies dumped in their midst, voicing a series of allegations against them. They were provided with comfortable accommodation and rations that exceeded those recommended for the civil population, all at public expense. They could come and go as they pleased, buying up all the sweets and other provisions in local shops and depriving the rest of the population. At church in Princetown many of them disgraced the country by walking out rather than standing to sing the national anthem. A packed meeting at Plymouth Guildhall on 25 April rowdily complained about the lenient treatment of the law-breakers housed at Princetown. They were described as mostly disloyal men, anarchists and preachers of a bastard Socialism who spread sedition and held political meetings that ended with a chorus of *The Red Flag*. They were slackers at work and many were even given railway passes so they could return home for an Easter holiday. Revd Riley, a non-conformist minister, tried to speak in moderation, but was shouted down. Strong views were also expressed in Parliament, and in April Mr Whiskard of the Home Office visited the centre to increase discipline and give more power to the warders.

From Frank's and the other conchies' perspective, life was rather different. They were roused at 6 a.m. and many had to work for ten hours in the fields and quarries in all weathers until 5 p.m. The work was made deliberately galling, with men told to dig a field by hand rather than use a plough, and eight men were yoked together to pull a roller rather than employ a horse. For this they were paid 8d a day, with a penny deducted for every half-hour of lateness or absence. On at least one occasion when a party went to the church in Princetown they were stoned by parishioners while the parson looked on. Some working parties were sent further afield, and one group were at Lyme Regis for tree-felling duties when a rumour went round the town that they had jeered at some soldiers. Several of the conchies were knocked to the ground and others had to flee for their lives.

That was on Friday 27 April, and on the following Monday another incident occurred which would have far-reaching consequences for Frank. It happened at the prison, when Sgt Screech, a policeman from Tiverton, came to arrest one of the inmates. Such visits were not uncommon, usually for some alleged trivial offence, but this time the conchies surrounded the constable to prevent him carrying out his purpose. He was jostled by the crowd and called on the warders for help.

The country was appalled, and Sir Kinloch Cooke asked in Parliament what was being done about the incident, which he described as a cowardly attack. *The Western Times* called it a 'display of pugilistic propensity', sarcastically adding, 'For men who vowed before tribunals that they would not lift a finger to protect mothers and sisters from the Huns, to betray a liking for at least a little violence is good news.' The government ordered an enquiry, to be conducted by Major Henry Terrell, a Member of Parliament and a leading light in the Committee on the Employment of Conscientious Objectors. At the public hearing, when called to give evidence, Frank Beale said that he had stood outside the melee and had tried to calm proceedings, but admitted that he had picked up a handful of stones, saying that he "had a feeling of alarm momentarily". Mr C. H. Norman, a journalist, leading member of the NCF and fellow inmate, better known to the populace as 'Comrade Norman, the peace crank', supported his claim of peaceful intent by saying that he didn't think Mr Beale would ever throw a stone.

The *Berks & Oxon Advertiser* reprinted one of the local press reports which sarcastically described Beale as 'a smooth spoken, obese individual, who is alleged to be one of the ring-leaders in the disturbances', who at the enquiry 'stood with his hands in his pockets while he told a plausible tale'. The incident was more than enough for Major Terrell to declare that the conditions to placement at the Work Centre had been broken, and ordered that Frank and several others should be recalled to the army. His reserve status was withdrawn on 19 May.

C. H. Norman refused military service, was court-martialled again and returned to prison, where he went on hunger strike, was forcibly fed and confined to a straitjacket. Frank, for whatever reason, gave up the fight and accepted transfer to the Royal Engineers. He travelled to Bletchley where he joined the Signal Service, finally putting on the khaki uniform. No doubt he comforted himself that his was a back office role, but all the scenarios that he had recited at his tribunal appearances were true, and he might yet be called on to fight.

No doubt life was hard for Frank as he underwent his basic training, with his superiors and fellow recruits well aware that he was a lapsed conchie. At least his mother was now granted a separation allowance of 9s per week, 3s 6d of which came from Frank's pay. Three months after leaving Dartmoor he was ordered to the front and travelled to Devonport docks. He was not headed for France, but rather for an obscure campaign in East Africa. On 16 August he boarded the *Ascanius*, an Australian troop transport ship that had recently been part of a convoy bringing to England a large consignment of Antipodean soldiers. Now it headed down the Channel bound for the southern hemisphere, returning home.

At Durban Frank changed ships and was taken by the *Ingora* up the east coast of the continent, landing at Dar es Salaam on 29 September. Once the capital of German East Africa, the town had been taken by the British in August 1916, the enemy retreating into the hinterland. A bitter and drawn-out guerrilla war followed, with General von Lettow-Vorbeck forcing the deployment of large numbers of colonial troops as he ranged across the continent. The GHQ for the British Empire forces was in Dar es Salaam, and as the *Ingora* entered the wide harbour Frank was struck by the beauty of the waterfront, with its white buildings set amongst mango and palm trees outlined against the blue of the African sky. Only the ruins of the Governor's Palace, the wreck of a German freighter and the large naval presence in the harbour indicated that there was a war on.

A more exotic location compared to Cholsey or Dartmoor was hard to imagine. The port echoed to the clanking of the steam cranes and the cry of the black rickshaw boys, while the air filled with the heady smells of overripe fruit, dead fish and manure. Behind the docks stretched a strange conglomeration of wide German boulevards, now adorned with English names, the poorer quarters of the Arabs and Africans, and the narrow fetid lanes and crumbling mud houses of the Indian town. Frank was directed to his billet and to his place of work in the Royal Engineers' Base Signal Depot. This was the army's main switchboard, where his skills would be used for both telegraph and wireless communications.

The climate in Dar es Salaam was humid, and as October progressed it became more so as the rain showers of the summer season began. Frank sweated in his khaki shorts on the coast, but things were much worse for the soldiers inland. The death rate amongst the troops was very high, with German losses estimated at 2,000 and those of the British Empire at 10,000, plus over 100,000 black bearers and civilians. However, only a minority

Fig. 13.4 Dar es Salaam as painted in 1926 by J. H. Pierneef

died fighting, with the big killers being typhoid, dysentery, malaria and more exotic infections such as sleeping sickness and blackwater fever.

On 24 November, like many of his colleagues in the Base Signal Depot, Frank was admitted to hospital with dysentery. The fever, severe stomach cramps and diarrhoea grew worse until he felt his whole inside dissolving, foul liquid pouring out both ends. At least he was better off than men in the field, who often just had their trouser legs tied up before being sent on the sometimes long journey to a dressing station. Treatment for the illness was primitive, concentrating on rehydration, and ten days later Frank took a turn for the worse. On 3 December a telegram was sent to his mother in Cholsey warning her that her son was dangerously ill. In fact he did not even last the night and died at 1.20 a.m.

When the second telegram arrived in Cholsey hot on the heels of the first, Keren was devastated to learn that her only child was dead, buried in a military cemetery thousands of miles from home. The following May his effects were returned to her, the remains of a life in a small parcel containing an identity disc, three cap badges, two keys, two safety razor strops and blades, a pair of nail scissors, a wrist watch and strap, gold locket, purse, wallet, pipe, fountain pen and some letters.

When the war was over Keren was sent her son's medals, the British and Victory decorations that were the right of every soldier who served in a theatre of war. Accompanying the silver and bronze discs was a scroll and a large circular bronze plaque bearing the name Frank Beale and the words 'He Died For Freedom And Honour'. No doubt in the place of these dubious heroic honours, she would have preferred that her son had remained a conscientious objector and lived. Those conchies who did last out the war found themselves forever reviled, with most job adverts declaring that such types need not apply, while Parliament withdrew their right to vote. Cholsey people may have been in two minds about how they now regarded Frank, but at least, to his mother's satisfaction, it was decided that his name would appear on the Roll of Honour in the parish church[1]. Aged 75, Keren died four years after this was unveiled, a small recompense for her sorrow.

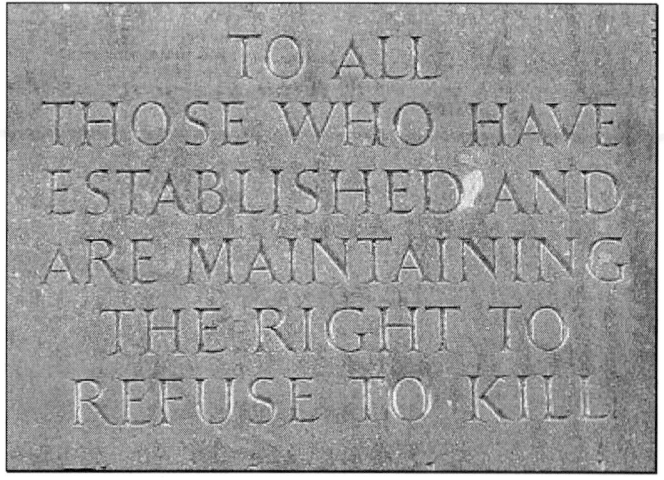

Fig. 13.5 The conscientious objectors' memorial in Tavistock Square

---

[1] See Fig. 14.7 for a picture of the Cholsey memorial.

Chapter 14 The War to End All Wars

Back on the Western Front through 1916, amongst those who had volunteered to fight, the death toll continued. The three kinsmen from the Queen's Own Oxfordshire Hussars, now all 2nd lieutenants in the Royal Berks, suffered in July of that year. Harold Gale and George Abbott left England with the 2/4th Battalion on 26 May and were then taken by train to the Merville area, halfway between Arras and Dunkirk. The next two months were split between spells in the trenches and at billets in the village of Laventie. On 16 July they moved to the trenches in preparation for an attack, when Harold was hit and invalided out. Back in England, a recipient of the Silver War Medal to show he had done his duty, he might have thought that his fighting days were over. In fact it wasn't the end for him and, after recovering, he returned to the war in May 1918 as a 1st lieutenant in the 8th Royal Berks. A month later he was again wounded, and taken to hospital in Rouen. His injuries were severe and, although he lived, he was declared unfit for further service in October.

July 1916 was, however, the end for Lt George Shrubb Abbott. In the middle of June Lt Abbott led a patrol out into no-mans-land to lay wire and report on the enemy's installations, and came back unharmed. Returning to Cholsey for a few days' leave at the beginning of July, he asked his father not to mourn should anything happen to him. Three days after Harold Gale was invalided out, George led his platoon over the top near to Laventie. The casualties were severe, with over 100 wounded and 38 killed, including three officers. Lt Abbott was a fearless leader, and almost burnt to death after the flares in his haversack caught fire. Saved by another officer, he directed his men on, trying to get through the enemy's barbed wire whilst under heavy machine gun fire. The efforts were in vain, so he led his men on, searching for the next gap, but was killed shortly afterwards. At the remembrance service held in Cholsey on Sunday 6 August, the church was full, as his father tried to come to terms with the loss of his only son, which came less than three years after the death of his wife.

Meanwhile, following its arrival in France from India in November 1914, the 2nd Battalion Royal Berks had been involved in several actions in Flanders, including the battle of Loos in September 1915. Cpl Alfred Alder was with the battalion all this time, and Lt William Gale joined the following month. Towards the end of March 1916 they moved to the Somme area as part of the build-up for a major offensive. William spent 20 days in hospital in May, but was back on duty in time for the big advance. The forthcoming attack was massive in scale and was designed to break a decisive hole in the German line, but it turned into a disaster for the allies. In an area south of

Arras, either side of the river, 1.2 million British and French troops were pitched against around 1.4 million Germans. By the end of the battle of the Somme four and a half months later, after over a million casualties altogether, the allies had advanced just six miles.

On the first day, 1 July 1916, the British Army suffered the worst day in its history, with 60,000 casualties. The British barrage had started seven days earlier, and the shell tonnage that fell on the German lines was far higher than anything ever seen before. So when the 2nd Battalion went over the top for their attack on Orvilliers at 7.30 a.m., they were quietly confident. At that time their strength was 24 officers and 800 other ranks, but as they tried to advance they were swept by a storm of rifle and machine gun bullets and men fell left and right. By nine o'clock only four officers and 386 other ranks were still standing. Lt Gale was one of those wounded. Of the four healthy sons of Joseph Gale at the outbreak of war, two were now dead and two wounded.

In some ways William was lucky to escape with just a wound, as the Somme saw the end for many other Cholsey men. Cpl Vincent Elijah Saunders was a mature man with the 5th Battalion, 37 years old and the son of Emily and Joseph, a labourer from Station Road in Cholsey. Vincent had been married for fourteen years and his family lived in Reading, where he worked in the biscuit factory. Vincent survived the battle of Loos the previous year and lived to fight at the Somme, which started when his unit attacked Orvilliers two days after the 2nd Battalion. As they advanced they found the ground strewn with the bodies of their fallen comrades and,

Fig. 14.1 A field kitchen during the battle of the Somme

although they made greater headway, the attack ended in confusion and they had to withdraw. Only six were killed, but 215 were wounded and 111 were missing. Vincent was one of those who died.

Walter Rowland Howse, a gardener and the nephew of John Howse, the farmer and Chequers' publican, was also in the attack and was one of those missing. After being hit he fell to the ground as the battle raged and his comrades drew further away. Unable to move, he lay in the mud for six days and nights, without food or water, feigning death whenever a German patrol passed by. Finally Walter was found and taken to a dressing station, where one leg was amputated. He was invalided home and treated in Ipswich Hospital, but the wounds and exposure had been too severe, and he died not long after his arrival. Walter's remains were brought to Cholsey and on Tuesday 1 August he was interred at a well-attended military funeral, watched over by the Cholsey members of the Volunteer Training Corps.

Earlier in the battle of the Somme, after a few more days in the trenches, the 5th Battalion were withdrawn, but were back at the beginning of August. At 3 a.m. on 8 August the Germans made a determined attack on the battalion's positions and succeeded in getting into the trench. They advanced with flame-throwers, but were driven out in hand-to-hand fighting. They again breached the defence at 5.30 a.m. and the defenders were driven along the trench about 50 yards before a barricade could be erected and the attack repulsed. Leading the courageous defence was Lt Francis Andrew Lloyd Edwards, but as he directed the erection of the barricade, he was fatally wounded in the head and died two days later.

Lt Edwards was 23 years old and the son of Charlotte and Capt Herbert Edwards RN. Francis' father had died when he was very young and the family eventually moved to Cholsey, settling in 'Broadlands', the large old house in West End. He was educated at Reading Grammar School and the City and Guilds College in Kensington, before joining up at the outbreak of war. Francis received a commission in the Devon Fortress Engineers and transferred to the Royal Berks in 1915. His mother and sister Nina were no doubt devastated when the awful news arrived at

Fig. 14.2 Pte Howse's gravestone

Broadlands in August 1916. The following month they learned that Francis had been posthumously awarded the Military Cross for his bravery.

After their disastrous losses of 1 July the 2nd Battalion were withdrawn to reorganise and re-man. Over the summer they were largely in reserve near Béthune with only a few spells back in the front line trenches. Pte Albert Cook, a 27-year-old horseman from Dry Farm in Cholsey, was killed in one of these on 21 September. In mid October they moved back to the Somme area and took part in an attack on the 23rd, suffering 218 casualties. Cpl Alfred Alder of Hithercroft Farm had now been in France for nearly two years and once again he survived this advance, only to be killed five days later as the battalion were withdrawing from the front line.

Several other Cholsey-related men in other regiments also died on the bloody Somme battlefield. Although Dudley Sydney Laurence came from Moulsford, his father Revd Frederick Spencer Laurence, the vicar of Moulsford, was also heavily involved with the parish of Cholsey. The Laurence Hall was built in the 1920s thanks to his benefaction, and his wife was for years the WI president and leader of the Guides and Brownies. Dudley joined the forces as soon as he was of age and, after serving as a cadet in the Officer Training Corps at Cambridge University, he was appointed on 24 October 1915 as a 2nd lieutenant with the Rifle Brigade. The following year he was attached to their 1st Battalion and landed in France on 20 June 1916, just in time for the battle of the Somme.

Platoon commanders like Dudley did not last long in the deadly trench warfare. They were expected to lead their men over the top and show by their own bravery what needed to be done, while the enemy specifically targeted the leaders. Dudley's first task, though, was to gain the respect of his men; not easy when he was a raw eighteen-year-old and they were mostly battle-hardened older soldiers. The average life expectancy for a junior officer on the front line was now just six weeks, but Lt Laurence lasted longer than many. He was killed in action on 23 October. Back home at Cranford House in Moulsford, a few days later, his parents received the awful telegram announcing the death of their only son.

The worry must have been a daily burden for many in the village, but it was particularly acute for Robert Brind, who was 88 years old and lived in Caps Lane, a retired shepherd and labourer. He had sired three sons, Thomas, George and Robert, who in turn produced eight, three and two sons respectively. All thirteen grandsons enlisted, and by this time one from each family had been killed. One of these was later recorded amongst Cholsey's fallen; Robert Charles Brind, a grocer's assistant and the son of Robert, died of wounds on the Somme on 9 September, aged 23 years.

* * *

At home the wartime restrictions and edicts from DORA increased. In 1916 the Whitsun and August Bank Holidays were cancelled to aid production, and even Guy Fawkes night was banned. Daylight saving, an idea judged crazy when first suggested, was introduced during the summer months, when the clocks were advanced one hour. Food prices increased further, with a 4lb loaf now costing 10d, compared to 6d at the start of the war, and butter, milk and sugar at double their previous price. The potato harvest was also poor, and their cost leapt twofold just between April and the end of the year.

Food production needed to increase. At the start of the war Britain imported 60 percent of its needs and, to begin with, the wheat, sugar and other foodstuffs continued to flow. But in 1916 the amount of shipping sunk by the *unterseebooten* (U-boats) began to rise, and a poor harvest in America and Russia also raised grain prices. For those with money, most things could still be bought, although increasingly supplies of butter, meat and tea often ran out, and a new word was used to describe the long lines waiting to be served by shops with scarce products: a 'queue'. Some were more than a hundred yards long, and generally they didn't disappear until 1918 when rationing was introduced. Of course reduced sales to customers meant lower turnover for shops, and towards the end of 1917 George Dix, Cholsey's grocer and baker, was declared bankrupt.

To help with the shortages, the government sought to raise production with the great patriotic allotment campaign. The Archbishop of Canterbury sanctioned Sunday labour, which put the fourth commandment on an equal footing with the sixth, thou shalt not kill, which was already in abeyance. In addition to those with provided allotments, as in Cholsey, throughout the land flower borders, tennis courts and other non-essential plots were dug up. Seeds were supplied at cost price and, in January 1917, John William (Bill) Money was the local representative of the Berkshire Agricultural Committees who arranged for the distribution of seed potatoes from Scotland. Those who took advantage of the offer and looked after the crop

Fig. 14.3 Bill Money as a Local Defence Volunteer

were mainly women and children, as conscription increased and the list of reserved occupations diminished. At a tribunal in May 1917, Boshers the builders asked for exemption for their last two workers, all that were left of the 55 who were employed before the war.

Travel was also becoming more and more difficult, as locomotives were taken off the railway for use in France and rails were ripped up to provide around 5,000 miles of additional track there. Sports events were cancelled, with racing, regattas, football and cricket all suspended. Increasingly everywhere took on a shabby look, both buildings and people, and personal sorrow and war weariness became the predominant expression. Pleasant distractions were rare, but one Cholsey incident in April 1917 brought the crowds out. An aeroplane from the depot at Port Meadow in Oxford developed engine trouble and made a forced landing near to Hithercroft Farm. The pilot was looked after by the farmer, Mrs Julia Stevenson, until the next day, when a second machine landed to help with the repairs. After a while both planes took off together, to the delight of the assembled bystanders.

Meanwhile in France the decimation of young men continued. By the end of the war, around one in ten would be dead, but the attrition rate was far higher for junior officers. This meant that middle and upper class families were hit harder than those of the workers, and Cholsey was no exception. One such family was that of Charlie and Mary Hansen, who occupied Blackall's Farm after the death of Stephen W. Cozens in 1912.

Carl Lauritz (known as Charlie) Hansen was born in Copenhagen in 1868, the son of a food merchant, and first came to England in 1885. Later he set up a business in Manchester importing Danish bacon, butter and beer, and that is where he met his English wife, Mary. Following restrictions on the import of Danish beer, he moved to London and set up the Danish Bacon Company in 1902. The company went from strength to strength and gradually grew into a worldwide organisation with Charlie as the CEO[1]. He commuted daily to London, but also ran a pig breeding enterprise employing Danish workers on his model farm, which stocked up to a thousand animals. He was said to be a good salesman, full of humour and optimism, but that must have been sorely tested after what happened to his two eldest sons.

Carl Friedrich Vilhelm Hansen, born in Denmark, was twenty years old at the outbreak of war, while his younger brother William George, who was born on the outskirts of London, was a year younger. In 1914 Carl became the joint manager of a subsidiary of his father's business, which was set up

---

[1] The Danish Bacon Company prospered through the twentieth century, but went into administration in March 2012.

in Hull to handle alternative supplies of bacon from America and elsewhere. William graduated from the Inns of Court Officer Training Corp in January 1916 and became a 2nd lieutenant in the 1/9th Battalion of the King's Liverpool Regiment, perhaps chosen because of his mother's Lancashire origins. Carl also joined up and became a full lieutenant in the 165th Company of the Machine Gun Company (MGC), which was attached to the same brigade as his brother.

Fig. 14.4 Lt Carl F. V. Hansen

Although they had spells in the front line trenches through the spring, it wasn't until later in the summer that they were involved in the attacks that made up the battle of the Somme. In the first half of August the battalion suffered about 300 casualties, without making any progress. On 25 September the brigade was involved in an attack on the town of Gueudecourt. The men went over the top at 12.35 p.m. in four waves, with the artillery laying down a creeping barrage 150 yards in front of the soldiers. The German trenches were reached with few casualties and subjugated through the afternoon, an advance of 1,000 yards on the old British front line. It was a victory, during which 28 men were killed, 129 wounded and 150 reported missing. Unfortunately, Lt William Hansen was one of the four officers who died. During the attack twelve guns from the 165th MGC accompanied the advance, but Carl Hansen emerged unscathed, obliged to write home to his parents with the awful news of his brother's death.

Soon afterwards the brigade moved to the Ypres Salient and through the winter and spring Carl endured various periods of front line duty, alternating with time in reserve. On 29 July 1917 the 165th MGC moved to their assembly positions in the trenches at Potijze Wood in preparation for the battle which became known as Passchendaele. Zero hour was 3.05 a.m. two days later and No. 1 section, led by Lt Hansen, went over the top with their four guns alongside the third wave of infantry. Their objectives were clearly defined in the earlier orders, with four precise locations specified where they were to set up their firing positions, but at Jasper Farm they met stiff opposition. Carl led the rush to subdue the Germans, but at 6.50 a.m. he was hit and seriously wounded. He clung to life for a few more hours, but died at 10 a.m., by which time his section had consolidated its new position.

Carl's father subsequently published a death notice in *The Times* which finished 'Peace, Perfect Peace', but it is doubtful that this was how he felt. Charlie Hansen took comfort from his two surviving sons Harold and

Fig. 14.5 Mary and Charlie Hansen c1938

Holger, and threw himself into his work in London and on the farm. After the war Blackall's welcomed coachloads of Danes visiting the model farm, a strange sight in deepest Berkshire. For 40 years Charlie steered the Danish Bacon Company through difficult periods of war and peace, finally dying one summer morning in 1942 as he walked around his fields.

Of course, the sheer number of soldiers meant that men of other ranks were more numerous than officers amongst Cholsey's fallen. Pte Rowland Butler was the son of Emily and William, an engine driver and general farm labourer, who moved to Cholsey sometime after 1911. Rowland volunteered and joined the 11th Battalion of the Worcester Regiment, who were sent to Salonika in November as part of a build-up of forces to aid the Serbians, who had been attacked by Bulgaria. It was a long time before they saw action, but in 1917 Rowland was hit and died of wounds on 8 May. A few days earlier L-Cpl Frank Alfred Spratley, the son of Cholsey's former policeman, also died of wounds near Salonika, aged nineteen.

The 5th Battalion Royal Berks spent the time after the battle of the Somme in the vicinity of Arras, in and out of the trenches. On 28 April 1917, during a successful advance designed to take some trenches from the enemy, Pte George Didcock, a railway platelayer aged 34 from West End in Cholsey, was killed. Six months later the end came for Ernest William Cook, a gamekeeper and brother of Albert, killed the previous year. He died during the battle of Cambrai, to the east of Arras, when a ferocious German counterattack forced a retreat that led to over 300 casualties. His wife Elizabeth was notified soon afterwards at their home at Ranger's Lodge in Charlbury, while his parents at Dry Farm, Cholsey, now had to live with the thought of two sons killed far away. Also in November 1917 L-Cpl Edward Hutt, 21, was killed in the second battle of Passchendaele, near to Ypres, while serving with the 12th Battalion Manchester Regiment. Before the war he had been a coal porter, working in his father's business. John Henry Hutt established Cholsey's main coal merchant business towards the end of the nineteenth century, while it was his wife Edith who sang so eloquently at the Baptist fund-raising event two years before Edward died[1].

---

[1] J.H. Hutt & Sons was still operating in Cholsey in 2013.

Fig. 14.6 A British soldier in a captured German trench

In March 1918 the deadlock on the Western Front was broken, when a massive German attack broke through the allied lines in several places. Deep inside France the offensive ran out of steam and the allies were able at last to use their superior forces in a mobile war. However, the high death rate continued. Amongst the Cholsey dead was Pte Fred Kimber, a waggoner at Green Hill, who was with the Sherwood Foresters near Ypres when he was killed in action on 18 April. Gunner William Joseph Ferris, a labourer and the son of Fanny and George, a coal merchant and retired sergeant in the Metropolitan Police, died of wounds in Flanders while serving with the Royal Garrison Artillery. His brother Ernest, who served with the Canadian Infantry, died six months later in the same area.

As autumn 1918 progressed there was little indication that the war was almost over as the bitter fighting continued. Pte Frank Rupert Butler, the brother of Rowland who died in 1917, was killed on 22 October soon after his unit had crossed the canal at Knokke in Belgium, aged nineteen. Eight days later, Pte Ernest William Dearlove died of wounds while serving with the 2/4th Battalion of the Royal Berks in Flanders. He was also nineteen, robbed of his life just twelve days before the war came to an end.

Through 1918 morale in Cholsey sank further as food rationing came in and more families were bereaved. To make matters worse, a terrible flu epidemic hit the country. The first occurrences that were confirmed as a new and virulent virus happened in June, followed by three waves of the epidemic which resulted in about 200,000 deaths in Britain over the next twelve months, mainly from pneumonia. Just like the deaths in the war, it seemed to be the young and healthy who were particularly hit, the older generation having gained some immunity from previous attacks. In

October all three teachers in the school went down with the disease and it had to close for a month, although happily all three recovered.

A particularly sad case happened earlier in the year, when the village constable contracted some form of influenza and could not shake it off. PC William Spratley had taken over in 1911 from his brother Ernest Spratley, who left to become a sergeant in Harwell. Perhaps it was the flu and the bronchitis that accompanied it that made him feel depressed, or the wartime duties that he was finding increasingly onerous at the age of 46. His wife Eliza Ann was nursing him, and on Saturday 30 March she gave him his breakfast and then at 9.30 a.m. set off from the police house to cycle into Wallingford to purchase more medicine. From the road she saw him at the window, and shouted for him to get back under the covers so as not to catch cold. An hour-and-a-half later she returned, to find him lying at the top of the stairs in a pool of blood, a long razor slash jagged across his throat.

Like everyone else she would have been urged to carry on in the face of awful tragedy. The shortage of men in the village was now acute, but for those working on the land there was some new help with the arrival in the parish of 60 German prisoners of war. They were put to work clearing ditches and water courses, and were generally seen to be well-behaved when they attended Sunday morning service alongside the other parishioners.

On Monday 11 November rumours started to circulate of the signing of an armistice in France, and in the early afternoon a confirmatory telegram arrived in Wallingford. Everybody stopped work, people flooded into the streets, the bells in all the churches round about began to ring, those with any sort of gun fired them into the air, while bugle calls and cheers emanated from wherever folk gathered to celebrate. Nobody could quite believe that after four years perhaps the bloodshed was over. Although the recent news from the front had said the Germans were retreating, the glad tidings nevertheless came as a welcome surprise. However, perhaps it could have been foretold. The car containing the assassinated archduke in Sarajevo in 1914 had carried the number plate 'A111 118'.

The next day in Wallingford handbills were printed and distributed to the surrounding villages advertising a proper celebration. Following an afternoon thanksgiving service on the Wednesday, local people gathered in the Market Place for the start of a procession at 6.30 p.m. Led by the local volunteers and band, a medley of vehicles adorned with Chinese lanterns and torches progressed around the town, while every house and shop front was covered in flags and bunting. An aeroplane mounted aboard a lorry displayed a sign 'the first machine to reach Berlin'; blacksmiths beat on a forge with red-hot iron; the gleaming steam fire engine carried the firemen in their smart uniforms; and many private conveyances followed, decorated with whatever had come to hand. On foot were hundreds of soldiers, sailors, Boy Scouts, Girl Guides and civilians of all sorts. Many were in fancy dress, with some of the girls wearing dresses and hats made from Union Jacks.

The noise was terrific and when the cavalcade reached the Kine Croft a huge bonfire was lit. The vast throng crowded round as close as they dared while rockets shot into the sky, fireworks exploded and the smiths fired their anvils. A great cheer went up when a cart carrying a straw effigy of the Kaiser backed up to the fire and he was cast into the flames. The band switched to dance music, and many of the young girls waltzed with the military men in the bright moonlight. It was a cold and frosty night, but nobody cared. According to the local paper:

> As the fire burnt itself slowly out, so the people felt that though their pageant was a little primitive and a little pagan, yet it was just a right method of relieving their pent-up feelings after the severe self-discipline and repression of more than four years of the greatest war in history.

However, in the cold light of the next morning and over the following weeks and months, there was no escaping the terrible aftermath of the conflict. What's more, the deaths from the war did not end with the armistice, as many of those invalided out succumbed to their wounds. For example, Albert Edward Silvester, the son of Henry and Ellen of Kentwood Farm, died six weeks later on Christmas Day 1918.

In statistical terms, the experience of the menfolk of Cholsey was typical. Britain mobilised around 10 million men to fight in the war, and of these around 10% died, while a further 20% or so were wounded. According to the census, in 1911 there were 376 males in Cholsey aged from 12 to 43, and hence of military age in 1914-18. The memorial plaque erected in St Mary's church in 1921 commemorates 41 fallen (26 of whom are mentioned above), rather more than 10%. No doubt many more returned maimed physically, and probably almost all were harmed in some way psychologically.

Technically the armistice was just a truce and the war did not officially end until the treaty between Germany and the allies was signed at Versailles on 28 June 1919. The Germans had little option but to agree to the onerous terms, which let the leaders go free but which, at French insistence, deprived Germany of much land and subjected the population to heavy financial reparations.

Because of the long negotiations, many soldiers were not demobbed until well into 1919 when it was certain that hostilities would not break out again, while others became part of the army of occupation. For some men the peace was more difficult to handle than the war, once the conditioning wore off and the pointlessness of it all became obvious. The government announced that 19 July would be 'Peace Day', with a victory parade in London and a day of celebration throughout the country. But a lot of

Fig. 14.7 The Great War memorial in St Mary's church

veterans refused to join in, feeling they were unappreciated, that a party was not appropriate when so many lay dead in France, and that the money would be better spent on helping those who had returned.

However, Peace Day went ahead, signalling a return to normal peacetime activities and concerns, and no doubt Cholsey joined in the festivities. People were preoccupied with how the last four years had changed society, but how much more had altered during the previous 100 years.

The old village way of life, which had endured for centuries, but was already on its way out in Edwardian times, had now disappeared completely. The aristocracy and landed gentry were no longer as powerful, and class mobility had improved, so that even a few working class men rose to wealth and prominence. Education was widespread, so that local gossip was now complemented by a knowledge of and interest in wider affairs. Democracy for all adults was a reality, although the votes granted to women in 1918 were still only for those aged 30 and above.

However, families who had lived within a few miles of each other for hundreds of years were now sadly dispersed across the country, or indeed the world, as access to cheap and fast transportation combined with the attractions of work elsewhere. The old convictions were replaced by uncertainties and constant change, and a generation of women remained spinsters for the rest of their lives after they lost their sweethearts in the Great War carnage. Folk songs that held people together were lost, village traditions died, and some of the camaraderie of large numbers of men and women working together in the fields disappeared.

Life for the average family in Cholsey had significantly improved over the past hundred years, but there was no denying that something had been lost as well.

Money, Inflation, and Imperial Units

Before decimalisation in 1971, a British pound (£) was made up of twenty shillings (*s*), and a shilling of twelve pence (*d*). Shillings and pence could be written as, for example, 3*s* 6*d*, 3/6*d* or 3/6, although in this book only the first form is used. During most of the period covered by this book, there were gold coins for £1 (a sovereign) and 10*s* (a half sovereign); silver coins for 2*s* 6*d* (half a crown), 2*s* (a florin), 1*s* (a bob), 6*d* (a tanner), 4*d* (a groat or a joey), and 3*d* (thru'penny bit); and bronze coins (known as coppers) for 1*d* (penny), ½*d* (ha'penny), and ¼*d* (a farthing).

A guinea was also a coin up until 1814, when it was worth £1 1*s*. The name stems from the country of origin of the gold used in the first machine-struck coin for £1 in 1663. A rise in the value of gold meant that it was worth more than its original face value.

Comparing the buying power of old currency with present-day money is fraught with difficulty, as it all depends what items make up the 'basket' of products and services being compared. However, very roughly, a Victorian £1 was worth, on average, around £100 in 2012, 1*s* worth £5, and a penny worth 40p. Using some measures there was disinflation of perhaps 20% at the beginning of our period, roughly level prices over the Victorian period, and inflation going into the Great War, leaving overall the value of money little changed. However, this general trend was dwarfed by periods of rising and falling prices in different decades.

Imperial units were used for measures of weight, length, area and volume:

16 ounces (oz) make 1 pound (lb)
14 pounds make 1 stone
8 stones make 1 hundredweight (cwt)
5 hundredweights make 1 quarter
4 quarters make 1 ton

12 inches make 1 foot (ft)
3 feet make 1 yard
22 yards make 1 chain (1 rod is ¼ chain)
10 chains make 1 furlong
8 furlongs make 1 mile

30¼ square feet make 1 pole, perch or square rod
40 poles make 1 rood
4 roods make 1 acre

5 fluid ounces make 1 gill
4 gills make 1 pint
2 pints make 1 quart
4 quarts make 1 gallon
8 gallons make 1 bushel

Comparing to metric measures, one pound is approximately 0.454 kilograms, one foot is 0.3048 metres, one acre is about 0.405 hectares and one pint is around 0.568 litres.

The temperatures used at the time were in degrees Fahrenheit. To convert to Celsius subtract 32, then multiply by 5 and divide by 9.

Chronology

Key events and the main focus of each chapter by date.

1819	Ejection of the Parish Clerk	
1820	Accession of George IV	
1830	Accession of William IV	
1830	Swing Riots	
1834	Establishment of Poor Law Unions	
1837	Accession of Queen Victoria	
1840	Opening of Cholsey's first railway station	
1845	Commutation of Tithes	
1851	Enclosures	
1856	Establishment of Berkshire Constabulary	
1865	Opening of the Wallingford branch line	
1870	Opening of the County Lunatic Asylum	
1887	Queen Victoria's Golden Jubilee	
1888	Establishment of the County Council	
1892	Opening of the new Cholsey station	
1894	Establishment of District and Parish Councils	
1901	Accession of Edward VII	
1910	Accession of George V	
1914	Outbreak of the Great War	
1918	Armistice	
1919	The formal end of the Great War	

Sources

Abbreviations
BRO   Berkshire Records Office
GRO   General Register Office
TNA   The National Archives

General

Judy & Stuart Dewey, *Change at Cholsey Again*, Pie Powder Press, Cholsey, 2001

Pamela Horn, *Labouring Life in the Victorian Countryside*, Alan Sutton Publishing, Gloucester, 1987

G. E. Mingay, *Rural Life in Victorian Britain*, Alan Sutton Publishing, Stroud, 1990

Neil Philip, *Victorian Village Life*, Albion, Oxfordshire, 1993

Censuses for 1841-1911, TNA via www.findmypast.co.uk and www.ancestry.co.uk

Cholsey Parish Baptisms, Marriages and Burials

General Register of Births, Marriages and Deaths and the index at www.FreeBMD.org.uk

International Genealogical Index

National Burial Index

Chapter 1 The Vicar and His Clerk

David Bentley, *English Criminal Justice in the Nineteenth Century*, Hambledon Press, London, 1998

Thomas Clutty, *Archbold's Practice of the Court of King's Bench in Personal Actions and Ejectment*, Sweet Stevens & Sons, London, 1835

Revd E. C. Hyde, *Notes from Old Cholsey*, Unpublished, 1931-40

Sabine Sutherland, *Shalfleet Parish and the Cottle Family*, Unpublished, 2004

Alumni Oxoniensis
Berkshire Chronicle 8 March 1828
Brightwell Parish Register, BRO
Cambridge Chronicle 5 November 1819
Cholsey Parish Churchwardens' Accounts, BRO D/P 38/5/2, 1800-47

Cholsey Parish List of Paupers, BRO D/P/38/19/5, 1849 and 1852

Cholsey Parish Memorial Inscriptions, Berkshire Family History Society

Cholsey Parish Overseers Accounts, BRO D/P/38/19/1, 1837-48

Cholsey Parish Vestry Minutes, BRO D/P/38/8/1, 1811-40

Cornwall Gazette 23 November 1833

Court of King's Bench Affidavits, TNA KB1/42/1/3 first bundle f7 and KB1/42/2 third bundle f103 and f135

Court of King's Bench Controlment Rolls, TNA KB29/480 Easter Term, 1820

Court of King's Bench Rule Books, TNA KB21/22 Trinity Term, 1820

Deeds of the Swan Inn, Robin and Ginnie Herbert, Swan Cottage

Indictment of Revd Wyatt Cottle before King's Bench, TNA KB11/77, Easter Term 1820

Jackson's Oxford Journal 23 October 1819, 13 November 1819, 2 December 1820, 8 March 1823, 2 June 1827, 8 March 1828, 21 July 1832, 30 March 1833, 17 June 1899

London Birth, Marriage and Death Index, www.ancestry.co.uk

Oxford Circuit Quarter Sessions Order Book, BRO Q/SO 12, 1820

Oxford Circuit Quarter Sessions Roll, BRO Q/SR 343, Michaelmas 1819

The Gentleman's Magazine, February 1816

The Morning Post, London 9 November 1819

Tithe Map for Cholsey, BRO D/QC 59/1, 1845

Wallingford Deanery Visitations, BRO D/RDW 3/1, 1812

Wills for Thomas Cottle and Wyatt Cottle, TNA PCC Wills online

Writ of Mandamus, Court of King's Bench Michaelmas 1820, TNA KB16/27/2 f37

Chapter 2 The Swing Riots

J. M. Beattie, *The First English Detectives: The Bow Street Runners and the Policing of London, 1750-1840*, OUP, Oxford, 2012

Jill Chambers, *Berkshire Machine Breakers*, Jill Chambers, Letchworth, 1999

P. H. Ditchfield and William Page, *Victoria County History Volume 3* pp296-302, 1923

Norman Fox, *Berkshire to Botany Bay,* Littlefield Publishing, Newbury

Eric Hobsbawm and George Rudé, *Captain Swing*, Phoenix Press, London, 2001

William Mavor, *General View of the Agriculture of Berkshire*, 1808

Berkshire Chronicle 22 January 1831, 15 and 22 December 1832

Jackson's Oxford Journal 22 January 1831, 7 April 1832, 16 March 1833, 8 August 1835

Letters from William Stone JP to the Home Secretary, TNA HO64/3 ff102, 206 and 230, 1832

OS Map Series 1, One inch to the Mile for Cholsey, 1830

OS Map 1:2500 for Cholsey, 1877

Reading Mercury 16 January 1830, 25 October 1830, 29 November 1830, 24 January 1831, 9 April 1832, 3 August 1835

Register of Electors for Berkshire for 1832, BRO D/ELMZ4

Wallingford Workhouse, www.workhouses.org.uk

Chapter 3 The Ilsley Family

Charles Bateson, *The Convict Ships*, Reed, New South Wales, 1974

Ian Brand, *The Convict Probation System: Van Diemen's Land 1839-54*, Blubber Head Press, Hobart, 1990

Barrie Charles, *Kill the Queen! The Eight Assassination Attempts on Queen Victoria*, Amberley Publishing, Stroud, 2012

Bonnie Hilsley, Great Great Great Granddaughter-in-law of James Ilsley, *Private Communication*, NSW, 2012

John Frederick Mortlock, *Experiences of a Convict Transported for Twenty-One years*, edited by G. A. Wilkes and A. G. Mitchell, Sydney University Press, Sydney, 1965

Shirley Muir, Great Great Granddaughter of William Stanley, *Private Communication*, Melbourne, 2012

Anthony Stokes, *Pit of Shame: The Real Ballad of Reading Gaol*, Waterside Press, Winchester, 2007

Christopher Sweeney, *Transported: In Place of Death*, Macmillan, Australia, 1981

Emma Elizabeth Thoyts, *History of the Royal Berkshire Militia*, Sulhampstead Park, 1897

Australian Birth, Marriage and Death Index, www.ancestry.co.uk

Berkshire Chronicle 4 January 1834, 7 March 1835, 2 and 9 March 1844, 13 April 1844, 10 July 1844, 3 July 1847, 22 September 1855, 14 June 1856, 18 April 1857

Berkshire Militia Return of Volunteers, BRO L/B4/1/1, 1855-57

Charles Wilkins in the Register of Assisted British Migrants, Victorian Archives VPRS14, 1846

Cholsey List of Paupers, BRO D/P/38/19/5, 1849 and 1852

Cholsey Overseers' Accounts and Vestry Minutes, BRO D/P/38/19/1, 1837-48

Colonial Times, Tasmania, 23 October 1848

Convict Musters, Tasmanian Archives, 1846 and 1849

Cornwall Chronicle for Tasmania 30 May 1849, 17 October 1849, 3 August 1850, 18 September 1852

Criminal Petitions for James Ilsley, March 1835, TNA HO17/18 Bv7

Criminal Registers, www.ancestry.co.uk, 1833-47

Henry Ilsley, Joseph Ilsley and John Pulbrook Convict Records, Tasmanian Archives Ident, CON14/1/28, Description CON18/1/43, Conduct CON33/1/63

Index to Criminal Petitions, TNA HO19/6, 1835

Jackson's Oxford Journal 7 May 1835, 2 July 1836, 13 August 1836, 20 July 1844, 2 June 1870, 13 April 1844

James Ilsley and Charles Wilkins Convict Entries, Queensland Convict Database

James Ilsley in the Convict Index, NSW Archives

Kerang Times & Swan Hill Gazette, Victoria 28 June 1878, 8 April 1887

Letter from Governor of Abingdon Gaol to the Home Secretary, TNA PC1/92 Box 4, July 1844

Leviathan Hulk Quarterly Returns, TNA HO8/44, 1835

Lloyd's Register of Shipping, 1835 and 1846

Millbank Prison Register of Convicts, TNA HO24/1, 1844

Prison Hulk Registers, www.ancestry.co.uk

Oxford Circuit Minute Books for Lent Assizes, TNA ASSI2/32, 1835

Oxford Circuit Minute Books for Summer Assizes, TNA ASSI2/33, 1844

Pentonville Register of Convicts, TNA HO24/16, 1844-46

Reading Mercury 9 March 1835, 18 April 1857

Surgeon's Log for the Maitland, TNA ADM101/46/3, 1846

Surgeon's Log for the Recovery, TNA ADM101/63/7, 1835-36

Surgeon's Log for the Sir Robert Peel, TNA ADM 101/68/3, 1844

Tasmanian Birth, Marriage and Death Index

Victoria Birth, Marriage and Death Index

Wallingford Poor Law Union Workhouse, www.workhouses.org.uk

Chapter 4 The Coming of the Railway

Edward Charles Davey, *Memoirs of an Oxfordshire Old Catholic Family and Its Connections from 1566 to 1897*, British Library, 1898

Brian Lingham, *The Railway Comes to Didcot*, Alan Sutton Publishing, Stroud, 1992

Revd H. W. Lloyd, *Happy Jack: A Workman on the Great Western Railway*, TNA RAIL 1014/16 f20, 1840

Sources

Mary Lobel (ed), *A History of the County of Oxford Vol. 7 Dorchester and Thame Hundreds*, Victoria County History, 1962

E. T. Macdermot, *History of the Great Western Railway*, Ian Allen, London, 1964

Andrew Roden, *Great Western Railway: A History*, Aurum Press, London, 2010

Alan Rosevear, *Responses of the Turnpikes to the Coming of the Railway: The Extension of the Great Western Railway to Steventon*, Reading Library qB/cQ, 1994

Adrian Vaughan, *Grub, Water & Relief: Tales of the Great Western 1835-92*, John Murray, London, 1985

Berkshire Chronicle 19 January 1839, 9 March 1839, 30 March 1839, 2 October 1840, 10 October 1840, 17 September 1842, 2 March 1878

Colonial Times, Tasmania 26 October 1847

Contracts and Bonds for the Construction of Moulsford Bridge and Section 4R of the Great Western Railway, TNA RAIL 252/393, 404, 405

Cornwall Chronicle, Tasmania 3 August 1850

Hulk Register for the Justitia, TNA HO9/3, 1841

Hulk Quarterly Returns for the Justitia, TNA HO8/67 and 68, 1841

Jackson's Oxford Journal 10 May 1823, 12 January 1839, 26 January 1839, 9 March 1839, 6 June 1840, 18 July 1840, 6 March 1841, 10 September 1842, 14 November 1863

Launceston Examiner, Tasmania 26 May 1849

Morning Post, London 17 August 1840

Petty Sessions Licensing Breaches, BRO PS/MN/1A/1/4-5, 1838

Proprietors' Meetings of the Great Western Railway, TNA RAIL250/64, 1838-40

Reading Mercury 14 July 1838

Surgeon's Log for the David Clarke, TNA ADM101/19/2, 1841

The Era 11 October 1840

The Times 6 October 1840, 5 March 1841

Will of Robert Davey, PCC, TNA PROB11/1670, 1823

Will of William Davey, PCC, TNA PROB11/1787, 1831

William Davey Application to Marry, Tasmanian Archives CON/52/1/2 p42, 1845

William Davey Appropriation List, Tasmanian Archives CON27/1/9

William Davey Conduct Record, Tasmanian Archives CON33/1/13

William Davey Description List, Tasmanian Archives CON18/1/29 p140

William Davey Indent, Tasmanian Archives CON14/1/9
William Davey in the Queensland Convict Database, 1841
William Davey in the Marriage and Death Registers for Tasmania, www.ancestry.co.uk

Chapter 5 Land Reform

James Caird, *English Agriculture in 1850-51*, Longman, London, 1852

Oliver Chester Jenks, *Parliamentary Enclosure in Berkshire, 1723 - 1883, and its Effect on the Poor*, PhD thesis, University of Reading, 2005

H. C. Prince, *The Tithe Surveys of the Mid-Nineteenth Century*, The Agricultural History Review Vol 7.1 pp 14-26, 1959

Ross Wordie (ed), *Enclosure in Berkshire*, Berks Record Society, Reading, 2000

Enclosure Award for Cholsey, BRO Q/RDC/90A, 1851

Enclosure Map for Cholsey, BRO Q/RDC/90B, 1851

Reading Mercury 5 April 1845, 10 February 1849, 7 July 1849, 15 September 1849, 13 October 1849, 15 December 1849, 22 December 1849

Tithe Apportionment for Cholsey, BRO IR/29/2/36, 1845

Tithe Map for Cholsey, BRO D/QC59, 1842

Chapter 6 Crime and Punishment

Sgt W. Indge, *A Short History of the Berkshire Constabulary*, 1956

Berks & Oxon Advertiser 28 December 1906

Berkshire Chronicle 13 June 1863, 16 December 1865, 3 March 1866, 13 July 1867, 20 July 1867, 4 July 1868, 3 June 1871, 15 July 1871

Berrow's Worcester Journal 20 December 1849

Cholsey Parish Monumental Inscriptions, Berkshire Family History Society

District Courts Martial Registers, TNA WO86/7, 1855

Jackson's Oxford Journal 30 September 1837, 20 May 1843, 22 August 1846, 23 June 1855, 4 July 1857, 11 September 1858, 13 June 1863, 16 December 1865, 3 March 1866, 13 July 1867, 20 July 1867, 23 May 1868, 4 July 1868, 27 May 1871, 3 June 1871, 15 July 1871, 31 August 1872, 10 November 1900

Lunatic Asylum General Statement Book, BRO DH10/A/4/1

Lunatic Asylum Monthly Wages, BRO DH10/C/2/2

Reading Mercury 22 September 1849, 15 December 1849, 30 March 1850, 4 August 1855, 9 February 1856, 29 March 1856, 5 April 1856, 2 May 1857, 22 June 1861, 20 October 1866

Chapter 7 The Growth of the Railway

Paul Karau & Chris Turner, *The Wallingford Branch*, Wild Swan Publications, Berks, 1982

Abingdon Herald 14 January 1893

Berks & Oxon Advertiser 4 March 1892, 13 January 1893

Berkshire Chronicle 29 March 1862, 12 April 1862, 9 July 1864, 21 January 1865, 13 January 1866, 13 December 1873, 2 March 1878, 11 February 1893

Daily News, London 11 January 1866

Jacksons Oxford Journal 5 April 1862, 22 November 1862, 11 July 1863, 16 January 1864, 23 January 1864, 20 February 1864, 9 July 1864, 16 July 1864, 6 August 1864, 20 August 1864, 21 January 1865, 20 January 1866, 7 July 1866 13 December 1873, 2 March 1878, 14 January 1893

Kentish Gazette 12 July 1864

Northampton Mercury 8 December 1849, 15 December 1849

Reading Mercury 23 February 1861, 10 July 1863, 13 February 1864, 14 May 1864, 2 July 1864, 9 July 1864, 18 February 1865, 12 August 1865, 14 October 1865, 13 January 1866, 7 April 1866, 27 February 1892

Report of the Inspecting Officers of the Board of Trade and of the Court of Inquiry Upon Accidents Which Occurred During the Year 1873, TNA RAIL1053/62 pp197-8

Chapter 8 The County Asylum

A History of Fair Mile Hospital, www.berkshirerecordoffice.org.uk

Berkshire Chronicle 25 April 1868, 13 January 1869, 14 August 1869, 28 August 1869, 4 September 1869, 1 January 1870, 7 January 1871, 4 March 1871, 4 November 1871, 20 April 1872, 2 November 1872, 2 March 1878

Coroner's Inquest Papers for William Goodyear, BRO COR/N/3/12/5, 1879

Hampshire Advertiser 11 August 1869

Jackson's Oxford Journal 19 October 1867, 23 November 1867, 28 March 1868, 30 May 1868, 16 January 1869, 20 March 1869, 10 April 1869, 1 May 1869, 14 August 1869, 21 August 1869, 28 August 1869, 1 January 1870, 14 January 1871, 20 April 1872, 10 July 1875, 21 September 1878, 5 October 1878, 14 June 1879, 28 July 1900

Moulsford Lunatic Asylum Case Books (Female), BRO D/H10/D2/2/1-3, 1871-79

Moulsford Lunatic Asylum Case Books (Male), BRO D/H10/D2/1/1, 1870-79

Moulsford Lunatic Asylum Monthly Wage Register, BRO D/H10/C/2/2/1-5, 1870-1900

Moulsford Lunatic Asylum Register of Admission (Paupers), BRO D/H10/D1/1/1/1, 1870-79

Moulsford Lunatic Asylum Register of Discharge (Paupers), BRO D/H10/D4/1/1/1, 1870-79

Note of Purchase of 9 Cottages by Moulsford Lunatic Asylum, BRO DH10/B/2/1, 1872

Parish Registers for Beenham, Moulsford, Stratfield Mortimer, Sutton Courtenay, BRO

Reading Mercury 3 July 1875, 18 January 1879

Wallingford Chronicle 13 August 1869, 20 August 1869, 27 August 1869, 3 September 1869

Will of William Cox, www.rootsweb.ancestry.com

Chapter 9 The Philandering Curate

Arthur Agassiz R.N., *A Short History of the English Branch of the Agassiz Family*, Oriental Press, Shanghai, 1907

Lewis Agassiz, *A Journey to Switzerland, and pedestrian tours in that country; including a sketch of its history and of the manners and customs of its inhabitants*, Elder Smith & Co, London, 1833

Col C. Field, *Britain's Sea Soldiers*, Lyceum Press, Liverpool, 1924

Joules Marcou, *Life, Letters, and Works of Louis Agassiz*, Macmillan, London, 1896

Sir John Smyth, *In This Sign Conquer*, Mowbray, London, 1968

Army Lists, 1809-84
Applications for Cadetship with the East India Company, British Library
Cholsey Board School Infants' Logbook, BRO C/EL/102/1, 1881-89
Crockford's Clerical Directory, 1890
Divorce Court File for Agassiz v Agassiz, TNA J77/706/1477, 1901
East India Register, 1811-60
Electoral Roll for Berkshire, BRO, 1886-89
Families in British India database, www.fibis.org
Incoming Passenger Lists for the UK, www.ancestry.com, 1892
Kelly's Directory for Berkshire and Oxfordshire, 1887
Madras Register of Births, Marriages and Deaths, British Library
Military Campaign Medals, www.ancestry.com, 1882
Moulsford Lunatic Asylum Chaplain's Journal, BRO DH10/E/1/4, 1887-88
Moulsford Lunatic Asylum General Statement Book, BRO DH10/A/4/4, 1887
Moulsford Lunatic Asylum Officers' Salaries, BRO DH10/C/2/1/1, 1887-88

Oxford Diocese Licensing Papers, Oxfordshire History Centre DIOC/1/B/2/B/7, 1884

Trewman's Exeter Flying Post 2 May 1866, 11 September 1872, 20 August 1873

Wallingford Times 24 June 1887

Will of Joseph Garnault, Probate Registry, 1872

Will of Sarah Eliza Agassiz, Probate Registry, 1884

Chapter 10 The Rise of Democracy

Ellis Roger Davies, *A History of the First Berkshire County Council*, 1974

Judy & Stuart Dewey and David Beasley, *Window on Wallingford*, Pie Powder Press, Cholsey, 1989

Berks & Oxon Advertiser 15 September to 13 October 1893, 7 December 1894, 21 December 1894, 28 December 1894, 27 June to 18 July 1902

Berkshire Chronicle 19 January 1889, 7 December 1894, 21 December 1894, 23 August to 6 September 1902

Cholsey Parish Council Minutes, Oxfordshire History Centre PC327/A1/1-2, 1894-1918

Cholsey School Logbook, BRO C/EL/101/2, 1904-08

Electoral Roll for Cholsey, BRO, 1894-96

Jackson's Oxford Journal 19 January 1889, 26 January 1889, 22 September 1894, 15 to 29 December 1894, 11 March 1899, 22 April 1899

Oxford Dictionary of Autobiography: Anna Munro

Reading Mercury 12 July 1902, 23 August to 6 September 1902, 18 October 1902, 7 March 1903

The Parish Council Act: What It Is and How It Works, The Fabian Society, Tract No. 53, London, 1894

Wallingford Rural District Council: A Record of Service, 5th March 1894 to 31st March 1974, 1974

Wallingford Rural District Council Minutes, BRO RDC/W/CA1/3-5, 1902-05

Wallingford Rural Sanitary Authority Minutes, BRO RDC/W/CA1/1, 1893-94

Chapter 11 The New Century

Berks & Oxon Advertiser 27 January 1899, 24 March 1899, 27 July 1900, 24 May 1901, 14 June 1901, 4 July 1902, 5 September 1913

Berkshire Chronicle 8 June 1907, 5 September 1913

Boer War Soldiers, www.findmypast.co.uk

Jackson's Oxford Journal 6 January 1900, 28 July 1900

Leeds Mercury 29 December 1900

Manchester Courier 21 August 1908

North Moreton Parish Register Transcript, 1906

Reading Mercury 2 February 1861, 3 March 1900, 10 March 1900, 25 May 1901, 1 June 1901, 15 June 1901

Results of the enquiry into the collision on 24 January 1899 at Wallingford Station, TNA RAIL 1053/88 pp72-76, 1899

The Graphic, London 29 December 1900

The Times 27 June 1902

Chapters 12 and 14 The Great War

David Bilton, *The Home Front in the Great War*, Leo Cooper, Barnsley, 2003

Geoff Bridger, *The Great War Handbook*, Pen & Sword, Barnsley, 2009

Adrian Keith-Falconer, *The Oxfordshire Hussars in the Great War 1914-18*, John Murray, London, 1927

F. Loraine Petr, *The Royal Berkshire Regiment Volume II 1914-18*, Royal Berks Regt, Reading, 1925

A. G. Russell, *For Your Tomorrow: The Men of Wallingford Who Died in the Two World Wars*, RusHawk Publishing, 2005

Reginald Spink, *The Story of the Danish Bacon Company 1902-77*, DBC, Welwyn Garden City, 1977

Army Service Record for Reginald Montague Griffith Hearmon, TNA WO363

Berks & Oxon Advertiser 31 July 1914 to 10 January 1919, June and July 1919

Carl Lauritz Hansen Biography, www.denstoredanske.dk

Cholsey School Logbook, BRO C/EL/101/2, 1914-18

Death Certificate for Alfred Abdey, GRO Wallingford 2C 353

F. A. L. Edwards, *University of London OTC Roll*

Old Abingdonians In Memorium, www.abingdon.org.uk

Queen's Own Oxfordshire Hussars records, Soldiers of Oxfordshire Museum

Reading Mercury 26 August 1916

Royal Navy Casualties, www.findmypast.co.uk

Soldiers Died in the Great War Database, www.findmypast.co.uk

The Commonwealth War Graves Commission database, www.cwgc.org

The London Gazette, Officer appointments, 1914-18

War Diary of the 9th Battalion of the Liverpool Regiment, www.9thkings.co.uk

War Diary of the 11th Battalion of the Worcester Regiment, TNA WO95/4874

War Diary of the 12th Battalion of the Manchester Regiment, TNA WO95/2012

War Diary of the 15th Battalion of the Hampshire Regiment, TNA WO95/2634

War Diary of the 250th Tunnelling Company of the Royal Engineers, TNA WO95/551

War Diary of the Battalions of the Royal Berkshire Regiment, The Rifles (Berkshire and Wiltshire) Museum, www.thewardrobe.org.uk

War Diary of the Queen's Own Oxfordshire Hussars, TNA WO95/1137

World War One Medal Cards, www.ancestry.co.uk

Chapter 13 The Conscientious Objector

Will Ellsworth-Jones, *We Will Not Fight*, Aurum Press, London, 2008

Lyn Smith and the Imperial War Museum, *Voices Against War*, Mainstream Publishing, London, 2009

Army Service Record for Frank Beale, www.ancestry.com

Berks & Oxon Advertiser 17 March 1916, 25 August 1916, 29 September 1916, 18 May 1917, 14 December 1917

British Postal Service Appointments, www.ancestry.com

Conscientious Objectors in Britain, www.ppu.org.uk

Exeter and Plymouth Gazette 10 May 1917, 19 July 1917

Hansard 22 March 1917

Interview with Donald Grant, a Great War Conscientious Objector, Imperial War Museum sound archive

Soldiers Died in the Great War Database, www.findmypast.co.uk

The Commonwealth War Graves Commission Database, www.cwgc.org

The Times 19 and 20 February 1917, 9 March 1917, 30 March 1917, 19 April 1917, 24 April 1917, 26 April 1917, 1 May 1917, 8 October 1917, 13 October 1917, 7 November 1917

Western Times 1 May 1917, 4 May 1917, 9 May 1917, 11 May 1917

World War One Medal Cards, www.ancestry.co.uk

Chapters 14 The War to End All Wars

The sources for Chapter 14 are included with Chapter 12.

Index

A

Abbott, George Shrub 185, 190, 211
Abdey, Alfred 184-186, 238
Abdey, Herbert John 193
Agassiz, Friedrich Wilhelm James Albert 147-160
Agassiz, Lewis 151, 236
Agassiz, Revd Robert 155
Alder, Alfred 187, 211, 214
Alder, John 186, 191, 192
Aldermaston 40, 118
Allnut, Mary 123
Allotments 94, 95, 167, 215
Arding, Richard 32
Arnould, Dr 99
Aston 105, 116
Aston Tirrold 42-44, 96, 176
Aston Upthorpe 42
Attwell, Martha 110

B

Bailey, Enoch 173
Baillie, William 91
Baldwin, Benjamin 172
Baldwin, Elijah 49, 68
Baldwin, Gadd 178
Baldwin, Matthew 68, 102
Band of Hope 196
Barn Elms 33, 42, 166
Barrett, Dr Charles 102, 104, 110-112, 131
Barrett, William 131
Barron, Dr John 144
Bartlett, Benjamin 115, 116
Basildon 42, 61, 63, 68, 95, 146
Beale or Beal, George 199

Beale, Frank 199- 209, 239
Beale, Joseph 199
Beehive, The 103, 104
Beeson, Fanny 177
Bennett, James 42, 44
Benson (or Bensington) 41, 44, 113
Bier Way 94
Blackstone, William 45, 46, 53
Blewbury 22, 186
Blunson, Ellen 141
Boer War 179, 181, 237
Bosher, Charles William 174
Bosher, John 130, 173
Bosher, Kerenhappuch 199
Bosher, Phyllis 20
Bosher, Robert 100, 101, 117
Bosher, Sally 101
Bosher, Thomas 117, 131
Boshers (the Builders) 216
Boulter, Harriett 110
Bowen, James 177
Bower, Annie 147, 155
Bower, William 147, 165
Boy Scouts 188, 221
Breach, Dr John 105, 106, 116
Brind, Robert 214
Brind, Robert Charles 214
Bristow, John 50
Brooker, Jeremiah 68
Brown, John 106, 107
Brown, William 61, 63
Brunel, Isambard Kingdom 81-85
Buckell, Anthony 166, 167
Bunce, George 145, 146
Butler, Frank Rupert 219
Butler, George 123, 124
Butler, Rowland 218
Button, Joseph 23, 24

C

Castell, Joseph	134
Cater, Henry Wormley	136
Cedar of Lebanon	19
Champion, William	31, 43, 64
Chequers, The	23, 27, 92, 157, 163, 174, 213
Chesterman, John	131
Cholera	162
Cholsey Brook	14, 34, 168
Cholsey Common	14, 41, 49
Cholsey Farm	33, 45, 49, 91
Cholsey Hill	14, 17, 33, 60, 95
Cholsey Manor	14
Cholsey Mill	94
Church of England Socialist League	200
Church Road (or The Causeway)	14, 17, 19, 22, 147
Church, George Bryden	123
Churchill, Winston	185, 186
Churchwarden	95, 229
Circuitt, Revd Richard William Perry	147, 157
Clayton, Walter	111
Clifford, George	103, 104, 108
Clifford, James	52, 108
Clifford, Maria	108
Clifford, Mary	104
Cloudsley, Alfred	102
Cock, James	45
Coleridge, Mr Justice John Taylor	52, 54
Coleridge, Samuel Taylor	52
Comtesse de Broc	37, 94
Constable	18, 102-104, 108, 126, 127, 132, 146, 176-178, 220
Cook, Albert	214
Cook, Ernest William	218
Costiff, James	115
Costiff, Mary Ann	135
Cottle, Revd Thomas	55, 230
Cottle, Revd Wyatt	17-30, 33, 37, 91, 230
Cottrell, George	162
Cove, Revd Edward	40
Cox, Frank	174
Cox, Henry	104, 107
Cox, Hester or Esther	139
Cox, Matilda	176
Cozens, Stephen	171, 173
Cozens, Stephen Willesley	164
Crake, Revd Augustine David	157
Cranford House	214
Crimean War	70, 100, 179
Cripps, John	45
Cross Keys, The	31
Crowmarsh	41

D

Danford, George	120
Danish Bacon Company	216, 218, 238
Dartmoor Prison	205
Davey, John	86-88
Davey, William	86-90, 233, 234
Dearlove, Ernest William	219
Dearlove, Thomas	63
Defence of the Realm Act	189, 194, 215
Didcock, George	218
Didcot	60, 77, 82, 120, 121, 125, 164, 178, 195, 232
Dix, George	196, 215
Dodd, Thomas	50
Dowsell, John	117, 118
Dowsell, William	118
Draper, Mary	198
Draper, Stephen	192, 193
Drove Lane (or Station Road)	13, 23, 33, 68, 94, 95, 115, 124, 178, 181, 185, 212
Dry Farm	214, 218
Dundas, Charles	38
Dunn, Dr Edwin	174
Durbridge, Edward	41
Durbridge, James	131

E

East End Farm 174, 175
East Ilsley 13, 50
East Moor 41, 95
Edney, Edward 79
Edwards, Capt (RN) Herbert 213
Edwards, Francis Andrew Lloyd 213
Elizabeth Cottages 192, 193, 198
Eltham, Heber 173
Evans, Revd Evan 20
Evans, Thomas 130
Eyston, Mr 45

F

Fair Mile Hospital – see Moulsford Lunatic Asylum
Farrar, Revd Augustus 166
Ferris, William Joseph 219
Ford, Ellen 162
Forty, The 13, 14, 21, 23, 33, 50, 78-80, 92, 96, 100, 101, 104, 178
French Horn, The 31

G

Gale, Harold 190, 211
Gale, Joseph John 185, 212
Gale, Leonard Franklin 185, 190
Gale, Ronald 190
Games, Lucretia 19
Garlick, Hannah 105
Garlick, Thomas 105
Garlick, William 52
Garnault, Joseph 149, 237
Gilland, Dr Robert 110, 111, 133
Girl Guides 188, 214, 221
Glass, PC John 102-104, 108
Good, Richard 60
Goodchild, William 41, 45
Goodyear, William 145, 146, 235
Goring 82, 115, 120, 121, 188
Goulburn, Mr 54
Graham, Sir James 64
Green, Edward Ferdinand 195
Greenaway, William 43
Greenhill 33, 49, 50, 105
Greenwood, William 31

H

Hansen, Carl Lauritz (Charlie) 216, 238
Hansen, William George 217
Hanson, Thomas 44
Happy Jack (John Starling) 79-81
Harding, Jane 138, 139
Hardy, Robert 22, 26
Hart-Dyke, Lt Col 200
Hazel, Revd James 31
Hearmon, Edward 166
Hearmon, Reginald Montague Griffiths 196
Hearmon, Sarah 175
Hearmon, Violet 197
Hearnes, Supt 176
Hedges, Major Francis Reade 184
Herbert, Thomas 42
Higgs, Matthew 103, 104
Higgs, Philip 103, 104
Hildesley family 50
Hillgreen 33
Hine, Thomas Henry 123
Hithercroft 33, 60, 101, 187, 199, 214, 216
Hodges, Thomas Howard 60
Honey Lane 13, 14, 33, 59, 96, 147, 176, 177, 192, 195, 198, 199
Hopkins, James 103, 104
Hopkins, Joseph 27
Horn Lane 14, 19, 23, 147, 155, 157, 162

Horn Lane – see also Wallingford Road
Horne, Dr 123
Horne, George 144
Horton, Hannah 109
Houlton, Henry 62
Howse, Elizabeth 174
Howse, John 174, 213
Howse, Walter Roland 213
Huggins, John 18-30
Hulcup, David 32, 43
Hulse, William 79
Hunt, Charles Hewitt 124, 166
Hunt, Harry Clark 189
Hunt, James 22, 27, 28
Hunt, John 21, 22, 42
Hunt, Joseph 27
Hutt, Edith 196, 218
Hutt, Edward 218
Hutt, John Henry 218

I

Ilges Lane 14, 49, 50, 59, 95, 101, 196
Ilsley Road 94
Ilsley, Henry 60, 73, 74, 232
Ilsley, James 49-59, 65, 71, 231, 232
Ilsley, John 70, 71
Ilsley, Joseph 67, 68, 73, 232
Ilsley, Sarah 50, 64, 68
Isolation Hospital 168

J

Javelin Men 51, 101
Jenkins, Thomas 114
Johnson, Robert 115
Jones, Susan 142, 143

K

Kearsey, Charles 103
Kearsey, Frederick 104
Keeling, William 32
Kensington, Lord 33
Kentwood Farm 23, 33, 188, 195, 221
Kimber, Fred 219
King George V 188, 227
Kirby, Mr 61-63
Kitchener, Lord 189

L

Langford, Louisa 145, 146
Larkcom, John 99
Laurence, Revd Frederick Spencer 214
Lay, Isaac William 171
Leonard, Thomas Barrett 53
Lewis, Charles 123
Little Stoke 50, 129, 130, 135, 137
Lloyd, Revd Henry William 78-81, 101, 133, 147
Local Government Acts 164
Lockie, Alfred 142
Lockup, The village 101
Lollingdon 33, 91, 96, 99

M

MacDonald, Ramsay 200
Manor Farm 33, 49, 157, 171-173, 178, 188
Mansell, Inspector 132
Marcham, Charles 49, 52
Marshall, Dr John Hedges 111, 132
Maunders, PC 126, 127
Melbourne, Lord 43, 45
Middlesex Imperial Yeomanry 188
Mill, Cholsey 14, 34, 118
Millbank Penitentiary 64, 232
Miller, PC Alfred 101, 102
Minshull, Louise 92
Minshull, Richard 18, 23, 24, 27, 29, 37

Minshulls Farm 33
Money, John William (Bill) 174
Moore, William 23, 24, 29
Morning Star, The 82, 137, 144
Morrell, George 123, 177, 178
Morrell, Revd Dr 133
Morrison, Charles 113
Morrison, James 94, 113, 147
Morse, Thomas 118
Moulsford 14, 29, 50, 60, 61, 63, 77, 79, 82, 94, 114, 120-122, 124, 125, 129, 132, 133, 135, 136, 138, 141, 143, 145, 174, 176, 188, 214, 233, 235, 236
Moulsford Lunatic Asylum 109, 111, 129-146, 157, 158, 164, 166, 167, 173, 174, 176
Moulsford station – see Wallingford Road station
Mulcay or Mulcahy, Hannah 109-111
Munday, Robert 85
Munro, Anna 169, 237

N

National Women's Temperance Association 196
Neal, Richard 99
Nelson, Dr William Bremmer 126, 163
Newton, Thomas 41
No Conscription Fellowship 200
Non-Combatant Corps 201, 204
Norcutt, George 166
Norfolk, Frederick 103, 104
North Moreton 117, 118, 175, 237

O

Oliver, W. G. 133
Overseer 95, 230, 232
Owen, Edwin Thomas 176

P

Palmer, James 89
Pancroft 33, 178
Pangbourne 61, 63, 68, 82
Pankhurst, Emmeline 169
Papist Way 82, 96, 137, 144, 173
Parish Council 165, 167, 227, 237
Parsons, William 49
Payne, George 33
Peedle, Elizabeth 131
Peel, Sir Robert 55, 64, 78, 232
Pentonville Penitentiary 64, 69, 232
Peters, Ann Eleanor 71
Pither, Thomas 27
Pitt, William 18
Pocock, Job 172
Poor Law 38, 46, 59, 161, 164, 167, 227, 232
Pope, Mark 123
Pope, William 42
Potts, John 31
Pound Farm 13, 14
Povey, William Francis 175
Powell, James 45
Pratt, Mary Ann 131
Pulbrook, John 60, 62-65, 232

Q

Queen Adelaide 84, 85
Queen's Own Oxfordshire Hussars 185, 186, 188, 190, 191, 211, 238
Queens College 94

R

Railway Tavern 85, 92, 94, 119, 178
Randall, John 45

Reading Gaol 40, 44, 51, 69, 101, 112
Reading Road 32, 61, 82, 124, 125, 173, 188
Red Lion 14, 163
Robards or Roberts, Richard 23, 24
Royal Berkshire Regiment 118, 130, 180, 184, 186, 189-193, 196, 211, 213, 218, 219, 231, 238
Royal Hotel – see Railway Tavern
Rumble, David 104
Rumble, Joseph 107
Rumbold, Anne 107
Russell, Bertrand 201
Russell, Lord John 55

S

Saunders, Vincent Elijah 212
Savage, Sarah 60
Saville, Alice Dorothy 176
Sawyer, Harriett Ann 116, 161
Sawyer, Lucy 161
Sawyer, William 116
Shaw, Alfred 122, 123
Shepherd, Charles 120
Silly Bridge 94, 113, 176
Slade, Charlotte 42
Slade, Henry 42
Slade, John 42
Smith, Bernard 20, 27
Smith, James 18, 20, 21, 27, 30
Smith, John 114, 116
Smith, Richard 126
Somerset, John 61, 63
South Moreton 60, 62, 63, 164
Speenhamland 35-37, 95
Spencer-Churchill, John Strange 186
Spokes, John 105
Spratley, Frank Alfred 218
Spratley, PC Ernest 176-178, 220
Spratley, PC William 220

St Mary's Church 14, 17, 31, 131, 174, 191, 221, 222
Stanley, Charlotte Amelia 67
Stanley, Sarah Eliza 66
Star Terrace 137, 173, 194
Starling, John (Happy Jack) 79
Station Hotel – see Railway Tavern
Station Road 13, 95, 178, 181, 185, 212
Station Road – see also Drove Lane
Stevens, Elisha 104
Stevenson, Julia 216
Stone, William 45, 47, 231
Stott, Edwin 134
Strange, William 102
Streatley 14, 42, 44, 45, 47, 61, 88, 146
Surveyor of Highways 96
Swan Inn 13, 19, 78, 103, 123, 125, 130, 166, 196, 230

T

Talbot, Jacob 89
Tatham, Thomas James 91
Taunton, Samuel 45, 46
Taylor, Maria 41
Thatcham 40
The Causeway – see Church Road
The Chestnuts 155, 157, 193
The Elms 124, 189
The Hazells 185
The Lees 178
Tinson, Jane 138
Tithes 91, 93, 227, 230, 234
Tomlin, Jane 131
Town Arms, The 131
Turner, George 102
Turner, Harry 193
Turner, Jasper 193
Turnpike, The 14, 31, 82, 87, 94, 113, 124, 130, 145
Turrill, James 140

Typhoid (or Enteric Fever)   161, 162, 180, 209

V

Vestry, The   230, 232
Vicars of Cholsey
   Augustine David Crake   157
   Evan Evans   20
   Henry William Lloyd   78-81, 101, 133, 147
   Richard William Perry Circuitt   157
   Wyatt Cottle   17-30, 33, 37, 91, 230
Vinden, William   130

W

Wakefield, William   32
Wallingford Road   14, 19, 23, 41, 94, 95, 126, 155, 157, 167, 193
Wallingford Road – see also Horn Lane
Wallingford Road (or Moulsford) station   82, 84-89, 113, 114, 118-120, 130
Wallingford Rural District Council   164, 168, 238
Wallingford Rural Sanitary District   161
Wallingford Volunteers   180, 181
Walter, Mr   53, 55
Walters, Arthur   180
Walters, Frederick   180
Ward, Arthur   121
Warren, Robert   135, 137
Warren, William   61, 63
Washbourne, Thomas Edward 45, 49, 50, 52, 91-93
Waterloo Tavern   130

Watlington   113, 131
Webb, PC James   132
Webb, Thomas   166
Wells, Bethia   108
Wells, Henry Watkin   166
West End   41, 117, 175, 178, 179, 213, 218
West Moor   41
Westfield Farm   33
Westfield Road   94-96, 180
White, Ann   60
White, James   102
Whittard, William   126, 127
Whittock, N   27
Wilcox, Shadrach   62, 63
Wilkins, Charles   60, 63, 64, 159, 231, 232
Willmott, Bessie   148
Wilson, Henry   61, 63
Winhurst   33
Winterbourn, William   44
Winterbrook 31-33, 40, 41, 43, 82, 94, 99, 126, 131, 166, 184, 185, 190
Wintle, Revd Thomas   94
Wise, William   68
Wood, William Bryan   93, 94
Woodward, Henry Francis   197, 198
Workhouse   89, 231, 232
Wormwood Scrubs   204
Wyatt, Mary Louisa   192
Wyatt, Robert   104

Y

Young, William   131, 132